When Baseball Met
Big Bill Haywood

When Baseball Met Big Bill Haywood

The Battle for Manchester, New Hampshire, 1912–1916

SCOTT C. ROPER *and*
STEPHANIE ABBOT ROPER

McFarland & Company, Inc., Publishers
Jefferson, North Carolina

LIBRARY OF CONGRESS CATALOGUING-IN-PUBLICATION DATA

Names: Roper, Scott C., author. | Roper, Stephanie Abbot, author.
Title: When baseball met Big Bill Haywood : the battle for Manchester, New Hampshire, 1912–1916 / Scott C. Roper and Stephanie Abbot Roper.
Description: Jefferson, North Carolina : McFarland & Company, Inc., Publishers, 2018. | Includes bibliographical references and index.
Identifiers: LCCN 2017043277 | ISBN 9781476665467 (softcover : acid free paper) ∞
Subjects: LCSH: Baseball—New Hampshire—Manchester—History. | Labor movement—New Hampshire—Manchester—History. | Textile industry—New Hampshire—Manchester—History. | Amoskeag Manufacturing Company—History. | Haywood, Big Bill, 1869–1928. | Manchester (N.H.)—History—20th century.
Classification: LCC GV875.N472 M376 2018 | DDC 796.35709742/8—dc23
LC record available at https://lccn.loc.gov/2017043277

BRITISH LIBRARY CATALOGUING DATA ARE AVAILABLE

ISBN (print) 978-1-4766-6546-7
ISBN (ebook) 978-1-4766-3091-5

© 2018 Scott C. Roper and Stephanie Abbot Roper. All rights reserved

No part of this book may be reproduced or transmitted in any form or by any means, electronic or mechanical, including photocopying or recording, or by any information storage and retrieval system, without permission in writing from the publisher.

Front cover: Dedication Day at Textile Field, September 8, 1913, featuring the Boston Red Sox and the Manufacturers League All-Stars (courtesy Manchester [New Hampshire] Historic Association)

Printed in the United States of America

McFarland & Company, Inc., Publishers
  Box 611, Jefferson, North Carolina 28640
    www.mcfarlandpub.com

Table of Contents

Acknowledgments	vii
Preface: Why Textile Field?	1
Introduction: The Amoskeag Manufacturing Company in an Age of Reform	9
1. A City on Edge	19
2. The Fight for Free Speech	27
3. Finding a Voice	37
4. Baseball Season at Last	48
5. The World Series and a "Last-Ditch Bogey Man"	59
6. Minor Leagues	65
7. Problems of Government	77
8. Textile Field	88
9. The Rise of the Eighth Ward	99
10. Manchester and the Red Sox	110
11. "Textile Field hath been Assailed!"	121
12. Amoskeag's Local Challenges	133
13. Rally Around the Flag	141
14. The End of Big Games	154

15. Amoskeag and the Federal League	167
16. Frank Knox's Manchester	178
17. The Demise of the Textiles	188
Epilogue: The Great Strike of 1922	199
Conclusion: Textile Field and the Progressive Movement in Manchester	209
Chapter Notes	215
Bibliography	232
Index	237

Acknowledgments

When we began this project in 1997, we thought we would answer some questions we had about a stadium in Manchester, New Hampshire. We had no idea that it would reveal the fascinating and complex story we found.

We could not have finished this book alone; many people, institutions, and forums have enabled its completion. We are particularly grateful to members of the NESTVAL Division of the Association of American Geographers, the Society for Baseball Research, the International Society for Landscape, Place, and Material Culture, and various faculty members of Castleton University who attended presentations of this material in 2005, 2006, 2013, and 2014, respectively, and who provided feedback on our findings. Equally important, we wish to thank faculty and administrators at Castleton University for their support through their encouragement, their advice and criticism: Adam Chill, Melisse Pinto, Judy Robinson, Jonathan Spiro, Patricia van der Spuy, Carrie Waara, Mike Austin, Ennis Duling, Honoree Fleming, Flo Keyes, Joe Mark, Dave Wolk, and particularly Andre Fleche, whose constructive comments and moral support have been greatly appreciated over the last several years.

Thanks are due the staffs of the Cornette Library at West Texas A&M University and the Coolidge Library at Castleton University for their patient help in locating materials, as well as the staffs of the Manchester Historic Association Research Center (especially Jeffrey Barraclough), Manchester City Clerk's Office, Manchester City Library, New Hampshire State Library in Concord, the Giamatti Research Center at the National Baseball Hall of Fame and Museum, the Iowa Women's Archives at the University of Iowa Libraries (particularly Janet Weaver), Minor League Baseball (notably Steve Densa and Tina Gust), the Baker-Berry and Rauner Special Collection Libraries at Dartmouth College, the Baker Library at Harvard University, the Rockefeller Library at

Brown University, the Geisel Library at Saint Anselm College, Rivier University's Regina Library, the Walter Peterson Library at Nashua Community College, and the Dimond Library at the University of New Hampshire.

And finally, we wish to thank students enrolled in the 2004 Baseball and Culture special topics class at West Texas A&M University, as well as our former colleagues in what was then the Department of History, Political Science, and Criminal Justice, for providing the impetus and encouragement to move forward with this research.

Preface: Why Textile Field?

Cultural geographers, architectural and social historians, and others who study material culture agree that cultural landscapes—imprints on the land that result from our interactions with environments and other people—can be read as texts. For instance, a building's design and location may suggest how the structure was used at a particular time, thereby revealing something about the economic, political, or social values of the people who built or used it. The existence of that building may even have symbolic meanings beyond its actual use. To understand those values and meanings, researchers might consider the building's physical form (materials, layout, and other architectural features), its location relative to similar structures or within a city or neighborhood, or the events surrounding the building's construction and use. In such cases, the building may even become of secondary importance, as it is just one piece of a much larger, often complex story.

This study began as an effort to understand why, in 1913, the Amoskeag Manufacturing Company of Manchester, New Hampshire, constructed Textile Field. Built mostly of concrete, steel, and brick, the $30,000 grandstand was a scaled-down version of what major-league baseball teams erected in major cities from Boston to St. Louis between 1909 and 1923. The fact that such a stadium was constructed in a community of only about 70,000 people was quite unusual, and indicates that something equally unusual was occurring in Manchester.

To understand Textile Field, then, one must understand the larger social, political, and economic conditions in Manchester at the time. In 1912, the Amoskeag Manufacturing Company employed between 15,500 and 17,000 people, and is believed to have been the largest cotton textile company in the world. The company's managers also realized that increased competition from factories in the American South threatened its future profitability. Confronted

Textile Field on Dedication Day, September 8, 1913 (courtesy Manchester [New Hampshire] Historic Association).

with the seeming inevitability that proximity to raw materials and lower labor costs would allow the industry to grow in the South, companies such as Amoskeag attempted to secure their future by reducing overhead, introducing efficiency measures to production, and influencing (as best they could) government programs and policies designed to protect them.

At the same time state and federal governments, responding to national social movements, seemingly became less aligned with textile corporations. Progressive reformers pushed for regulations to protect workers and consumers, threatening to saddle the industry with added costs. Workers, meanwhile, demanded not only safer working conditions, but also reduced working hours and to be paid a living wage. In response to all of these conditions, and particularly in an effort to escape government regulation of their industry, Amoskeag turned to benevolence programs designed to improve living conditions for workers. The construction of Textile Field was part of that effort.

But Textile Field owes its existence to immigration and anti-union sentiments as well. Amoskeag was an open shop—it banned union activity among most of its workers—in a city it had planned and controlled since the 1830s. Its workforce included many poorly paid immigrants, including Greeks and others from southern Europe who were, unfairly, associated with socialism, anarchism, and even terrorism. For proof of these immigrants' supposed anti-American character, some observers pointed to the violent 1912 strike of 24,000 workers at the American Woolen Company in Lawrence, Massachusetts, which had been led by immigrants from southern Europe. Making matters worse, the workers walked off their jobs with the help of the Industrial Workers of the World, a radical labor union that itself was associated with socialism and anarchism and, in the eyes of many people, had threatened the social order in labor movements across the American West.

To avoid a situation similar to the one in Lawrence, Amoskeag turned to baseball among other programs. At the national level, the game's most ardent supporters asserted that baseball was purely an American game. In what later became known as the baseball creed, they suggested that baseball's supposedly democratic principles and competitive nature held the power to Americanize immigrants—not only direct participants in the game, but those watching the game from the stands as well. At the same time in New England, Boston's major-league baseball teams suddenly became highly competitive, winning the World Series five times over a seven-year period. The popularity of the Boston Red Sox—who won four of those titles after opening their new concrete-and-steel ballpark, Fenway Park, in 1912—combined with the tenets of the baseball creed, gave manufacturers in Manchester the idea to create a city baseball league and Amoskeag, specifically, the impetus to construct a professional-caliber stadium for the league.

In effect, then, the construction of Textile Field represents Amoskeag's need to control external and internal factors affecting the company. Once built, Textile Field, and local baseball in general, had to remain under Amoskeag's control. Unfortunately for Amoskeag, a regional minor league took notice of Manchester's baseball renaissance in 1912 and attempted to place a minor-league team in the city in each of the next three years. As a result, the period from Textile Field's completion in 1913 to the end of 1915 was marked by numerous "battles" between Amoskeag and the New England League, the most notable of which resulted in a boycott of the city by all of organized baseball—from the lowest minor leagues to the teams of the American and National Leagues—in 1914. Just as the Manufacturers League was a failure, attempts at placing an independent league were negated due to Amoskeag's requirement for undisputed control over its workers and its stadium—a requirement that sometimes brought Amoskeag into conflict with the city's merchants and professionals.

Although part of our focus is on Textile Field and, more generally, baseball in Manchester between 1912 and 1916, the baseball stadium itself actually comprises a relatively small part of this study. Rather, we use the ballpark as a window onto the larger social history of urban New Hampshire during the Progressive Era. Researchers including Tamara Hareven, Randolph Langenbach, Daniel Creamer and Charles Coulter, Robert Macieski, and Arthur Kenison have contributed much to our reading of the social and economic conditions of Manchester as they related to Amoskeag in the early twentieth century, not to mention the rise of corporate benevolence in the city. They have added to our understanding of Amoskeag's increasingly questionable financial condition in its last three decades, working conditions (including the use of child labor) in the mills, its decision to invest in corporate benevolence programs to improve and control its workers' lives, and the mixed reception those programs received from Amoskeag workers. Andrea Tone's work on early twentieth-century corporate benevolence likewise provides an excellent view into the motivations of American corporations in creating benevolence programs, particularly as a way to control labor costs and deflect government intervention into corporate affairs. Our work adds to theirs by relating many of the political, economic, social, and cultural forces—some local, some regional or national, and some international—that shaped Manchester and informed the decisions of Amoskeag and other companies in New England during the Progressive Era.[1]

Obviously, given the importance of corporate and social history to this study, the history of immigration and labor is also of vital significance—so significant that regional historian Joseph Conforti has called for a "narrative of how New England developed not only as a Puritan-Yankee city on a hill but also as an ethnic city by the mill."[2] Luckily, from Robert Paul McCaffery's analysis of German culture and identity in Manchester and Lawrence between 1870 and 1942, to Gary Samson's documentation of French-Canadian immigrant life in Manchester, to Ardis Cameron's study of women in Lawrence between 1860 and 1912, to Bruce Watson's narrative of the Bread and Roses Strike in Lawrence, the cities of the Merrimack Valley are well studied. Yet despite the connections between the two textile cities, no recent author has connected the 1912 Lawrence strike to the events that transpired between 1912 and 1916 in Manchester. Meanwhile, American labor historians who focus on the strike or the Industrial Workers of the World rarely consider the wider impact of either on New England outside of Lawrence.[3] Although we do not pretend to answer Conforti's call for a complete narrative of the "ethnic city by the mill," we do hope to add to our collective understanding of how immigrants, native attitudes toward ethnicity and nationality, and labor movements in general helped to shape cities like Manchester in the Progressive Era.

Our study also reveals the controlling nature of Amoskeag in its relationships with local, state, and national governments, social movements, and media. Writers and academics who have studied the histories of Amoskeag and New Hampshire generally have refrained from analyzing the company's relationship with state government, despite Amoskeag's obvious attempts to scare voters in the elections of 1912 and possible effort to influence the state legislature's choice of United States Senator in 1913. With the notable exception of James Wright's *The Progressive Yankees,* researchers typically have not considered the purpose or effects of Amoskeag's control over local media in Manchester, nor how the company's own newspaper seems to have been an attempt to compete more directly with the left-leaning newspapers that suddenly emerged in 1912.[4] And no one has written about the importance of baseball or the Boston Red Sox to Progressive and Republican efforts to sway the hearts and minds of the local population, particularly among media outlets.

At the same time, this project remains a study of baseball in Progressive-Era New Hampshire. Admittedly, a number of baseball scholars have considered topics similar to this one. Steven Riess's *Touching Base* is the most obvious of these. In that work, Riess considers relationships among progressivism, urban problems and conditions, and the baseball creed in Atlanta, New York, and Chicago during the early twentieth century. In their wide-ranging *Baseball: The People's Game,* Dorothy Seymour Mills and Harold Seymour likewise document the use of baseball to "Americanize" European immigrant workers in the face of radical trade unions such as the Industrial Workers of the World, as well as the inclusion of baseball in corporate-welfare programs across the United States in the early twentieth century. Both of these efforts relate well to studies of leisure time in an increasingly industrialized, urban age, including Roy Rosenzweig's classic study of Worcester, Massachusetts, between 1870 and 1920. In that time and place, workers were able to protect leisure time from the incursions of corporations and well-meaning social groups who promoted temperance, parks, playgrounds, and "Safe and Sane" Fourth of July movements. This study connects the works of Riess, Seymour, and Rosenzweig by documenting Amoskeag's corporate attempts to focus worker attitudes and leisure time on Americanizing activities in an effort to keep them from radicalizing and striking against the Amoskeag Manufacturing Company.[5]

Researchers Neil Sullivan and Bruce Kuklick both consider the local social, political, and economic factors that influenced, or were influenced by, the construction of, activities inside, and alteration or destruction of New York's Yankee Stadium and Philadelphia's Shibe Park. Like those authors, we are interested in the people and politics associated with a sporting property—and with the development of the property itself—than with baseball. At the same time, this book is not quite as focused on stadium architecture as, for instance, Michael Gershman's *Diamonds*, which documents the evolution of professional baseball parks in the United States. Rather, what we hope to add to existing scholarship is an understanding of how one New Hampshire corporation used baseball and the construction of a modern stadium to Americanize its immigrant workers in response to a perceived threat from labor unions.[6]

Finally, we would be remiss if we did not mention studies of specific baseball leagues that existed in the period between 1912 and 1916. As both Sullivan and Seymour have shown, this was a tumultuous period for professional baseball in general, and particularly for minor leagues. Both the rise of a renegade third major league, known as the Federal League, and the onset of World War I in Europe brought financial problems to both major and minor leagues. The New England League, in particular, saw hardships during this period, eventually seeking out a merger with another Eastern Association to create the Eastern League. In his history of the New England League, Charlie Bevis recounts many of the events and circumstances that preceded and led to the merger. Sullivan, Seymour Mills and Seymour, and Bevis provide excellent overviews of professional baseball in the early twentieth century, but in being regional or national in scope, these studies often ignore local, non-professional perspectives. For instance, Bevis tends to emphasize the motivations and interests of the New England League's owners and president. Financial solvency, obviously, was of paramount importance to them, and that fact made placing a team in Textile Field an appealing venture. Yet the Amoskeag Manufacturing Company saw the situation quite differently: the company was willing to lose money in constructing Textile Field to control its workforce, and company officials saw the New England League as a threat to its control. Thus, our study adds to those of Bevis, Sullivan, Seymour Mills and Seymour, and others by providing a local, alternative perspective relating to the events surrounding professional baseball's difficulties in the 1910s.[7]

While this is partly a story of baseball and the construction and control of Manchester's Textile Field, it is also the story of, among others, Pearl McGill, an Iowa teenager whose work with IWW members in Lawrence helped to precipitate anti-government and anti-industry protests in Manchester. It is the story of Michael Healy, Manchester's baseball-loving Chief of Police whose desire to "keep the peace" challenged the First Amendment rights of protestors. It is the story of Frank Knox, whose attempts to create a mouthpiece for New Hampshire's progressive movement eventually resulted in perhaps the most important newspaper in the state, the *Manchester Union-Leader*. It is the story of Adolph Wagner, the passionate German immigrant who helped his section of West Manchester to transcend ethnic barriers and unify in its fight for better and safer living conditions. And it is the story of John "Phenomenal" Smith, Fred Lake, and John Carney, major-league baseball players in the nineteenth century who at various times played minor-league ball in Manchester, but found their ways back to the city in various roles during the early 20th century.

To tell their stories and those of others, we have organized this book conceptually into three parts. After an introduction to the Amoskeag Manufacturing Company in the context of the Progressive Era, the first five chapters describe the unrest in Manchester from before the Lawrence strike until the state and national elections of 1912. Amoskeag's apparent loss of control over local, state, and national politics only worsened that year as the radicalism of Lawrence infiltrated Manchester. The police force already watched some immigrant groups with suspicion. But its reactions against IWW members and other socialists in the city were so controversial that the police inadvertently caused the creation of the New Hampshire Free Speech Alliance, a short-lived organization that, like similar IWW-supported groups in the West, successfully focused public attention on Amoskeag's control over the Manchester Police Chief. Presumed radicalism among immigrants, combined with inroads made by state progressives in creating a new city newspaper, the *Manchester Leader,* as well as the success of the Boston Red Sox in 1912, led Amoskeag to promote baseball as a way by which to settle worker unease while also promoting American values.

Chapters 6 through 14 detail Amoskeag's attempts to regain control over its city and its workforce through baseball. After the 1912 elections, as the company's hold over state and local government seemed to slip, the New England League suddenly found its interest in placing a team in Manchester renewed. But Amoskeag rejected the league's overtures, particularly after the Amoskeag Textile Club began construction on a new, state-of-the-art grandstand. The new grandstand provided an ongoing story to attract readers to the club's new semi-monthly newspaper, the *Amoskeag Bulletin,* as did the company's success in bringing the Boston Red Sox to Textile Field for an exhibition game against a local all-star team in 1913. The results of this movement were not a panacea for most of the city's problems, however. For instance, the construction of Textile Field did nothing to alleviate inadequate roads, unreliable firefighting services, or unsafe places for children, particularly in those parts of the city in which Amoskeag held little economic interest. Meanwhile, as the Amoskeag Manufacturing Company worked to reassert its influence over the state legislature and find new ways to Americanize its workforce, the club's antagonism toward the New England League resulted in an unprecedented move: a boycott of Manchester by all of professional baseball. The boycott ended only after Amoskeag permitted the New England League to move a team into Textile Field, but on terms dictated by Amoskeag.

As we discuss in the final chapters, the disastrous 1914 season—which saw the failure of the New England League club, college football, and various exhibition games against well-known barnstorming and professional baseball teams in Manchester—led the Amoskeag Textile Club to drop out of the Manufacturers League and eschew future "big games." In fact, the club finally seemed willing to rent Textile Field to the New England League. But infighting among league owners and problems finding a buyer for the Manchester team led to delays. During this time an "outlaw" third major league, the Federal League, briefly considered creating a new minor league with one of its teams in Manchester, bringing its anti-trust fight against organized baseball to Textile Field. This effort failed, and despite the Amoskeag Textile Club's full cooperation with the New England League team in 1915, bad feelings toward the city and dishonesty among league owners led to the loss of Manchester's minor-league club.

Introduction: The Amoskeag Manufacturing Company in an Age of Reform

Early on the morning of April 14, 1913, officials of the Amoskeag Textile Club gathered in foul territory on the south side of Textile Field in Manchester, New Hampshire. Two weeks earlier a group of 25 workers had started construction on a new $30,000 grandstand, and already they had completed the concrete foundation. According to the club's newspaper, the *Amoskeag Bulletin*, the purpose of the gathering was accomplished at 7:50 A.M. when Frank Lyons, a popular member of the club's baseball team, installed the first brick for the new structure.[1]

The event was significant not only for the Amoskeag Textile Club, but for its parent corporation as well. With this act, the Amoskeag Manufacturing Company signaled its commitment to "welfare work," the betterment of social conditions for its employees. When Amoskeag's official history later proclaimed Textile Field to be the "largest and finest resort of athletic sports in New England outside Boston," it did so with good reason: of all similar structures in New England at the time of its construction, only Harvard Stadium and Boston's Fenway Park could claim to have been built of concrete and steel. In fact, though its seating deck was made of wood, making it technically a hybrid rather than a true concrete-and-steel stadium, local newspapers such as the *Manchester Daily Mirror and American* described it as "concrete and brick, fireproof throughout." As such, the Textile Field grandstand was one of the first in the country outside of a major American city or college campus to be built otherwise of permanent "fireproof" materials.[2]

More subtly, the grandstand represents the social and political climates of the time in which it was constructed. Since its founding in 1831, Amoskeag had controlled Manchester and its growth. By 1912, progressive reforms and left-leaning social movements throughout the United States threatened that control. As trust-busters, muckraking journalists, and other reformers sought to restore political power to the less privileged, discontented workers organized into unions and sometimes-radical political groups. Perhaps the most feared of these was the Industrial Workers of the World, a union that combined elements of socialism and anarchism to overtly threaten the established political, economic, and social order. In this context, Amoskeag's corporate-welfare program represents an effort to reclaim control over its workforce, Manchester's populace, and ultimately, local, state, and even federal government.[3] Inspired in part by the success of the Boston Red Sox, Amoskeag would make baseball one of the most visible parts of that program.

Between 1912 and 1916, the Amoskeag Manufacturing Company was among the most powerful businesses in New England. These years represent the textile corporation's peak, when it employed between 15,500 and 17,000 workers and boasted thirty major mills and many smaller buildings totaling 8,000,000 square feet of floor space. The entire complex lined the Merrimack River for a mile and a half below the Amoskeag Falls, essentially defining the city of Manchester, New Hampshire. It consisted of 74 separate cloth-making departments, three dye houses, 24 mechanical and electrical departments, three steam-power plants, and a hydroelectric station, and by 1915 was turning out cloth at a rate of 50 miles per hour.[4]

From its incorporation in 1831 to World War I, Amoskeag's planners created an industrial landscape remarkable for its "organic unity and visual continuity." As Tamara Hareven and Randolph Langenbach described it:

> The millyard was open at each end, with tree-lined canals and railroad tracks running through its entire length on two different levels above the river. Instead of a long, straight avenue, however, a gentle curve softened the rigor of the design, dividing the millyard into identifiable spaces. These carefully designed and meticulously maintained spaces were a supreme confidence in the unbounded confidence of the Victorian Age, a confidence rooted in the belief not only in continuing material progress but in the ability to overcome almost any social problem in the headlong rush for industrial improvement.[5]

Furthermore, through its distribution of the 26,000 acres of land it acquired, as well as the options it retained on land donated to churches, and through the fact that the company kept technical ownership over at least part of Manchester's park system, Amoskeag retained nearly total control over the city and its development. Prior to the company's closure in 1935 and ultimate demise in 1936, no new industry could be established in Manchester without Amoskeag's consent, and the company took an active role in planning and constructing the city's industrial plants.⁶ As a result, most factories built between 1838 and 1900—even those built by and for other companies—resembled the Amoskeag mills in design and materials.

Amoskeag's management planned other aspects of Manchester as well. One of its engineers, Ezekiel Straw, designed the city's roadways and grid. Periodic land sales ensured that the new downtown would be concentrated along Elm Street, and that residential neighborhoods would develop in particular areas around the city as well. Land sales occurred with an "elaborate set of restrictions and rules that controlled the nature of private development," so that all buildings erected in Manchester were limited in size, concentration, and sometimes in construction materials used.⁷

Manchester's layout reflected Amoskeag management's initial desire to create a utopian environment for its workers, just as was being attempted in Lowell, Massachusetts. As in Lowell, Amoskeag's early workforce was made up primarily of young, unmarried women from New England's rural communities,

Manchester from Ste. Marie Church, looking southeast, probably in the early 1900s. The southern section of the Amoskeag Millyard and the Granite Street Bridge are visible in the distance (courtesy Manchester [New Hampshire] Historic Association).

most living in corporate-owned boarding houses under strict rules governing their behavior. By the 1850s, Amoskeag had ended its utopian experiment. Mill girls were replaced by immigrant laborers—men as well as women, primarily from Ireland—who would work for less money and were less likely to leave the company. Before the end of the Civil War, Amoskeag had begun recruiting migrants from Quebec, where land scarcity, overpopulation, farming problems, and poverty provided incentive for many men and women to move elsewhere in search of work. Eventually, the company came to see French Canadians as ideal because, according to stereotype, they worked hard and were unlikely to strike or cause labor problems. As a result, their numbers grew considerably, though other nationalities continued to appear in the city as well. English, Scottish, German and Swedish groups arrived in the late 1860s and 1870s; and in smaller numbers, Poles, Italians, Greeks, and others in the 1890s and early 1900s.[8]

With each wave of immigration, Amoskeag opened new areas of the city to development, encouraging the geographical segregation of most groups within particular ethnic neighborhoods. Even so, neighborhood boundaries often blurred, and fights among members of different groups were common in those boundary zones, particularly in the city's parks. This fact, as well as Amoskeag management's fear that its employees would unionize and strike, necessitated that the company maintain strict political and social control over Manchester and at least some influence over state government. One typically could find Amoskeag overseers and other employees holding positions on the Board of Aldermen or the Police Commission, and management's close ties to the police force sometimes led to accusations that the Chief of Police was controlled by the company.[9]

By 1912 Manchester was a multiethnic, polyglot city. It boasted three daily newspapers, the English-language *Manchester Union* and *Manchester Daily Mirror and American* and the French-language *L'Avenir National*, as well as numerous weekly and monthly newspapers published in English, French, German, and Greek. Both the *Mirror* and the *Union* supported Republican causes and generally reinforced the positions of the Amoskeag Manufacturing Company. *L'Avenir National* tended to support Amoskeag, the Catholic Church, and most things Quebecois. Those hoping for an alternate perspective had to seek out newspapers such as the *Boston Journal*, a politically progressive daily read by approximately 10,000 people in New Hampshire.[10]

Although Manchester's media outlets helped to insulate Amoskeag from negative publicity, the Progressive Era took a toll on the company, threatening its power at every level. In 1909, for example, photographer Lewis Hine traveled throughout New England gathering evidence for the National Child Labor

Committee, which sought to document the practice of child labor. One of his targets was the Amoskeag Manufacturing Company. Hine was able to sneak into Amoskeag, where he photographed and spoke with several of the children he found in the spinning rooms. He also took photographs of children leaving the millyard for lunch and at the end of the workday. His work was cited by several state and national organizations in their efforts to force the state to abolish the practice of child labor.[11]

That Hine's efforts received the attention they did is attributable in part to the political and social atmosphere of the Progressive Era. During the first two decades of the twentieth century, progressive reformers worked to improve schools, introduce business principles to farming, conserve forests, and save Americans from what were believed to be the city's corrupting influences. Their aim was to create "a class of people representing the best of American traditions—people who have sufficient means of wholesome recreation, who maintain strong churches, who develop a satisfying home life and who are content with the work and the life of the farm."[12] In urban areas of New England, the

Lewis Hine photograph of a child laborer, one of many he took outside or inside the Amoskeag Millyard. Hine's caption reads, "This boy works in Mill No. 1, Amoskeag Mfg. Co., Manchester, N.H., May 26, 1909" (National Child Labor Committee Collection, Prints and Photographs Division, Library of Congress, LOT 7479, v. 2, no. 0793).

creation of such a class was compounded by the lack of open spaces and the number of people whose traditions seemed anything but American. With this obstacle in mind, progressives strove to eliminate monopolies and government corruption, pushed for education and English-language training for immigrants, supported the creation of parks and other recreational spaces, attempted to establish minimum wage standards and daily and weekly work-hour limitations, and hoped to abolish child labor. But for businesses such as Amoskeag, the fact that reformers were willing to use state and federal governments against corporations to accomplish these goals was the most worrisome part of the progressive movement.[13]

Robert P. Bass was among the most important of New Hampshire's progressive leaders. Born in 1873, Bass, a Republican, had represented the town of Peterborough in the state assembly for two terms (1905–1909), and in 1908 was elected to the state senate despite opposition from more established members of his own party. Bass fought for environmental causes, particularly relating to forestry, and against government corruption and the consolidation of corporate power. He was particularly proud of the direct primary bill, designed to make the selection of party candidates for public office more transparent by giving voters a role in the process.[14]

In 1910 Bass was elected to a two-year term as Governor of New Hampshire. Immediately he set out to bring extensive progressive reforms to the state, demanding the creation of permanent tax and public utilities commissions, better support of local schools by the state, full funding of state colleges, and state aid for highways, among many other programs and regulations. Of particular concern to Manchester's industries were Bass's calls for employer's liability, workmen's compensation, state-conducted factory inspections, a more effective Bureau of Labor, women's suffrage (which would have empowered a large part of Amoskeag's workforce), stronger child labor laws, and laws requiring the full disclosure of campaign contributions and expenditures and prohibiting corporate political contributions.[15] All three daily newspapers in Manchester opposed Bass and his progressive agenda.

With the dawn of the progressive movement, Amoskeag's future was far from assured. Competition from the American South made matters worse. By the early 20th century, Southern laborers worked for less money than their New England counterparts, giving Southern factories a distinct competitive advantage over the North. Moreover, Southern mills tended to be newer and, as a result, were more likely to be equipped with modern, automated looms.[16] Amoskeag shareholders were aware of the potential competitive disadvantage at least as early as 1886, when the company completed construction of the Jefferson Mill, a large mill building near the north end of the millyard. Even so, the company continued to increase capacity until 1922, perhaps hoping that market forces in the South would bring about wage parity between the two regions.[17]

The obsolescence of its machinery did become problematic after 1922, and scholars believe it to have contributed to the demise of the Amoskeag Manufacturing Company in the 1930s. However, between 1912 and 1916, Amoskeag's machinery was not obsolete. In fact, the construction and outfitting of the Bag Mill (1915) and the Coolidge Mill (1909, containing one-fifth of the company's cotton spindles), as well as several other buildings between 1890 and 1915, ensured that much of the equipment used by Amoskeag employees was relatively new during the period of this study.

Still, as a result of the South's advantages, the Amoskeag Manufacturing Company saw an overall decline in its operating profits—made even more pronounced after accounting for the company's dividend payments—in the first decade of the twentieth century. One solution to this problem came in May 1911, when the company was reorganized as a trust. Legally, this action allowed the company's shareholders to avoid paying taxes on their holdings. But it also coincided with a five-for-one stock split, which increased shareholder dividends by about one-and-a-half times and divided stocks into "common" and "preferred" categories. By selling common stock and holding on to preferred, shareholders could make back their investment while maintaining first claim to future profits, thereby protecting themselves against the expected decline of the New England textile industry.[18]

The reorganization of 1911 also affected employees of Amoskeag. In keeping with business practices of the period, Amoskeag attempted to reduce costs by increasing efficiency. One outcome was the establishment of a central employment office, which took much of the personnel decision-making power out of the hands of low-level managers and put it under the direct control of a single personnel department. This department created a system of employment records by which the company kept track of an employee's history, recording hirings, complaints, firings, union activities, blacklistings, and ethnicity. This allowed for increased top-down control over all aspects of the workforce.[19]

Amoskeag's need to control workers and costs meant that Manchester did not welcome most labor unions, particularly the Industrial Workers of the World. The IWW was founded in 1905 by socialists, radical union leaders, and others who felt that the American Federation of Labor, in the words of cofounder Eugene Debs, had "long since outgrown its usefulness" and had come under control of American capitalists.[20] The new union operated under the assumption that the interests of labor and capital were diametrically opposed. The IWW's advocacy for the overthrow of the wealthy and powerful and the redistribution of wealth to benefit laborers led some to brand the group anarchist, a charge that union leaders typically did not deny.

In January 1912, the IWW already was well known for its disruptive activities in the American West, particularly those relating to its defense of members' First Amendment rights. But the union's stature in New England grew almost overnight with the start of the so-called Bread and Roses Strike in Lawrence, Massachusetts. The strike lasted more than three months, involved more than 20,000 operatives of the American Woolen Company, and brought to light the impoverished living conditions of immigrant workers, the extreme discontent of the laboring class, and the willingness of state and local governments to protect corporations by violent means. Some observers even feared—or hoped— that the strike was the beginning of a revolution that would shake America's economic, political, and social foundations, particularly after its spread to Lowell. Every major industrial city in New England felt the strike's repercussions, including Manchester.

Amoskeag responded to the erosion of its power and the threats posed by both the progressives and the Industrial Workers of the World by expanding its welfare programs. Nationally, large companies from Ford Motor Company to General Electric implemented multiple forms of corporate benevolence for a variety of reasons. In Amoskeag's case, these reasons included a desire to ward off forced progressive reforms, Americanize an immigrant workforce, promote a common identity among workers, and control free time.[21] In theory at least, these last three goals, if successful, would encourage loyalty to Amoskeag and keep workers from becoming radicalized and joining groups such as the IWW. In fact, Amoskeag's welfare programs became known nationally as "The Finest Answer to I.W.W.-ism" thanks to publications such as *The Square Deal*, which in 1915 republished an article that had appeared under the same title in a New Bedford, Massachusetts newspaper the previous year.[22]

Though by no means the only one, baseball was among the most important and visible reminders of Amoskeag's commitment to welfare work. The company baseball team played against other local factories once per week from spring to autumn. The *Amoskeag Bulletin* and city newspapers published scores and other news relating to the team, and encouraged fans to turn out in support of their ball club. By sponsoring entertainment on Saturday afternoons, the Amoskeag Textile Club provided a diversion on the one half-day—besides Sundays, a day on which playing baseball still was illegal in New Hampshire— during which Amoskeag was closed. Plus, the game was promoted as being peculiarly American: it was believed to engender American democratic values, and was open to anyone regardless of ethnicity or class.

Admittedly, Amoskeag's baseball program was aimed at men more than women. This makes sense; as historian Andrea Tone has noted, men were considered to be more likely to unionize and strike than women.[23] But the Lawrence strike showed that women, too, were willing to strike, and could be quite effective in that role. As a result, baseball was but one of many welfare programs that Amoskeag initiated for its employees. Some, such as classes in cooking and domestic arts, were aimed at women and girls. Others, such as bowling and basketball leagues, programs promoting home ownership, and sponsorship of local Boy Scout troops, were meant for men and boys. Still others were aimed at both sexes, including English courses for foreign-born workers, opportunities to participate in theatrical productions, construction of a children's playground, and the organization of picnics and other outings.

Baseball could only be effective as a corporate-benevolence program if Amoskeag, through the Amoskeag Textile Club, maintained complete control over the game in Manchester. In this regard, Textile Field was especially important. The club was public in its assertions of ownership and control of the ballpark, particularly in its efforts to exclude the New England League, a class-B minor-league, from Manchester. Implicit in Amoskeag's efforts was the idea that the club had built a professional-caliber stadium—better than some stadiums then in use at the major-league level—for its use and that of other city teams. Accordingly, Amoskeag felt it had a responsibility to protect Manchester residents from the New England League, whose executives were believed to be neither reputable nor trustworthy, and whose owners were more interested in profit than in advancing Amoskeag's goals of controlling leisure time and Americanizing workers. Only when the New England League agreed to Amoskeag's terms would the Amoskeag Textile Club cooperate with the league and allow a team to call Textile Field home. The ultimate failure of this collaboration seemingly proved what Amoskeag officials had argued all along: that the New England League could not be trusted.

Textile Field and the associated pride in this state-of-the-art stadium was supposed to help Amoskeag in its effort to control its workers and the city of Manchester. Temporarily at least, the ballpark proved to be a fine-enough answer to IWW-ism and allowed Amoskeag to block the New England League from operating a team in Manchester. But ultimately, the company only delayed the inevitable march away from its unmitigated control over the city and its people.

1

A City on Edge

On January 12, 1912, approximately 500 weavers and spinners employed by the American Woolen Company in Lawrence, Massachusetts, received their first paychecks of the year. As a result of a new state law, their workweek had been reduced from 56 to 54 hours. But the workers, many of them Italian immigrants living at the edge of poverty, found that their weekly pay had been reduced as well. They walked off their jobs and encouraged other workers to join them. By invitation, the Industrial Workers of the World (IWW), or "Wobblies," sent Joseph J. Ettor to help organize the work stoppage. Within four days, the strikers reportedly numbered 15,000, clashes with police were common, and Governor Eugene Foss had called out the Massachusetts state militia to restore order.[1]

The Lawrence strike would have important consequences north of the state border in New Hampshire. If the strike expanded to cities such as Manchester, the profitability of the Amoskeag Manufacturing Company, which relied on low-wage employees in the production of cotton textiles, would be threatened. The participation of the IWW and ethnic minorities in that strike caused even more fear in the New Hampshire city, however. By the end of the year, Amoskeag faced protests, two new newspapers that opposed its policies, and threats to its dominance over state and local government. Initially, the company would turn to its police chief to help restore the peace.

Manchester residents kept close tabs on the Lawrence strike. Informal regional community networks, many of them ethnic in nature, meant that strikers in Lawrence were able to inform their compatriots in Manchester, Lowell, Fall River, and elsewhere about conditions through friends, families, and social clubs. Newspapers also carried accounts of the strike, though from a different perspective. For instance, most mainstream newspapers across the United States, including both the *Manchester Union* and the *Manchester Daily Mirror and American*, reported that the Lawrence strike was caused by Italians, Poles, Belgians, Syrians, and other foreign immigrants who did not speak English.[2]

By contrast, perhaps because it did represent an ethnic community within an English-speaking city, Manchester's French-language daily took a more sympathetic tone at the start of the strike. *L'Avenir National* informed readers about underreported stories such as the soup kitchens established by the IWW to help the starving families of Lawrence, and about movements growing on Manchester's West Side to raise money for the strikers.[3] A January 20 editorial suggests the reasons behind newspaper's position to that point:

> [Average wages of] as little as $6 per week, including those of supervising employees such as overseers and foremen, are not exactly what one can call "living wages."... [T]his is in a time when the cost of living is higher than it has ever been and in the time of year when needs are greatest. If these facts are true, the Lawrence strikers certainly deserve the public's sympathy. They merit more than sympathy, but also financial help to end the hunger that so cruelly spurs them on and to aid in the triumph of right and justice.[4]

On January 29, however, the Lawrence strike turned violent. That day, as an estimated 20,000 strikers clashed with police and militia troops, an unknown assailant shot and killed bystander Anna LoPizzo. Shortly thereafter, in an unrelated event, a Massachusetts National Guard soldier wielding a bayonet fatally stabbed 18-year-old John Rami.[5] Newspapers and city officials in Lawrence and throughout New England blamed the violence on Joseph Ettor and fellow IWW organizer and poet Arturo Giovannitti, claiming that their "fiery speeches" had incited the riot that led to LoPizzo's and Rami's deaths.[6]

With the escalation of violence in late January, *L'Avenir* turned against the Lawrence strikers. Following the lead of New England's powerful Catholic clergy, which dominated Manchester's sizeable French Canadian community, the newspaper labeled Ettor and the IWW as social agitators and terrorists, and claimed that as a result of the union's work, Lawrence had descended into a state of anarchy.[7]

Both the *Union* and the *Mirror* also weighed in with editorials concerning the strike. The *Mirror* proclaimed that the "great strike ... shows what happens when our immigrant importations run up against the American standard of living." The point, the *Mirror* argued, was that the disparity between living conditions in eastern Europe and the United States was too great, and new immigrants were unwilling to wait as long as had earlier groups to accumulate wealth and rise from the working class. The Lawrence strike was the inevitable result.[8]

The *Union* took a harsher tone than did the *Mirror*, railing against the foreign-born strikers in terms of law and order. "The state of Massachusetts will be the first to insist upon the restoration of order, of respect for and obedience to the law," its editor wrote. "If there are those among the new-comers to America who do not understand this fundamental principle, they must first be made to understand it and yield to it."[9]

Despite the generally negative press and the blame placed on Lawrence's immigrants, the work stoppage in Lawrence mobilized Manchester's working-class residents. On January 25, a committee representing the Manchester Cigarmakers' Union Local 192—which consisted primarily of Belgian-born employees of the 7-20-4 Cigar Factory adjacent to the Amoskeag Millyard, and represented perhaps the highest-paid artisans in Manchester—reported that it had found "much suffering [in Lawrence] from destitution because of the strike." Within five days the group reportedly had raised $560 to aid strikers' families, according to the *Mirror,* and was working to solicit aid from among Manchester's fifteen other labor unions.[10]

Employees at local shoe factories were at least as supportive as those at the cigar factory. On February 1 the *Mirror* reported that employees of the C. E. Green, George P. Craft, and H. B. Reed factories had "netted a good sum" for Lawrence workers, and that employees of another unnamed shoe factory had donated more than "the receipts in all other places."[11] This news came less than a week after 75 Greek operatives in the city's McElwain shoe factory walked off their jobs in protest of their ten-and-a-half-hour workdays.[12]

Unions and social clubs also hosted events to benefit the Lawrence strikers. The local Socialist Party sponsored a talk, entitled "The War of the Classes," at the hall of Club Jolliet by national socialist leader and former IWW member Ben Wilson, and raised an additional $25 to benefit strikers' families in Lawrence.[13] The Recreation Club, based in the French Canadian neighborhoods of the West Side, also raised money, sending $75 to Lawrence by the end of January.[14]

One of the most eagerly anticipated events was scheduled for the evening of February 1, when Joseph Ettor himself was to speak in Manchester at the invitation of the Cigarmakers' Union. Had the union's plans come to pass, Ettor would have spoken at the Polish Hall on Chestnut Street between 7:00 and 8:00, then at 8:15 he would have appeared for a speech at Stark Hall on the West Side. Once finished, he was to return to the Polish Hall for a third engagement.[15] Ettor never arrived in Manchester, however, for he, Arturo Giovannitti, and picketer Joseph Caruso were arrested in Lawrence for the murder of Anna LoPizzo.[16]

At the time of the Lawrence strike, Manchester was not a union-free city. But the list of unions operating in Manchester included no advocate for textile workers, and the Amoskeag Manufacturing Company, with more than 15,500 employees working 58 hours per week, was determined to maintain that condition. The company looked to Police Chief Michael J. Healy to maintain order.

Healy's position within the police department relied upon the support given him by the city's three-member Police Commission, and the commission often included representatives of, or at least sympathizers with, the Amoskeag Manufacturing Company. In 1912, for example, the commission consisted of Thomas R. Varick, Peter A. Farrell, and Edward B. Woodbury. Farrell was a clerk for a business at 831 Elm Street, but Varick and Woodbury both had ties to Amoskeag. Woodbury, the Commission's chairman, worked for the company as a clerk. Varick, meanwhile, was a well-respected business owner who, in the 1890s, had leased land from Amoskeag and transformed it into Varick Park, a multipurpose sporting venue favored by track, bicycle, and baseball enthusiasts. Amoskeag's Boston-based treasurer, Frederick C. Dumaine, kept close contact with Varick and Healy, among others, to understand "what was going on in Manchester."[17] Clearly, Amoskeag was in a position to influence the activities of the city's police chief.

Police Chief Michael J. Healy in the 1890s. Healy, a lawyer by trade, worked on behalf of the Amoskeag Manufacturing Company to keep law and order in Manchester. In the process, he particularly targeted the Greek community (courtesy Manchester [New Hampshire] Historic Association).

Chief Healy, the man in whom the commission entrusted authority over the city's police force, was born in County Kerry, Ireland, on March 28, 1857. At the age of six, he moved with his family to Manchester, where his father found work as a laborer. After graduating from Manchester High School, the younger Healy attended the College of the Holy Cross in Worcester and, subsequently, Boston College, earning a law degree. He returned to Manchester, and by 1888 had joined the Manchester Police Department as a sergeant. The 1892 city directory lists Healy as "Marshal." By 1895, he was the city's first Chief of Police.[18]

During his 49 years as a member of the Manchester Police Department, Healy actively promoted a strict agenda of law and order. One of his more controversial tactics for controlling criminal behavior was the so-called "Healy Method" or "Healy License System," which he perfected in the 1890s when the sale of alcohol within city limits was illegal. Healy allowed the sale of liquor, controlling it by issuing monthly summonses for saloonkeepers to appear in the city's police court. With the chief often acting as prosecutor, the court would find the saloonkeeper guilty of selling alcohol and levy a fine. In this way, saloonkeepers could sell alcohol, the city received a steady income, and Healy appeared to be enforcing the law. In one example, between April 1895 and March 1897, storekeeper Timothy Lynch was taken to court monthly and fined a total of $1,578.54. Through this method, estimated the *Union*, the city collected about $60,000 in fines each year during the 1890s. Healy continued this practice into the 1930s, except during Prohibition, bringing in about $100,000 per year in fines.[19]

Healy also tracked specific immigrant groups in his enforcement of the law, particularly the Greek immigrants who began to arrive in the city after 1900. Between July 1, 1911, and June 30, 1912, police department log books list 2,180 incidents investigated by Manchester police officers. In most of those, officers did not list the ethnicity of either the suspect or the complainant. On July 21, for example, the police log states, "Man exposes self to two women"—records indicate no ethnicity. However, in forty-nine cases, particularly in those involving violence or robbery or where an accuser's credibility was doubted, police recorded the ethnicity of those involved: 30 Greeks, seven Poles, three "Chinaman," two Italians, two Jews, and one each Russian, "Turk," "Scotch," Belgian, and German. The record indicates that "Polish women" had items stolen from them, that a "Chinaman fell and broke his hip," and that "a Greek" was "exposing his person" to women about 5:00 every afternoon. Despite the preponderance of English, Irish, and particularly French surnames in the police record, the police never identified anyone by those ethnic labels—on July 1, 1911, for example, Fred Lasarge's alleged drunkenness and report of being the victim of a hit-and-run was not accompanied by a description of Lasarge's ethnicity.

While no complete studies of Manchester poverty rates in 1912 are known to have been undertaken, researchers including Daniel Creamer and Charles Coulter (1939) and Tamara Hareven (1982) have noted the low wages that existed in Manchester, particularly among the large numbers of part-time employees who worked for Amoskeag. Police records support this likelihood. More than one-third of all police investigations in the year ending June 30, 1912, involved robbery: animals, clothing, food and milk, and money in particular. Not all cases of robbery were driven by necessity; for example, in one instance the police report indicates that a group of boys, upon seeing a police officer, immediately fled, and in the process dropped a bag containing six empty bottles of the soft drink Moxie. Yet reports in which "Greeks" were said to "be stealing wood and coal," or in which bottles of milk—in one case, a saucer of milk left for a cat—were stolen from local porches, were all too common.[20]

A government study of the Lawrence strike published in 1912 also provides a glimpse into Manchester's poverty and nutritional issues. In 1908 and 1910, about one-fifth of all children born in Manchester died before their first birthday (212 and 193 per 1,000 births, respectively). In 1909, that number exceeded one-quarter (263 per 1,000). In 1910 the city's mortality rate for children five years and under was 69.2 per 1,000; in fact, children under five years old accounted for more than 40 percent of all deaths in the entire city. Among the 35 American cities listed in the report, all with a population of 50,000 or more, Manchester typically ranked among the worst—and in some cases, absolute worst—in these categories.[21]

Considering the poverty in Manchester, Healy and the managers of the Amoskeag Manufacturing Company had reason to worry about possible social unrest. That so many of the city's residents were eastern and southern Europeans also appears to have been of concern. According to stereotypes that seemed to be reinforced by accounts of the Lawrence strikes, groups of poor, ethnic minorities with little to lose and little understanding of the supposedly leveling effects of American democracy were dangerous. Americanized immigrants and children of immigrants, they believed, would follow orders and accept the existing power structures. However, they feared that the radical socialist movements associated with the Industrial Workers of the World were sure to appeal to the "less civil" peoples of the Mediterranean.

In fact, Healy may already have believed that the city's Greek population fit that profile. One incident less than seven years earlier surely made him wary of the Greeks: the baseball riot of 1905.

Manchester's Fifth Ward encompassed less than 135 acres in 1905, but it may have been the city's most ethnically diverse section. Within a few blocks one might encounter people speaking any one of perhaps a dozen languages, including German, Polish, Romanian, Russian, Lithuanian, Italian, French, Greek, Yiddish, and English (albeit sometimes with an Irish brogue). The most sizable of the groups, and particularly the second- and third-generation Irish, tended to congregate in their own neighborhoods.

Well-established ethnic groups generally stayed away from recently arrived ones. Greeks, in particular, were objects of distrust and scorn. Greek immigrants became targets of more established working-class residents in 1903, when a small number of Greek shoe workers came to Manchester from Massachusetts as strikebreakers. Worse, shortly after their arrival, the strikebreakers themselves went on strike, drawing the attention of Chief Healy and the Manchester Police Department.[22]

The customs and activities of the young, male-dominated, Greek-speaking group also came under public scrutiny. According to one local newspaper, members of the city's newest immigrant group "insist on obstructing the sidewalk in the neighborhood where they live, and pedestrians who are obliged to go that way deem it necessary to walk out into the street to get by." Reportedly, women were at particular risk, for Greek men allegedly "insist on grabbing hold of them and hugging them. Some have been so bold as to kiss them. Girls on their way to work in the shoe shops have been menaced by them, and some will not go to work without escort."[23]

But cross-cultural encounters were inevitable, particularly in the city's parks during the summer months. Thus, on a hot July evening in 1905, Nicholas Pantackos and John Koutripos sat with other members of Manchester's growing Greek community on Park Common. Nearby, a group of English-speaking men with Irish surnames played baseball. The Greeks had little interest in or understanding of the game; they wished to keep to themselves and relax after a day at work in the shoe factories.

Unfortunately, Park Common was not a large park, and as they played, the ballplayers twice hit the immigrants with baseballs. Although these actions could have been accidental, a reporter for the *Union* implied that the Greek men had been hit on purpose. When the Greek immigrants "remonstrated with their assailants," one of the ballplayers threw a ball back at Koutripos, hitting him in the mouth and breaking a tooth. Thus began a full-scale riot. One ballplayer hit Pantackos over the head with a baseball bat, and when other Greeks pulled out their knives, "their opponents made use of clubs and bricks with telling effect. The crowd began to gather and everybody got into the fight. Anyone who looked like a Greek was smashed by the mob."

Soon the combatants and observers totaled a reported 2,000 people. The mob chased the Greek immigrants into nearby homes, from which some were able to toss bricks and other objects down onto the attackers. An entire squad of police officers arrived on the scene to restore order, arresting several people and causing the remainder to disperse. In this instance, the police were "inclined to believe that the Greeks are not entirely to blame in the trouble," and the next day charged only two participants, John Sullivan and William Sweeney, with crimes.[24]

But the real threat—the one that may have made Healy take notice of the Greek community—came the following evening. That night, 150 Greek immigrants marched to the common and sat on the grass, daring anyone they met to attack them. One even threatened to contact other Greek immigrants working in Lowell and Lawrence and invite them to Manchester. This show of Greek nationalism in a city of immigrants was particularly dangerous to Amoskeag, which demanded that employees—many of them immigrants—be loyal to the company rather than to a particular cultural group. In the end, Chief Healy sent a squad of police officers to the scene to disperse the Greek protestors, arresting one man in the process for obstructing the sidewalk.[25]

By 1912, Amoskeag and the city's shoe factories were heavily dependent on laborers from eastern and southern Europe. Healy could not keep immigrants from coming to the city, but he could stop other activities that seemingly threatened the peace. Thus, when he learned that the IWW would send other Lawrence strike organizers to speak in Manchester in Joseph Ettor's place on February 1, the Chief of Police was determined to stop the proceedings. In the coming weeks, Healy would witness union tactics that were not unlike those that the IWW had employed in Fresno, Spokane, and elsewhere in the West. Healy's own response, while certainly less severe, was not much different from the actions of his Western counterparts. In the process of battling the IWW in Manchester, however, he would help to instigate the New Hampshire "Free Speech Movement" of 1912. This movement stood as a direct threat to the power Amoskeag and Healy wielded over the city.

2

The Fight for Free Speech

Ora Pearl McGill arrived in Manchester for the first time on January 4, 1912. The seventeen-year-old Iowa native known as Pearl was in town to speak about labor issues, probably as part of an effort to raise money for striking button-makers in Muscatine, Iowa. After her talk she ran into a local printer, Jesse Markee, who introduced himself as a relative of hers through her mother's family. "It nearly took me off my feet," she wrote of the encounter. The two dined together and spoke about Iowa and family. They probably also spoke about labor issues, for Markee was an organizer and active member of the International Typographical Union of North America Local 152, an American Federation of Labor-affiliated organization that had managed to unionize most of the city's printing employees. But while McGill enjoyed her dinner with Markee, and though she found New Hampshire "beautiful" with "lots of pine forests," in her brief time in New England she found difficulty in acclimating to the region. "I don't like the people out here very well," she wrote her parents and siblings. "They are funny."[1]

McGill's path to Manchester began in 1910 when, at the age of sixteen, she left her parents' farm for Muscatine to earn money for teacher training school. Soon after her arrival there, factory workers went on strike, and she found herself serving as recording secretary for the Juvenile Sewers and Carriers Union. McGill later was recruited by the Women's Trade Union League to publicize and raise funds for the union, and traveled to Chicago, New York, and eventually Boston for that cause. She still hoped to teach one day. But in the meantime she became a dedicated organizer and a socialist, vowing to her parents that "as long as I live people will know something about the class war, unless it is settled before I die, and I would die for the just cause of starving out of work people of my Nation, the Working Class, if necessary."[2]

Soon after her first trip to Manchester, Pearl McGill's life took another turn. With the start of the Bread and Roses Strike on January 12, McGill made her way to Lawrence. Thanks to her socialist credentials and experience in Muscatine, she was enlisted by IWW leader Elizabeth Gurley Flynn and others to help organize the movement there. Owing to both competition and deep philosophical differences between the Wobblies and the American Federation of Labor, with which the Women's Trade Union League was affiliated, the AFL revoked the young Iowan's membership for her involvement in the Lawrence strike. Even so, she sustained her fundraising efforts for the Muscatine button workers when not working on behalf of the Lawrence strikers. She also continued to hone her speaking skills at events throughout New England, most notably in a talk before an estimated crowd of 1,100 people at a Baptist church in Boston.[3]

Left to right: Pearl McGill, Elodre Coppens, and William Trautmann in Lowell, early 1912. McGill made several appearances in Manchester during the Lawrence Bread and Roses Strike, helping to touch off the Free Speech fights when Chief Michael Healy denied her and two others their right to free speech. Trautmann, a co-founder of the Industrial Workers of the World, kept close watch on events in Manchester from Lowell (Bain Collection, Prints & Photographs Division, Library of Congress, LC-B2-1317-12).

2. The Fight for Free Speech

Pearl McGill's involvement in the Lawrence strike led her back to Manchester in February 1912, this time to raise awareness of and funds to support the Lawrence strike. When Joseph Ettor and Arturo Giovannitti were arrested for the death of Anna LoPizzo at the end of January, Ettor was about to embark on a one-day, three-engagement tour of Manchester to speak about recent events in Lawrence. After Ettor's arrest, the IWW chose McGill and two other strike leaders, Robert Laurence and Thomas Halliday, to travel to Manchester in his place.

The mere announcement of IWW-affiliated speakers in Manchester motivated Chief Healy to intervene personally. Acting in the best interests of the Amoskeag Manufacturing Company, Healy worked to control free speech—and, by extension, Manchester's workers. Therefore, he barred McGill and her compatriots from speaking in the city. Healy's actions not only led to the creation of the New Hampshire Free Speech Alliance, an IWW-inspired statewide movement to protect worker free-speech rights, but also to calls for Healy's removal and questions about Amoskeag's influence over Manchester's police department.

Manchester's Belgian cigarmakers were undoubtedly among the most radical of Manchester's immigrants, and their union's position supporting the Lawrence strikers seems obvious given that the Lawrence Local 20 chapter of the IWW, founded in 1906, had held its meetings in that city's Franco-Belgian Hall even before the strike.[4] Nevertheless, prior to the deaths of Anna LoPizzo and John Rami in Lawrence, apparently no one in Manchester questioned the cigarmakers' plans to sponsor fundraising events and speeches for the Lawrence strikers.

On the morning of February 1, Joseph Ettor's arrest and heightened tensions in Lawrence caused Chief Healy to summon John Kubilia, the janitor of the Polish Club on Chestnut Street, and Gerard Pellens, president of the Recreation Club which had rented Stark Hall to the cigar makers, to his office. Reportedly, neither man realized for what purpose the Cigarmakers' Union had rented the halls, despite the coverage that the pending events had received in the *Mirror* and *L'Avenir National*. Healy told Pellens that "Manchester was a peaceful city, that he wanted no trouble, and that he was going to send two officers over to the hall" that night in case the Wobblies pressed forward with their meeting. To Kubilia, the chief suggested that he "not let the hall." When Kubilia responded that he already had taken their money and could be sued, Healy told him, "No matter. If they sue you they will have to sue me." After thinking about the issue, the janitor agreed not to rent the hall.[5]

When McGill, Laurence, and Halliday arrived in Manchester, members of the Cigarmakers' Union met them at the train station and took them to the

Polish Club. There, a police officer informed them that their talk had been cancelled. When the group attempted to organize an open-air meeting across the street, the officer, feeling outnumbered, called to the police station for help. By the time Chief Healy arrived with several more officers, Laurence had started speaking and refused to stop. Two officers confronted Laurence, one of them telling the Massachusetts resident, "You are an interloper, you have no right here. You are a foreigner." Subsequently, they arrested him for obstructing the sidewalk.[6]

Unsure what to do next, the crowd milled around in front of the hall until Manchester resident Fred Wolf, a New Hampshire organizer of the Industrial Workers of the World and a member of the Socialist Labor Party, suggested that the meeting reconvene at a shop on Lowell Street. The group filled the room to capacity, but Healy and the several police officers who followed informed the group that they did not have the proper permits to gather there, even though the shop constituted private property. The leaders then engaged in a public dialogue with Healy, asking him whether or not the citizens of Manchester had a right to be heard. "I am the citizens," Healy was said to have responded. He also told McGill directly that as an Iowan, she was an "interloper, pure and simple," with no right to speak in Manchester. When McGill asked the chief whether or not they could collect donations on the streets in a manner similar to that of the Salvation Army at Christmas and Thanksgiving, Healy said that they could, and told her that canvassing the city in this manner likely would raise more money than would a mass meeting. Healy also permitted Wolf to read a call for assistance from the Lawrence strike leaders and to collect money from the crowd. When the organizers collected eleven dollars, but wanted fifteen, the chief denied their request to read the document again, and instead contributed four dollars from his own pocket. Finally, the group voted to adjourn the meeting. Only McGill dissented, complaining that it was the first time in her life that she had been denied the right to speak in public.[7]

After this confrontation, Healy arrived at Stark Hall to inform those who had gathered there that the meeting had been called off. Halliday and Wolf, meanwhile, went to the police station to check on Laurence. The night watchman at the station refused them access to their comrade, alleging that the prisoner wanted neither bail nor visitors. (Laurence later denied this and claimed that during the night, a police officer entered his cell and beat him with a rubber hose.) Next, they called on the local newspapers, issuing a statement in which they accused Healy of acting as a "czar" and of violating the group's constitutional right of free speech—something that had not been done even in Lawrence, they claimed. They also spoke with Healy on February 2, threatening to obtain an injunction preventing him from stopping their next meeting. Healy responded, "There is nothing to stop you from getting such an injunction." But, he asked, who would enforce it?[8] With these actions, the New Hampshire Free Speech Alliance was born.

The Free Speech movement in New Hampshire mirrored the IWW's passive-resistance efforts in the American West. In the years before the Lawrence strike, the group's speakers often took positions on street corners in Western cities, the "seditious, unpatriotic, and threating" tones of their speeches alarming local business and political leaders. The street-corner oration, in fact, became one of the union's most effective means of promoting IWW goals and recruiting new members. Then, in Montana in 1909, in response to the group's unionizing activities, the Missoula city council banned soapbox orators from speaking in the streets. Union members defied the ban and, in the name of "free speech," set out to fill local jails, clog court dockets, and otherwise tax the government institutions assigned with maintaining law and order. This scene played itself out in about thirty cities over the next seven years. In Spokane, Washington, for example, after police arrested one protestor for speaking without a permit, the union initiated around-the-clock street meetings. Before long, "the city jail held every local IWW leader," and more than 400 Wobblies were imprisoned before the conflict's end, taxing the city's budget and infrastructure.[9]

With each attempt at passive resistance, the IWW found reactions from local police, government officials, and even mobs to be more and more violent. In public places, IWW representatives were jeered or beaten. Jails could be even less safe. In Spokane over a 110-day period, 334 of the 400 Wobblies in prison were treated in the local hospital a total of more than 1,600 times. In Fresno, California, where no statute actually forbade street speaking, the local police chief arrested IWW speakers anyway, denying them adequate clothing, heat, or food, and in one case subjecting jailed prisoners to a half hour of 150-pound-pressurized water from a fire department's pressure hose.[10]

In the minds of IWW leaders, violent displays such as these only aided their cause. According to one editorial in the IWW newspaper *The Industrial Worker*, the Free Speech Movement signified "a distrust of legal methods of obtaining redress for wrongs inflicted upon" workers. In their protests, workers "do not stand upon their constitutional rights," for, according to the newspaper, they "have no rights save those which their organized power enforces." They also distrusted jury trials, because "one of the prerequisites for jury service is property holding and property owners as a class are opposed to the proletaire." But they sought jury trials nevertheless, usually through means of peaceful resistance, because of their expense, as "the tenderest spot of Capitalism [is] the pocketbook." Ultimately, the IWW saw "propertiless toilers" as creating their own system of morals and ethics, rules and regulations, separate from those of the owners of capital.[11] For good reason, then, New England mill owners came to see the IWW as a threat—just as IWW leaders hoped they would.

More than anyone, William D. "Big Bill" Haywood personified the union. At five foot eleven and 240 pounds, with a scarred and pockmarked face and sometimes wearing a patch over his missing right eye, Haywood, the forty-three-year-old national leader of the IWW, was an imposing figure who had earned a reputation as a fierce opponent and effective agitator. He had been active in organizing miners' strikes in the American West before co-founding the IWW in 1905. Two years later, in a nationally celebrated trial in which Clarence Darrow defended him, Haywood was acquitted in the murder of former Idaho governor Frank Steunenberg.[12] He arrived in Lawrence on January 24 to great fanfare in the media, and according to the *Union* was seen in Manchester "incognito from time to time" during the week before February 5, "directing the campaign for the sympathizers."[13] Chief Healy himself, in defending his activities against the IWW, later stated, "Manchester is not ready, I believe, to welcome men like Bill Hayward [sic]."[14]

In the days after their first showdown with the Manchester police, the New Hampshire Free Speech Alliance set to work. On February 3, two organizers met with Mayor E. C. Smith, requesting the right to hold meetings "in the interest of the Lawrence strikers."[15] The mayor deferred to the Police Commission, angering Fred Wolf. "I want to be understood on that point I make no threat," he told the mayor. "This fight is for free speech and free assemblage. The chief of police has taken a position against these things and his action invites a protest and a fight to a finish, and we intend to make a protest and a fight that will go to the finish even if it brings on a condition like that in Spokane in 1910 and the one in Lawrence today."[16]

In a letter describing conditions in Lawrence, Pearl McGill told her parents, "you can't believe what the papers say about this strike, for they don't belong to us. They belong to our enemy, the Capitalist Class."[17] Even in Manchester, local newspapers worked against the Wobblies. The *Union* regularly printed the home addresses of IWW and alliance operatives and sympathizers who lived in Manchester. The *Mirror* went so far as to publish a statement to the effect that the local police department and the city's newspapers "work in harmony," and defended the newspaper's policy of voluntarily withholding stories from the public.[18]

For their parts, McGill, the Wobblies, and the Free Speech Alliance seemed to take delight in manipulating local reporters using the establishment's fears of Bill Haywood. In one instance, the Cigarmakers' Union convinced Chief Healy to allow McGill to organize a daytime meeting to raise money for

Muscatine button makers. When covering the meeting, a *Union* reporter noticed that Haywood's name was mentioned by a group of attendees, and that one of the men at the meeting resembled Haywood. When he asked McGill if Haywood was in attendance, McGill claimed that he was, and introduced a man to the reporter as "Mr. Haywood." After talking with him for a while, the man left and McGill told the reporter that that had not been Haywood, a fact that the presumed Bill Haywood later confirmed. When the reporter asked for the man's name, he answered, "I haven't any," and refused to speak any more.[19]

Little is known about Thomas Halliday, one of the men who accompanied McGill to Manchester to speak in Joseph Ettor's place in early February. *The Industrial Worker* described him as a "quiet, blue-eyed weaver, 30 years of age, an Englishman by birth; but in this country since a mere child." In mid–1912 he, Haywood, and six other people would be indicted for conspiracy, Halliday's crime being to write a proclamation on behalf of the Lawrence strikers that indicated their willingness to "rise in armed revolt against their oppressors if the present state of affairs is allowed to continue in Lawrence."[20]

On February 17, despite his work in Massachusetts, Halliday returned to Manchester to join in an IWW-style street-corner protest. During the day, the New Hampshire Free Speech Alliance distributed pamphlets advertising that "the suppression of free speech and assemblage, the brutality of the police department, the powers of officialdom used against the working class, the real reason for suppressing the established rights of free speech and assemblage would be discussed by prominent speakers, including a leader of the Lawrence strikers."[21] At about 7:00, before what the IWW claimed was a crowd of 4,000 people, but which local newspapers merely described as "very large," Halliday, Fred Wolf, and five other men arrived at the corner of Mechanic and Elm Street. About thirty police officers met them there.

As protestor George Howie placed a chair on the corner, and with Healy watching, Captain Thomas Steele ordered the police to form a line separating the demonstrators from the crowd. When Fred Wolf climbed onto the chair in an effort to speak, the chief sent two patrolmen to arrest him. After Wolf, John Burke stepped onto the chair and began to explain the principles of the IWW, but was likewise arrested. Lorenz Kierdorf, Nathan Jacobs, and John Hock also took turns on the chair and ended up in police custody. Finally, Thomas Halliday climbed onto the chair and, after complaining that the city resembled Czarist Russia more than the United States, was arrested. The chair promptly disappeared, and when others stepped forward to speak, the police dispersed the crowd.[22]

Healy charged the group of speakers with disorderly conduct. Rather than request the full penalty permitted under the law, he asked the court "that a fine be imposed that would show the men that while they had some rights there were others that they did not have." Each was released on $300 bail, but eventually fined $15.39, and required to post $100 bonds "to keep the peace."[23] For good measure, the *Union* published the home addresses and occupations of the six men as well as those of Sebastian Gartner, Charles Hoffmeister, Sylvester de Nutte, and Julius de Cook, the four men who paid the protestors' bail.[24] It also carried a threat from John J. Balam, who claimed to have taken part in IWW protests in Spokane and Fresno and was now in Lawrence. "I can tell you," said Balam, referring to the IWW's Western efforts, "that those demonstrations will be mild [compared] to what will take place in that little New Hampshire mill city if the authorities see fit to refuse us the privilege of speaking on the street corners."[25]

Healy, for his part, told the press, "We are not going to have any disturbances here if we can help it, and we are going to try mighty hard to prevent trouble. The people here are all satisfied and do not want to strike." In response, *The Industrial Worker* backed Balam's threats, stating that Healy's actions are "more likely to start trouble—such as flooding the jail of Manchester and forcing the right of free speech." The IWW promised that, once some of its Western endeavors were out of the way, "we will send some men to Manchester to see what manner of a place it is that can boast that the people are all satisfied. It surely must be Heaven on Earth and that is what we are looking for."[26]

In the meantime, the street-corner protest provided impetus for organizers to turn the Free Speech Alliance of New Hampshire into a formal organization. On February 19 the group met to elect officers and appoint a committee to visit local churches and labor organizations in an effort to gain support for "the constitutional right of free speech and peaceable assemblage." Members planned to issue a nationwide appeal for funds to finance their campaign and to take their grievances directly to the Manchester Police Commission and Governor Robert Bass. They also resolved

> that we, the Free Speech Alliance of Manchester, inspired by the heroic struggles of our forefathers against oppression and tyranny, do hereby protest against the czar-like action of Chief Healy. We call the attention of all thinking people to the fact that the Chief Healy action is a return to the brute principle that "Might is Right." And we call upon all patriotic citizens to arouse in their right, and in their might of unconquerable numbers, and show Chief Healy that the constitutional rights of American citizens must not and shall not be abridged.[27]

Just a week before the Free Speech street-corner protest, Healy began to see signs that the IWW was disrupting businesses in Manchester. When Greek operatives at the McElwain shoe factory went on strike, the police cracked down on them violently. The strikers, who had adopted the IWW technique of picketing by this time, protested to local media, complaining that police were treating them as anarchists and depriving them of their civil rights.[28] The IWW, meanwhile, claimed to be leading the strike, which, they asserted, had involved 500 workers—far more than the handful reported in local newspapers. In fact, events in Manchester were so worrisome to state officials that the Adjutant General of the New Hampshire National Guard traveled to Lawrence to study the methods by which Massachusetts troops kept order.[29]

Despite such worries, the mayor's office did grant a permit to the Free Speech Alliance to hold a legal "mass meeting" on February 23. Perhaps 10,000 people gathered on Hanover Common and stood in the cold winter air to listen to Pearl McGill, Alliance president John P. Burke, and Massachusetts Socialist Party secretary James F. Carey speak about the Lawrence strike, and about socioeconomic and power inequality among the classes in general. Burke opened the meeting by indicating its purpose: to solicit aid for the Lawrence strikers. McGill followed Burke, initially drawing a distinction between Manchester's workers and employers in her remark that the wintry common "seemed hardly like the place that would be chosen by the officers of the mills to announce an increase of wages from." But other than that comment, she concentrated the majority of her speech on working conditions in Lawrence: the riches that were promised to induce immigrants to leave Europe, the low wages that met them in Lawrence, and the rampant malnutrition among children.

Carey spoke last. In a speech noted for its wit and satire, he implored workers to advocate for their rights peacefully and at the ballot box. "My friends," he told the crowd, "every time you get a policeman's club over your head, you are getting the echo of your own vote." But Carey specifically asked the crowd not to blame Healy for recent problems. "The police do what they are told to do. They have power because you vote it to them." He also criticized judges and condemned the two major political parties, stating that the problems in Lawrence can be traced to both Democrats and Republicans and that both parties exist to protect the mill owners, not the workers. Finally, he concluded with an explanation of the principles of the Socialist Party, which promised to protect workers' interests.

At the end of the night, the group had collected $108.31 for the Lawrence strikers. Just prior to the event, the police did investigate a complaint, apparently from Amoskeag employees, "that a crowd of Greeks insult the girls while returning from work at 6 o'clock evenings on Granite Street."[30] Yet Healy stayed away from the mass meeting, and sent only three plainclothes policemen to observe the proceedings.[31] Bill Haywood claimed victory in Manchester, stating, "This is only one more feather in the hat of the IWW in the free speech campaign. Our middle name is Free Speech and we have won every fight so far." *The Industrial Worker* concurred, noting that "the winning of the free speech fight with such ease shows that the authorities of the eastern cities have some slight brain power," unlike the "breed of animal that infests the official chairs upon the Pacific Coast."[32]

With that, Manchester's newspapers went silent with regard to the Free Speech Alliance. Generally, since the media tended to support Amoskeag's interests, they ignored potential conflicts to those interests, including ones that would undermine Amoskeag's anti-union agenda. Therefore, the Alliance would not be heard from again—at least not in print media—until the end of April.

3

Finding a Voice

At the time of the Lawrence strike, the Industrial Workers of the World sold a poster parodying the capitalist system; it was available by mail through *The Industrial Worker*. The poster showed a human pyramid topped with a bag of money. Below the money is a level signifying kings, rulers, and politicians with the caption, "We rule you." The next level down represents religion: "We fool you." Beneath that, the military is denoted next to the words, "We shoot at you." Next is a group of men and women drinking and feasting around the table; they represented the bourgeoisie, and were accompanied by the caption, "We eat for you." Finally, holding up the entire pyramid is a group of laborers—some suffering, some in revolt—with the captions, "We work for all—We feed all."[1]

If anything had become clear to the most radical of Manchester's pro-labor forces by early February, it was that the IWW poster may have described conditions in their own city. Certainly Manchester's newspapers, police force, and government in general seemed to exist to protect the capitalist system. From their perspective the managers of Amoskeag controlled city government, and through Chief Michael Healy, the police. The police, in turn, kept workers from organizing and expressing their discontent with social and economic conditions in Manchester. Religion, most notably the many churches that had benefitted greatly from Amoskeag's generosity, served the status quo by asking workers to remain patient and docile, in return for which they would "inherit the earth" in the afterlife. And most disturbingly, Manchester's newspapers seemed to occupy their own level as pillars that actively supported Amoskeag, Chief Healy, religious institutions, and the bourgeoisie.

Although they did not agree with the political aims or overall social interpretations of groups such as the IWW, members of both the American Federation of Labor and New Hampshire's burgeoning progressive movement also saw

Manchester's corporations, media, and police chief as impediments to practical reform. Progressives felt that only by altering portions of social, political, and economic systems could a working-class revolution be avoided. They hoped to build a new political party that could facilitate those reforms, but were frustrated by their inability to convey their message to a larger audience. Union advocates in Manchester likewise worked toward reform, but they found their efforts blocked by many of the same elements that obstructed both radicals and progressives, most notably the pro–Amoskeag newspapers which promoted the idea that Manchester's economic fortunes depended entirely on Amoskeag's.

Thus, as the Lawrence strike waged on, three separate movements sought a platform from which to amplify their calls for reform. Representing the American Federation of Labor and the progressive movement, respectively, both printer Jesse Markee and Governor Robert Bass initiated plans to start new newspapers in Manchester. The most radical reformers, on the other hand, continued to press their case against the establishment through the New Hampshire Free Speech Alliance's battle with Chief Healy, despite the fact that no pro-reform newspaper yet existed in the city.

By early February, many observers saw the Lawrence strike less as a simple work stoppage than a revolution, an attempt at social upheaval directed by the IWW at the behest of southern and eastern Europeans. After a trip to Lawrence, an official immigration inspector from Manchester summarized his observations: "Everybody now recognizes that this strike is led and dominated by the Socialist leaders of the state and nation ... [and that it is] part of the worldwide revolution being built and solidified by socialism."[2] Manchester's weekly French-language newspaper *Le Canado-Americain* concurred, claiming that the labor movement in Lawrence "is no longer a strike[,] it is a revolution" that espoused the principles of socialism and anarchy.[3] But perhaps to insulate Manchester from broader trends, local media still tried to downplay actual events. At various times throughout February newspapers claimed, erroneously, that up to half of the Lawrence strikers had returned to work. Moreover, in their reports the strike had developed into "a racial fight" between loyal English-speaking operatives and an un–American "foreign element."[4]

To some extent, newspapers were correct to suggest that events in Lawrence had taken on an ethnic or "racial" tone. Even though both Joseph Ettor and Bill Haywood asked workers to ignore ethnic affiliations and work together as a socioeconomic class, the IWW actually did organize workers by nationality—each ethnic group met separately and elected its own representatives to the general strike committee.[5] This probably suited the strikers well, for conditions in the Lawrence mills had promoted ethnic competition. As historian Ardis Cameron has shown, in its employment practices the American

3. Finding a Voice

The Rev. Thomas Chalmers and family, around the time of the Bread and Roses Strike. Chalmers, Pastor for the First Congregational Church in Manchester, became one of the city's leading progressive voices during and after the Lawrence unrest (courtesy Manchester [New Hampshire] Historic Association).

Woolen Company "sought to exacerbate ethnic divisions in an attempt to undercut unity on the shop floor and prevent unionization" by controlling their numbers on the shop floor and even by threatening to replace workers with ones from other ethnic groups.[6] Thus if revolution did come to Manchester, Lawrence provided a plausible blueprint that workers could follow.

The belief that the troubles in Lawrence were entirely ethnic in origin, however, merely played into popularly held stereotypes based in the idea that a person's character was determined by the environment into which he or she was born. For instance, in mid–February, after a visit to Lawrence, The Rev. Thomas Chalmers described this perspective at a service at Manchester's First Congregational Church:

> New England is an industrial section. Its industries and its climate call for the rugged races of northern Europe or Canada. It is sheer cruelty to encourage the gardening, vine-growing population of the soft, mild climate of the Mediterranean to emigrate to mill centers in New England, with the promise of increasing their happiness. They are bound to suffer, and their suffering will fill them with discontent and wrath.

Chalmers, to be fair, was more hopeful about Manchester. "We have an unquestionably better and more intelligent class of labor and less wretchedness," he claimed.[7] Nevertheless, beliefs such as this about ethnicity and labor, repeated and expounded upon in editorials published in Manchester's daily and weekly newspapers, concealed the true nature of the Lawrence strike. Quite simply, Lawrence workers—for that matter, most New England textile workers—were underpaid, many to the point of living well below the poverty line. Poles, Syrians, Italians, and Lithuanians were the most poorly paid of Lawrence's textile workers. But this situation was not inevitable. Factory managers themselves—not the workers' "natural" predilection to work—created pay disparity among different groups, even after these groups were enticed to move to New England by promises of high wages.[8] In fact, Chalmers believed that despite ethnic tensions, employer-employee relations could be strengthened through direct communication and understanding, and that less-radical unions such as the American Federation of Labor—but emphatically not the IWW—could help bring about better communications.[9]

Despite the ethnic divide, the tide of public opinion eventually did turn against capital and in favor of the Lawrence strikers. On February 10, after adopting a proposal made by an Italian socialist who had seen the tactic employed in Europe, strikers began sending their children to be cared for by families in New York City. That day, nurse Margaret Sanger arrived in Lawrence to personally escort 119 children to New York, where newspapers reported first-hand accounts of their impoverished and undernourished appearances. A week later, another 150 departed from Lawrence, some destined for New York, some for Barre, Vermont, and some for Manchester. On March 9, after additional children had been sent to Philadelphia and elsewhere, the Stark Club sponsored the transportation of another eighteen, as well as about a dozen strikers, to Manchester, where 52 members of the Cigarmakers' Union met them at the depot.[10]

3. Finding a Voice

The tactic worked so well that Lawrence officials attempted to halt the exodus on the pretense of child neglect, banning the practice outright on February 22. When a group of socialists arrived in Lawrence to take about 150 children to Philadelphia, police responded by beating the activists, the children, and the children's mothers. Women "were furious over the 'Russianized' actions of Lawrence officials.... City leaders were held accountable for the attacks on women, several of whom were pregnant, but women also used the event to highlight the plight of mothers and children."[11] The actions came just three days after Lawrence policemen beat 100 women picketers with clubs. Some industrial advocates claimed that the strike committee had been "cowardly ... to send out women pickets" with whom the police had to be more gentle than they would with men. Notwithstanding, most of the country responded to these events with tremendous disapproval. The image of the American Woolen Company and the Lawrence Police Department suffered considerably in the aftermath of the brutality, and both Congress and the Governor of Massachusetts launched inquiries.[12]

Amoskeag officials must have recognized the shift in popular opinion toward mill ownership. As the strike wore on and the company feared losing control over its workforce, managers worked to reestablish the trust of workers and, more generally, the public in Manchester. Manchester's newspaper publishers attempted to assist the company by distancing themselves from the brutality in Lawrence. Even so, they continued to carry stories antithetical to progressive and pro-union causes.

However, Jesse Markee saw an opportunity. The 54-year-old printer was already encouraged by what his union had accomplished in Manchester: raises of a dollar per week for members of Typographical Workers Local 152 in 1912 and the promise of another dollar per week in the two years after that, a successful printing boycott of anti-union businesses after the Park Theater fired its stage hands for organizing, pro-union messages flashed by spotlight onto the curtain at the Auditorium Theater, overflowing crowds at meetings of Local 152, and success at convincing local merchants to use only union printers for their printing needs. He sensed that Amoskeag's employees were frustrated by their inability to unionize and the lack of an outlet by which to promote the union cause. He also seems to have feared that without guidance, Amoskeag workers might follow the path of the Lawrence strikers toward the Industrial Workers of the World. A pro–American Federation of Labor newspaper, he believed, would provide them with the voice they needed while leading them away from the radical worldview of the IWW.

Markee appears to have been well qualified to run a newspaper. Born in 1858 in Muscatine County, Iowa, he already worked for the *Wilton Chronicle* by the time he was ten years old. By 1877 he had found his way to Eldon where he briefly owned the *Western News,* but closed the newspaper in the spring of 1878. By the early 1890s was working in Toledo, Ohio, where he remained even after his first wife, Mattie, died in 1892. Eight years later he was a printer in Toledo where, according to the federal census, he owned his own house and was busy raising four sons and two daughters with his second wife, Louisa.[13]

According to city directories, Markee moved to Manchester in 1909 to work for the *Manchester Daily Mirror.* Unfortunately he left no record indicating why he chose to take a job in New Hampshire. Regardless, Markee became active with American Federation of Labor-affiliated Typographical Workers Local 152 soon thereafter, at a time when the group's meetings often could not attract a quorum. The Iowa native quickly rose through the local union's ranks, and by 1911 he was the local's primary reporting agent for its parent union, the International Typographical Union of North America. But in his time with the union he also became increasingly aware of the power that corporations held over workers in New Hampshire. "Union labor has desired a few shares of stock in the New Hampshire legislature," he wrote in 1911, "but it is alleged that the Boston and Maine Railroad and a cotton mill corporation have controlling interests therein, and have taken all the stock out of the market."[14] Although he did not say it, the "cotton mill corporation" undoubtedly was Amoskeag.

In early 1912, the "general rousing up of unionism in the town" that resulted from the Lawrence strike and was so clear in his union's success led Markee to unveil his idea: a four-page, six-column weekly newspaper for the city's workers, one that espoused "American Federation [of Labor] principles.'"[15] To finance it, the newspaper would accept advertising from unionized and pro-union businesses in Manchester. Although he planned to write editorials and cover selected local stories relating to the AFL cause, he also hoped to publish national stories, particularly ones that could be reprinted from other AFL publications. In this way, Jesse Markee sought to further the union cause in Manchester, and at the same time break Amoskeag's stranglehold over state and local government.

As the Lawrence strike dragged on and Markee set his plans for a newspaper into motion, Robert Bass had other, though not unrelated, concerns. Over his short career, and sometimes despite the objections of the Amoskeag Manufacturing Company and the Boston and Maine Railroad, the 38-year-old New Hampshire governor could point to many progressive reforms that he had helped spearhead. By mid–February, however, some reformers must have been disappointed with Bass. On January 20, before the Lawrence strike became violent, he had married Edith Bird, the daughter of Massachusetts manufacturer and former Democrat-turned-Progressive Charles Sumner Bird. Thereafter he left for a lengthy honeymoon in the South, escaping, if unintentionally, the problems that appeared in New Hampshire in the wake of the Bread and Roses Strike. Making matters worse, on February 10, while Bass was still on his honeymoon, a letter that he and six other Republican governors had signed was released, urging Theodore Roosevelt to run for the Republican presidential nomination against incumbent William Howard Taft. According to political scientist James Wright, "Bass's Roosevelt appeal immediately started a splintering of the progressive organization in New Hampshire."[16]

Bass had long recognized that many of the "old political leaders" in the Republican Party were openly antagonistic to progressive ideas.[17] He probably also realized that his decision to support Roosevelt would not be met with universal approval, especially among Republicans. Still, the governor hoped to rally the voting public around the progressive cause. However, the state's most significant English-language dailies, the *Manchester Union* and the *Manchester Mirror and American*, were as antagonistic to Roosevelt and progressivism as was the state's Republican leadership. In fact, *Union* owner and publisher Rosecrans Pillsbury was himself a mill owner who once ran for governor, while *Mirror* publisher Henry Putney was a frequent target of progressive criticism for favoring the Boston and Maine Railroad when he served as the state's railroad commissioner. Both men actively supported the Republican Party; neither newspaper had shown any recent support for Bass or progressivism. Even *L'Avenir National* opposed the progressives, partly because of Bass's failure to appoint French Canadians to prominent state political posts.[18]

With no newspaper willing to support his cause, Bass decided to finance his own progressive newspaper. He sent his older brother, newspaper correspondent John Foster Bass, to Michigan to meet with Frank Knox, a seasoned veteran of the newspaper business. By 1912 the 38-year-old Boston native was Secretary Treasurer and General Manager of the Sault News Printing Company. Like the New Hampshire governor, Knox supported Theodore Roosevelt, at least in part because the publisher had served under Roosevelt's command as a Rough Rider during the Spanish-American War. He had been corresponding with Robert Bass for some time about the national progressive movement.[19]

Over the next few months, Bass and his brother completed a series of background checks on Knox, and Bass invited the Michigan newspaperman and his business partner, John Muehling, to start a progressive newspaper in Manchester. Knox agreed, but only if Bass would use his influence to help raise $25,000 to finance the new venture. The governor assured Knox that financing would not be a problem; in fact, Bass put up at least $15,000 of his own money. While Bass located other investors, Knox worked to establish the *Manchester*

Leader and its parent corporation, the Leader Publishing Company, in time for the autumn election season.[20]

By early March, as Knox and Markee worked toward the creation of their newspapers, Amoskeag officials continued to worry about what *could* happen in Manchester. At some point during the strike Amoskeag hired the Burns Detective Agency of Boston to measure worker attitudes toward the company. The agency reported that workers displayed minor levels of discontent, but a strike was unlikely.[21] Even so, problems remained elsewhere in Manchester. The cigarmakers had been radicalized, and the working public was sympathetic enough with their Lawrence brethren that the union was able to raise an estimated $40,000 for Lawrence strikers.[22] Greek shoe workers at McElwain continued to strike, apparently with the help of the IWW, though Manchester newspapers continued to conceal the Wobblies' involvement. Police even arrested, to the delight of the *Daily Mirror,* eight McElwain strike leaders for "interfering in lawful business." Shortly after, two Syrian scabs complained to the police that a group of Greeks had "threatened to annihilate them if they continued their work in the shoe shops."[23]

Meanwhile, the city received, from an unlikely source, some criticism for its handling of free-speech protestors. The Reverend Chalmers noted that Chief Healy "may have made a mistake in forbidding the strike sympathizers the right of free speech in this city." His mild complaint was not based on the morality of denying protestors their First Amendment rights; he was not, after all, particularly sympathetic to the IWW. Rather, he disapproved of Healy's actions because "he has attracted attention to this city of a kind that we would have been just as well without."[24]

Perhaps because of these issues and similar ones in other communities, on March 9 management teams representing textile mills throughout New England met in Boston, where they voted to increase wages by between five and seven percent. According to the *Mirror*, the raise was approved by every mill with an office in Boston, and was "due partly to the situation in Lawrence."[25] Five days later, the Lawrence strike ended.

The Amoskeag Manufacturing Company was among the corporations to increase wages for its employees. This was not the company's first attempt to placate its workers that year, nor would it be the last. On February 2, one day after Chief Healy had closed down the Polish and Stark halls to IWW speakers, Amoskeag had already announced that it planned to donate Rock Rimmon, a natural stone formation and park on Manchester's West Side, to the city, as well as a "fine level tract which will be laid out for a playground" closer to the millyard.[26] Then, on March 11, four days before the end of the Lawrence strike, the company declared that it would increase wages by five percent, though this was not enough to alleviate worker discontent in one of the company's factories. At the end of March, 1,000 weavers, coiler boys, and card strippers walked off their jobs, something that Jesse Markee remarked was once "counted among the impossibilities" but had been made possible by the Lawrence strike. To avoid the problems of Lawrence, which by this time had spread to Lowell, Amoskeag responded with another pay increase. As of April 1, employee pay rose by 11 percent over what it had been before the start of the Bread and Roses Strike, a gross increase of approximately $825,000 distributed among more than 15,500 textile workers.[27] When the details of the increase reached William Trautmann, an IWW representative leading strikers in Lowell, he stated to reporters that the IWW "planted seed in Manchester some time ago. The workers are now gathering the harvest."[28]

Amoskeag did even more, announcing on March 18 and again on April 1 that the company would help its employees to purchase homes. According to the *Manchester Mirror*:

> The city of Manchester, in many ways the child and creation of the Amoskeag Manufacturing company, is to again be made the beneficiary of this magnificent corporation, which has already deeded to the city no less than seven parks and numerous sites for public buildings. This time it is not the city in its corporate capacity which is to be made the recipient of the company's beneficence, but the employes [sic] of the company....

To any worker employed by the company for at least five years, Amoskeag offered a plot of land on the city's West Side. Each 50-by-100 foot lot was located between Coolidge Avenue and Rock Rimmon. So long as the employee constructed a house consisting of no more than two tenements within a year of purchasing the lot and lived in one of the tenements, the company would provide up to two interest-free mortgages to the owner, each worth one-half of the purchase price. If the owner remained in Amoskeag's employ for five years, the second mortgage would be forgiven for a dollar. After another five years, Amoskeag would forgive the first mortgage for a dollar as well. About 200 workers took advantage of Amoskeag's offer, and the program allowed the company to boast of its "progressive" attitude toward workers, thereby improving its reputation as a benevolent paternalist employer among workers and the public at large.[29]

As the Lawrence strike concluded, the New Hampshire Free Speech Alliance submitted a petition to the Police Commission requesting the removal of Michael Healy as Chief of Police based on the events of early February. The commission held a public hearing on the matter on April 29, with local attorney Mederic Guilbeault representing the Alliance and Healy representing himself.

Chairman Thomas Varick opened the hearing by asking the secretary to read the complaint, after which Attorney Guilbeault reiterated the points mentioned therein: that the Chief of Police had abridged the free-speech rights of protestors by denying them access to the Polish and Stark halls or the right to speak at a privately owned shop on February 1; that he subsequently prevented meetings at other locations later in February; and that Healy's actions had been "arbitrary and without justice," violating rights of free speech and assembly guaranteed in both the state constitution and in the federal Bill of Rights. "The abridgements of such fundamental American rights as those of free speech and public assemblage is a serious matter in any community," Guilbeault remarked.

Healy did not offer an opening statement.

The Free Speech Alliance then sent eleven witnesses, including seven members of the Cigarmakers' Union, to testify in support of its case. Together they spoke about the events of February 1, as well as other occasions later that month when "they themselves were arrested for disturbing the peace and were hauled before the city court." Both John Kubilia, the janitor of the Polish hall, and Gerard Pellens, president of the Recreation Club, explained how Healy had approached them and that, as a result, they had closed their buildings to the cigarmakers.

After the Alliance concluded its testimony, Healy addressed the commissioners on his own behalf. He did not offer any witnesses to rebut the petitioners' claims. Instead, he explained that while he had spoken to Kubilia about closing the Polish hall, no evidence had been presented to show that he had ordered the Polish hall locked; Kubilia did this of his own accord. Regarding the closing of Stark Hall, Healy pointed out that in his testimony, Pellens admitted that "he himself had entered the hall and announced that the meeting had been abandoned," a fact corroborated by one of the other witnesses. The meeting at the shop was prevented because city ordinances "prohibited the holding of public gatherings in any building without first obtaining the sanction of the superintendent of buildings and the chief of the fire department." In other words, Healy was simply enforcing the law, adding that he "did not propose to let agitators walk over him." Healy apparently stopped other meetings as well, including one at Club Jolliet on Concord Street where, he pointed out, the assembly had been proposed by Socialist Party members, not the cigarmakers. If the club wished to keep Bill Haywood from speaking there, Healy told the commission, its members had that right.

Guilbeault then addressed the commission by criticizing Healy's actions, stating that the chief should "take the matter more seriously; that the chief did not seem to realize that the petitioners were citizens." He also noted that while it was true that Chief Healy had to enforce the law, it "was also true that the average citizen was not a bomb thrower. That the average citizen had a guarantee of free speech and assemblage, not for the majority but for the whole people." Besides that, Guilbeault claimed, city ordinances do not actually prohibit meetings, so Healy had exceeded his authority. Furthermore, if the Chamber of Commerce and the Salvation Army can meet and raise funds in Manchester, he asked, then why not peaceful protestors attempting to support the Lawrence strikers? The attorney concluded by emphasizing the final point of the Alliance's petition: that Chief Healy should be removed.[30]

The Police Commission adjourned the hearing and took the Alliance's request to remove Healy "under advisement," but ultimately did nothing to reprimand the chief for his actions. Displeased, the Alliance promised to bring its case to Governor Bass himself, eventually submitting a petition for a hearing on July 30. The governor, however, was busy with a number of other issues, some of them relating to the future of the progressive movement in New Hampshire. Over the next six months, as the Free Speech Movement seemingly died down, Amoskeag worked to reestablish its power over Manchester. Bass and the Executive Council would not hear the Alliance's petition until the end of October, by which time Amoskeag had found a new solution to its city's problems: baseball.

4

Baseball Season at Last

In April, after a tension-filled winter, many of Manchester's residents welcomed a new baseball season. Early that month the Saint Anselm College team began practicing under the tutelage of head coach George M. Cassidy and his assistant, John F. Smith, who worked with the club's pitchers.[1] Not long after, Boston's two major-league baseball teams opened their seasons. The Boston Braves were as bad as ever, quickly dropping to last place in the National League. The Red Sox showed more promise, winning their first three games in New York. The American Leaguers also were beginning their first season in Fenway Park, a new concrete-and-steel stadium that was said to be much safer and more convenient for fans than the more fire-prone, less structurally sound wooden grandstands of the past.[2]

As typically happened each year, local sports writers sought out Smith for his opinions about the upcoming major-league season. Smith often helped coach local baseball teams during the day while working nights as a patrolman for Chief Michael Healy's police force. But the respect accorded the 47-year-old policeman once known by the nickname "Phenomenal" came from his baseball experience: from 1884 to 1892 he pitched in 139 games for seven major-league baseball teams, winning 54 games against 74 losses.[3] He spent several more seasons as a player-manager in the minor leagues before settling permanently in Manchester. In response to their queries, Smith picked the Philadelphia Athletics to win the 1912 American League pennant, and felt that the New York Giants, Philadelphia Phillies, and Pittsburgh Pirates would compete for the National League flag.[4]

Phenomenal Smith played an important role in promoting baseball in Manchester after 1901. So, too, did the Boston Red Sox, who—despite Smith's proclamations—won the 1912 American League pennant. In fact, baseball proved such an effective diversion for so much of the population that by mid-year, the manufacturing companies of Manchester, including Amoskeag and some of the shoe factories that had been beset by strikes, formed their own league. In doing so, the companies hoped to employ the baseball creed—the idea that baseball would Americanize the city's immigrant labor force, making them less likely to unionize and strike.

Born in Philadelphia in 1864, Officer John F. Smith's path to Manchester was long and complicated. In 1884, at the age of nineteen, he signed his first major-league contract with the Philadelphia Athletics of the American Association. By this time, the five-foot-six-and-a-half-inch-tall lefthander already had earned the nickname "Phenomenal." His stay in Philadelphia was brief, lasting only one game, but he managed to catch on with six other major-league clubs over the next eight years. In the early 1890s, he moved into a comfortable career in the minor leagues as an outfielder and manager. By 1899, when he played for and managed the Portland club of the New England League, he was a distinguished and highly respected baseball veteran known by local fans simply as "Phenom."[5]

Smith's move to Manchester came in 1901 at the invitation of local minor-league investors from the New England League who were grateful for his actions as Portland's manager at the end of the 1899 season. The story began on August 31, 1899, in a New England League game between Taunton, Massachusetts and Manchester at Manchester's Varick Park, constructed on Amoskeag-owned land just five years earlier by Thomas Varick. Less than three weeks prior, clubs representing Pawtucket, Rhode Island and Brockton, Massachusetts, had disbanded, leaving Taunton as the least stable of the league's four remaining clubs. At about the same time,

Taunton management found that it could not pay its players, among them future major-league pitching star Christy Mathewson. The demise of Taunton would have meant the failure of the entire league. Therefore, the players took over the team and played out the schedule, splitting gate receipts among themselves.

For its second-to-last series of the season, Taunton arrived in Manchester without a catcher's mask. With no catcher, Taunton would be forced to forfeit its game with Manchester, which was in a tight pennant race with Newport, Rhode Island. Manchester player-manager Fred Lake agreed to permit the Taunton catcher to use his mask. Then, in the ninth inning of a game that Taunton led 12–6, Lake took his mask and protector with him to the Manchester bench, either trying to force the Taunton club to forfeit a game that it seemed sure to win or, according to the *Union*, forcing Taunton's catcher to take a position farther away from home plate than catchers typically took. The catcher requested use of the items, but Lake refused to give them up. The

Taunton player took his regular position behind the plate anyway, ready for the first pitch. For the remainder of the game, which Taunton won, Manchester fans openly rooted against the home club.

After Mathewson lost the September 1 game, 5–3, Taunton left town for three games against Newport, and players' anger at Lake led to rumors that Taunton would "lay down" in its three remaining games against Manchester's closest competitor. If Newport were to win all three games, Manchester would place second for the league pennant. Luckily for Fred Lake, his team's only remaining opponent was Portland, whose players—led by captain John "Phenom" Smith—felt that Newport had mistreated their own club in a recent series.

Prior to the season's final day, Smith and his players plotted with Fred Lake's team to help Manchester capture the pennant. Instead of two games as scheduled, the clubs agreed to play *six* games at Varick Park, all on September 4. Should Manchester win all six, it would win the championship by a game and a half over Newport.

As expected, Taunton lost all three of its games to Newport. Smith's Portland team, meanwhile, proceeded to throw each of its games in Manchester. In the first, Portland merely played one bad inning, but in subsequent contests "the ball playing gradually developed into a regular farce." Manchester outscored Portland, 54 to 28, in the first five games. "It was really amusing to see how foolish players acted," reported a *Union* correspondent. "It was silly ball." The two clubs started a sixth game as well, but Portland forfeited the game in the second inning when a minor melee erupted after a close play. Exhausted yet satisfied, Manchester seemingly had won the pennant and, as far as anyone knew, set a record for the most professional games played between two clubs in one day.

However, the series did not secure the pennant for Manchester after all. Although the *Mirror* supported the home team, the *Union* claimed openly that the teams had not engaged in "honest ball." "The weather was fine and the attendance good," the newspaper reported. "Honest ball would have been vastly appreciated. Still, the local fans should feel grateful to the Portland friends for their willingness to drop the series in order that the pennant might come this way." Meanwhile, after Newport disputed the final results, New England League president Timothy Murnane issued a statement to the effect that "the games … between Portland and Manchester will do the game no good, and the league will never countenance such proceedings.…" One of the league's directors called the series a "black eye for the sport," and demanded an investigation into the matter. Manchester's mayor suggested his city's team and Newport decide the league pennant with a playoff series, but Murnane disagreed.[6] Instead, the league granted the pennant to Newport.[7]

John "Phenomenal" Smith, center (seated), surrounded by his 1902 Manchester New England League baseball club. As player-manager of Portland club 1899, Smith allegedly conspired with Manchester's Fred Lake to throw the 1899 New England League pennant in favor of Manchester. He became Manchester's manager in 1901, and within a few years had joined Michael Healy's police force (National Baseball Hall of Fame Library, Cooperstown, New York).

The New England League suspended operations for the 1900 season. That year, Phenom Smith managed a club in Norfolk, Virginia, taking Christy Mathewson with him and helping the young pitcher perfect his mechanics before selling his contract to the New York Giants of the National League.[8] In 1901, when the New England League was reorganized, a group of Manchester residents reestablished the local club and hired Smith as the team's captain and right-fielder.[9] Manchester finished second to Portland in the standings.

The following season Smith led the league in batting with a .369 average as he helped Manchester to win—legitimately—a New England League championship.[10] Attendance dipped in 1903, but the club remained in Manchester until the middle of the 1905 season when, due to poor patronage at Varick Park, it moved to Lawrence.[11] Smith went with the team as manager, but by that time he was only a part-time player. Always popular with Manchester fans, the former Portland manager who, according to the *Union*, conspired to "throw" the 1899 New England League championship, had become a Manchester police officer.[12]

Like Smith's teams in the first years of the twentieth century, both Saint Anselm College and Manchester High School played home games at Varick Park, while St. Joseph's High School played at Derryfield Park, east of the city along Bridge Street. Saint Anselm opened the 1912 baseball season with exhibition losses against Lawrence, Lowell, and Worcester, three New England League clubs that the college team could not have been expected to defeat. Yet the season was a success, the college winning more than it lost. Manchester High School, meanwhile, began the season with a victory over Lawrence High School, and ended up winning the Triangular League pennant. St. Joseph's was less successful, but nevertheless had the support of the city's large Roman Catholic population.

The excitement surrounding Saint Anselm College, St. Joseph's High School, and Manchester High School actually did seem to divert attention from the winter's labor problems. The *Union* and *Mirror* covered the schools heavily, as they did Phillips Exeter Academy, which played several of its contests against college teams. Although most Manchester residents had no direct ties to the school, Exeter's season was perhaps the most impressive; behind coach John Carney, the team lost only to the Harvard varsity and, on the last day, to archrival Phillips Andover Academy.[13]

The attention paid to local high-school and college nines is significant. White Anglo-Saxon Americans saw baseball as a purely rural and American game. Because it "typified all that was best" in American society, in the words of historian Steven Riess, it supposedly could "teach children 'traditional' American values" and "help newcomers assimilate into the dominant WASP culture through their participation in the sport and its rituals." According to this "baseball creed," crowds consisted of people from "all walks of life," professional team owners operated their franchises for the public benefit, and anyone with sufficient talent and perseverance could play the game. At the professional level, the players themselves were considered to be the "*most* virtuous and should serve as role models for all Americans." In addition, fans would be encouraged to root for a common local team, thereby encouraging community, hometown pride, and boosterism among even disparate peoples.[14]

Though it lacked a name, the baseball creed permeated American culture, and had appeared in American baseball novels and short stories since the Civil War. Baseball fiction promoted the idea of equal opportunity for all, regardless of class or ethnicity. Researcher Clarence Jenkins found that the "hard work and honesty which were [believed necessary] to open the door to success in the American democracy were translated into diligent training and fair play in the game of baseball and its fiction." Those with no knowledge of the English language still could participate in the game, though many works of fiction from that period depict both African Americans and those who retained any characteristics of foreign culture in negative, even stereotyped, ways.[15]

Former pitcher and executive Albert G. Spalding explained the creed in his 1911 history of baseball. In attempting to prove that baseball was an American game that had been invented in Cooperstown, New York by Abner Doubleday, Spaulding cited several supposed traits of the game that made it American:

> The genius of our institutions is democratic; Base Ball is a democratic game. The spirit of our national life is combative; Base Ball is a combative game. We are a cosmopolitan people, knowing no arbitrary class distinctions, acknowledging none. The son of a President of the United States would as soon play ball with Patsy Flannigan as with Lawrence Lionel Livingstone, provided only that Patsy could put up the right article.

Furthermore, Spalding suggested that even though "Base Ball is War!," it is a "bloodless battle" in which "foes of the minute past are friends of the minute present." It was also the "only form of field sport known where spectators have an important part and actually participate in the game," affecting the outcome through their common goal of rooting for the home team.[16]

In Manchester, evidence already suggested the baseball creed's validity. *L'Avenir National,* for instance, printed standings and box scores for the American, National, International, and New England Leagues as well as for local high schools and colleges. It also noted those occasions when employees from different Amoskeag Manufacturing Company divisions engaged each other in a game of baseball at Varick Park after work.[17]

The Manchester Police Department also found that the popularity of baseball affected its work. In the months prior to June 30, 1912, the department received nine complaints related to amateur baseball. In light of the 1905 baseball riot involving Greek immigrants who likely had no knowledge of the game, perhaps the two most promising cases were ones involving children. The police responded to one complaint of child laborers playing ball during lunch outside the Amoskeag millyard, and to another involving a "Greek" who, "while playing ball in the back street," had broken a window.[18] Could the city's immigrants be unified by an "American" game after all—and if so, could Amoskeag somehow use this unity to influence its workers?

In mid–May, apparently noting the success of the 1912 baseball season, Amoskeag officials floated the idea of forming a manufacturers baseball league in conjunction with other Manchester industries. The company hired Henry S. Bingham, the former president of the Manufacturers League of Providence,

Rhode Island, to initiate the venture, and on May 15 Bingham met with representatives of several Manchester-based companies to discuss the possibility. Noted the *Mirror,* "With no [New England] league team in Manchester and the schedule of the high schools and college team gradually being played off the fans of the city will only be too glad to turn out and witness the contests."[19] By May 27 the W. H. McElwain and F. M. Hoyt shoe factories along with the Stark Mills had joined Amoskeag as league members.[20]

On May 30, representatives of the four companies met at City Hall to officially organize the Manufacturers League. The group appointed William B. McKay, foreman of Amoskeag's print works, as league president, and Bingham as official scorekeeper.[21] The league continued to solicit other teams from among the city's major employers, and finally enticed the H. B. Reed Company to join. By early June, the organization had devised a set of bylaws and could boast eight teams: the Amoskeags, Starks, Reeds, Beacons (of the F. M. Hoyt Company), and the Midlands, Eurekas, Norfolks, and Hancocks representing four separate divisions of the McElwain factory.[22]

To be eligible to play in the league, players had to have been employed in one of the member companies as of May 28, 1912. That rule supposedly gave factories little flexibility in the decision to use ringers—employees hired because of their exceptional baseball skills. Perhaps due to the lack of time, Amoskeag does not appear to have hired many ringers. Left fielder Ernest Bond, for example, originally was hired as a weaver in 1906 at the age of fourteen. Nineteen-year-old Bill Donovan, a catcher, joined the company two years after Bond, while shortstop Albert Greager—whose employment records list him as "German," though the 1910 census indicates his place of birth as New Hampshire—was hired in 1900 as a sixteen-year-old pin setter. In fact, among the Amoskeag employee records identified as belonging to Amoskeag baseball players in 1912, the only worker who seems to have been recruited specifically to play baseball was Willard G. Taber, a twenty-three-year-old pitcher from Columbus, Ohio. Taber was hired as a flannel inspector on May 15, 1912, just thirteen days before the league's eligibility deadline.[23]

The first games of the inaugural Manufacturers League season took place after the end of the workday on Saturday, June 15, 1912. As the *Mirror* reported, "Three of the contests were exciting and well contested, and the teams give promise of providing plenty of exhilarating sport on Saturday afternoons throughout the summer months.... [The Amoskeag-Reed game] was well contested, and interest never flagged." The *Mirror* also reported that, in addition to playing a competitive, entertaining game, participants fulfilled their duties as role models under the baseball creed: "The players on both teams are true sportsmen, and played a clean game."

In other games that day, the Hancocks beat the Midlands, 6–4 in an "exceptionally fast and exciting game" in which players "attended strictly to business, setting an example in discipline and sportsmanlike conduct to the average professional outfit," while the Starks defeated the Eurekas 7–6 in an "even and well fought" game. The only "uneven contest" of the day occurred at Varick Park, where the Beacons defeated the Norfolks, 34–6. Even so, the *Mirror* reported that the Beacons had benefited from "constant practice" and "more experienced players," and that the Norfolks had "put up a good game" considering those facts.[24]

Varick Park, located between the Greek neighborhoods of the Fifth Ward and the Hoyt Shoe Company's Beacon factory on the East Side, was only one of the fields used by the Manufacturers League on opening day. The Stark-Eureka game took place on the North End Grounds, a poorly maintained grounds in which high grass, trees, and rock outcroppings interfered with play. Meanwhile, the Midlands and Hancocks played at the Barry Playground, a field on the south side near the McElwain factory about which nothing—positive or negative—ever was reported in the newspapers.[25]

A fourth grounds, at the Rock Rimmon park on the West Side, debuted that day in the Amoskeag-Reed game. The Amoskeag Manufacturing Company claimed it was "one of the finest diamonds in the country," or at least "in this section of New England." Prior to the season's first games, 25 workmen had constructed benches for players and, under the shade of pine trees, a wooden bleacher section for spectators. The dirt diamond was rolled smooth, the field oriented with home plate to the south so that "the sun will cause little interference with the outfielders," and a "huge backstop" erected at "the required distance back of the catchers' box" behind home plate. To mark foul territory, chalk lines extended from home plate to the outfield where they met two poles, each flying an American flag.

The Amoskeag Manufacturing Company took tremendous pride in the Rock Rimmon grounds, and the *Mirror* commended the "Enterprise and Liberality of the Amoskeag Company" in a headline reporting the improvements. Yet Amoskeag deflected some of the credit to the Amoskeag Textile Club.[26] The Textile Club, known less formally as the "ATC," was established in 1910 by 350 Amoskeag employees during a company outing to Hampton Beach. Initially its purpose remained unstated, though membership was limited to employees in supervisory positions. By 1912 its objectives had come to include the advancement of "the acquaintanceship of the employees of the Amoskeag Manufacturing Company with each other," the provision of recreational opportunities for its members, and the promotion of "athletics and healthy sports." In other words, the club was an ideal testing ground for the baseball creed.

The ATC finally drew up articles of incorporation on June 28, 1912, and adopted bylaws on August 12. Voting ("active") members and officers had to be employees of the Amoskeag Manufacturing Company, though associate and honorary members were permitted all of the other rights and privileges associated with membership. Not surprisingly, members were required to be citizens of the United States.[27] The Americanization of immigrants clearly was an important if unstated objective. In writing about the club in his 1915 Amoskeag-sponsored history of the company, George Waldo Browne noted:

> It has already been remarked that the Amoskeag Manufacturing Company has always employed a high class of labor, and the very fact makes it more necessary to keep pace with the changing conditions of affairs. Where in former years the help employed was mainly from among the people at home, to-day the rank and file of the employees are aliens from strange lands, who labor under many disadvantages unknown to those earlier employed.[28]

Researchers Daniel Creamer and Charles Coulter, writing in 1939, found that company control over the club "was assured by the company agent's [son, William Parker Straw] serving as president in its formative years. Certainly the club's program in many respects was closely correlated with the company's needs and not unrelated to the workers' interests as [managers] ... conceived them at that time."[29] Thus, between 1912 and 1922 the club would oversee a Textile School, organize baseball, bowling, and basketball leagues, sponsor cooking classes, educational talks, and courses to teach employees English, and organize four local troops of Boy Scouts. Through its educational and athletic endeavors, Browne argued, the Textile Club would help immigrants to become good citizens of the United States.[30] He did not mention that as good American citizens, immigrants were expected to be loyal to Amoskeag.

The 1912 Manufacturers League season was more successful than anyone had dared to imagine, netting $18.78 for each player in the league and a bonus of $25.00 for scorekeeper Henry Bingham.[31] In reality, the profits meant nothing; after all, the Amoskeag Manufacturing Company provided land and capital outlay for the improvement of the league's baseball diamonds, meaning that between the company and its textile club, the venture probably lost money. More important was what the profits represented: attendees, or people who would benefit from exposure to baseball. Initially by the end of June, attendance dipped to between 200 and 500, leading the *Union* to blame the use of "players who will leave the game open to protest"—in other words, ringers whose eligibility to play in the league was questionable. Yet the league's popularity rebounded in July, particularly once it began imposing fines on teams that did not report their scores to the local newspapers in a timely fashion. On July 22, the Amoskeags defeated the Beacons, 11–5, in front of more than 3,000 spectators, "amid the ringing of cowbells, blowing of horns and the waving of banners...." The *Mirror* noted, "Not since the old days ... has there been such a scene at Varick park, and the Amoskeag aggregation deserves all the laurels that go with a clean, well-earned victory."[32] Still, at the end of August, the Beacons and the Amoskeags remained tied for first place, each with ten wins against one loss. Even with an admission fee of ten cents, crowds swelled to over 3,500 on Labor Day weekend.

The Beacons seemingly won the league championship on September 7 when the club defeated the Reeds, 15–6, while Amoskeag could manage only a rain-shortened, eight-inning tie against the Midlands team in front of 5,000 fans. However, the Amoskeag Textile Club protested the result of its game, suggesting that the league championship should not be decided by the weather, and the Midlands-Amoskeag game was replayed a week later. In the ensuing contest, Midlands defeated Amoskeag, 2–0, in front of 5,500 spectators, giving the league pennant to the Beacons.[33]

On September 21, 1912, the results were made official. At 2:00 that afternoon, automobiles carried the Beacons and the Amoskeags onto the Varick Park field, where they were met by cheers emanating from about 3,000 fans who had gathered to watch an upcoming exhibition game between the two teams. Each club was accompanied by a band, and after the players disembarked from their vehicles the Beacon band took up a position in the "southerly part of the grandstand, where lively tunes were played during the afternoon." The Amoskeag band remained in their truck, which was parked to the north of the grandstand and from which it "played enlivening music." Players representing all of the teams in the league then competed in a number of field events to demonstrate their baseball proficiency and general athletic prowess.

Following these events, as spectators strained to listen, William McKay presented Beacons manager Francis Hurley with the league pennant and a wood-mounted silver shield donated to the league by the John B. Varick Company. After Hurley thanked the league for the pennant and trophy, the Beacon band struck up a march and, followed by the Beacons, Amoskeags, and members of other league teams, proceeded to center field. There, Hurley and his players removed their caps and raised their pennant on the flagpole.[34]

The large crowds of fans who attended the Manufacturers League games in 1912 encouraged ATC officials to believe that local baseball might aid in the Americanization of Amoskeag employees. Meanwhile, with the season over and with the Boston Braves out of the pennant chase, Manchester baseball fans turned their attention to the Boston Red Sox. The American Leaguers had already clinched the pennant on their way to a 105-win season, and by the end of the month the World Series matchup had been set: the Red Sox would open the best-of-seven series against the Giants at New York's Polo Grounds on October 8, then move to Boston for the second game the next day. All of Manchester looked forward to the series, but perhaps no one anticipated it more than Frank Knox.

5

The World Series and a "Last-Ditch Bogey Man"

Despite the clouds and possibility of rain, fans began to arrive at Boston's Fenway Park early on the morning of October 9, 1912. At 9:18, when the park's ticket office opened, the crowd already had grown to an estimated 5,000 people, all of them anticipating the second game of the World Series between the Red Sox and the New York Giants.[1] By noontime the group had grown and filled the stands, though the game did not start until after 2:00. To amuse those in attendance, the Royal Rooters, the unofficial fan club of Boston's two major-league baseball teams, led the crowd in songs which included fan-favorites "Tessie" and "Sweet Adeline."[2]

The game ranked among the most exciting in the brief history of the World Series. According to the *New York Times*, "the Giants and the Red Sox battled to an eleven inning tie in a see-saw, topsy-turvy game with thrills of delight and pangs of disappointment."[3] Boston scored three runs in the first inning against Giants ace Christy Mathewson, Phenomenal Smith's one-time protégé. The Giants, however, scored single runs in the second and fourth innings against Boston starter Ray Collins. Harry Hooper of the Red Sox tallied the game's sixth run on Steve Yerkes's triple in the bottom of the fifth inning. A combination of singles, doubles, and Red Sox errors led to three Giants runs in the eighth inning, giving New York a 5–4 lead. Boston responded with a run in the eighth, and after a scoreless ninth the game went into extra innings. In the tenth, Fred Merkle scored the go-ahead run for the Giants.[4] Tris Speaker tied the game in the bottom half of the inning with an inside-the-park home run. The two teams played a scoreless eleventh inning before umpire Silk O'Loughlin called the game due to darkness.[5]

Back in Manchester, fans gathered on Hanover Street, drawn there by the sounds of "barkers." Receiving their information via telegraph, three men used megaphones to relay a play-by-play account of the World Series game to the growing crowd. This was Frank Knox's public introduction of the new *Manchester Leader*. In the first edition of the newspaper, which appeared on the evening of October 10, the *Leader* claimed that the crowd outside its offices numbered "thousands," including "fully 50 women and girls." The estimated size of the crowd may have been exaggerated, but as more people stopped, a police officer was summoned to clear a path for pedestrians and vehicles. "It was a Red Sox crowd," reported the city's newest newspaper; "the tension was terrific during the last four innings, and men yelled at nothing in their excitement."⁶

Despite the presence of a police officer at the *Leader* event, Chief Michael J. Healy and several other members of the city's police force were not in Manchester. They were, in fact, at Fenway Park.⁷ Even as Healy enjoyed the World Series from his seat in Boston, however, trouble seemed to be brewing at home. Not only had Knox and John Muehling established a Progressive newspaper in time for the November elections; but so, too, had Jesse Markee begun to publish his own pro-labor newspaper, the *Manchester Advocate*. Furthermore, Governor

Boston's Fenway Park, 1914. Built in 1912, the concrete-and-steel ballpark would play an important role in the Amoskeag Manufacturing Company's efforts to promote baseball among its employees, culminating in the construction of Textile Field in 1913 (Bain Collection, Prints and Photographs Division, Library of Congress, LC-B2-2447-10).

5. The World Series and a "Last-Ditch Bogey Man" 61

Robert Bass finally planned to convene what the press termed "Free Speech Hearings," to be held just days before the November elections and in which Healy was to be the central figure. What promised to be a chaotic political season became more so because of the Amoskeag Manufacturing Company, which saw its own attempt to insert itself into the election backfire dramatically.

Considering the high degree of interest in baseball among Manchester residents, the *Leader*'s promotion of the Red Sox-Giants game could not have been mere coincidence. Knox and Muehling arrived in Manchester in early September, just as the Manufacturers League ended its season and the Red Sox clinched the American League pennant. Neither man could have failed to note the popularity of baseball in Manchester when they arrived. When on September 6 Robert Bass announced that he had changed his party affiliation from Republican to Progressive, Knox knew that his newspaper had to support the new party.[8] The publisher needed to find a way to promote his newspaper to the masses, and baseball's most important annual event seemed ideal for that purpose.

When it finally appeared, the *Leader* assumed an identity unlike that of any of Manchester's other newspapers. At one cent per issue, the paper—advertised as "New Hampshire's Popular Penny Newspaper"—cost half as much as either the *Union* or the *Mirror*, making it more affordable to the average worker. It printed large-type, front-page headlines just under the masthead, much more easily read than the smaller headlines found in the city's other newspapers. It also espoused Progressive Party politics, as an editorial printed in the first issue demonstrates:

> The Progressive party is the party of YOUNG MEN, and Progressives are young at seventy.
> The Progressive party is the party of OPTIMISM.
> The Progressive party is the party of HOPEFULNESS FOR THE FUTURE.
> The Progressive party is the only party that DARES TO FIGHT THE BOSSES, and the creator of the boss system, ENTRENCHED PRIVILEGE.
> The Progressive party is the only party with a DEFINITE PROGRAM FOR THE CONTROL OF THE TRUSTS.
> The Progressive party believes in the protective tariff but demands that its benefits shall be equally distributed between employer and employee. It would PASS PROSPERITY AROUND.
> The Progressive party has a DEFINITE PROGRAM for the relief of social and economic ills, the existence of which is indisputable, but which have been ignored by both republican and democratic parties.

These words appeared in an editorial inside the newspaper's first issue. The front page, on the other hand, was emblazoned with a headline, "RED SOX–GIANTS BATTLE." The paper also carried a front-page recap of the game, which had not ended when the issue first went to press, and included a photograph of the crowd listening for World Series updates outside the *Leader*'s offices. "The Manchester fans were told of all the happenings on the field of play within five seconds of their occurrence," read the caption beneath the photograph.[9] The next several issues followed a similar pattern: "WOOD FACES GIANTS" (October 11); "RED SOX TAKE LEAD" (October 12); "SOX AND GIANTS BATTLE IN SIXTH GAME; OBRIEN KNOCKED OUT" (October 14); and "SOX-GIANTS IN FINAL" (October 16). The only issue in which the Red Sox shared a headline came on October 15, after Theodore Roosevelt was shot while campaigning for the presidency: "ROOSEVELT WOUND SERIOUS; GIANTS KNOCK WOOD OUT." Roosevelt's picture appeared just under the Giants–Red Sox line score. In the end, the Red Sox defeated the Giants, four games to three, with one tie. During that stretch, the *Leader* claimed a circulation of between 18,000 and more than 25,000 copies. Knox's skill at using the World Series to promote the *Leader* quickly and dramatically made his newspaper a very powerful voice in Manchester. The publishers of the *Union* and the *Mirror*, as well as the managers of Manchester's major industries, had reason to worry.

To Jesse Markee's delight, the *Leader* also announced that its printing department would be a closed shop. That meant more jobs for union workers in Manchester, of course; but it also furthered the union cause in Manchester. Markee's own weekly, the *Manchester Advocate*, had first appeared in June, and through it Markee was able to oppose the anti-labor tactics of the Amoskeag Manufacturing Company. He did not wish to destroy the company; he readily admitted that the "removal of the Amoskeag from Manchester would be a serious calamity to the city and state" and that "Manchester would be off the map were it not for the Amoskeag."[10] But he did hope to promote the unionization of Amoskeag's workforce—just as long as that union was not the IWW. Markee, like other American Federation of Labor supporters, was a vocal critic of the IWW for what he saw as its anarchist, destructive activities. Perhaps that is why the paper never ran any stories or editorials about the complaints that the Free Speech Alliance brought against Chief Healy.

The Free Speech Alliance's April appearance before the Manchester Police Commission had resulted in no action against Chief Healy. Believing that the "police commission did not act with justice ... [and that] their decision was arbitrary and unjustifiable," thirty members of the Alliance met with Bass and the Executive Council on October 31.[11] The hearings revealed little new about the events of the previous winter. Healy denied having stopped any of the February meetings other than the one instigated by Wolf at a private shop. The owners of the Polish and Stark halls had merely refused to open their doors, he contended; the Chief did not intimidate them into closing the halls to protestors. Officers arrived on the scene only to preserve order.[12] Perhaps subtly invoking the tragedy at New York's Triangle Shirtwaist Factory in 1911, he claimed to have stopped the meeting at the shop for fear of fire, as "the shop was wooden and everybody was smoking." And besides, he told the Executive Council, the group had no permit to meet in the shop.[13] He also noted that trouble had arisen at the Polish Club earlier that evening, though he failed to mention the role of the Manchester Police Department in helping to create that situation. Bass, meanwhile, pressed Healy about whether or not the Police Commission had had any influence over Healy's behavior that evening. "No, the Commissioners have nothing to do with my enforcement of the law," the Chief responded, visibly angered by Bass's question. "They can't instruct me."[14]

If Bass had wanted to use the Free Speech Hearings for political advantage, he did not succeed. Not surprisingly, the *Union* ignored the hearings. The *Advocate* also ignored the hearings, likely because Jesse Markee did not want to ally the paper with either the IWW or the New Hampshire Socialist Party. Even the pro–Bass *Leader* relegated its report to page eight.

In fact, Amoskeag itself had upstaged the Free Speech Hearings, but not in the way its managers had hoped. Rather, Manchester still was abuzz over a desperate statement attributed to longtime Amoskeag agent Herman Straw that had appeared in state Republican political ads on October 28. In the statement, which appeared in all of Manchester's daily newspapers, Straw indicated that a Democratic victory in the November elections would force American manufacturers to "reduce the cost of making their goods or discontinue their manufacture"—in other words, companies like Amoskeag would have to reduce wages or close altogether.[15] Hovey E. Slayton of Manchester's F. M. Hoyt Shoe Company concurred, adding, "it will surely result in a readjustment of the wage condition or else the shoe business of the American manufacturer will be greatly curtailed."[16] Pointing out Straw's statement, the *Mirror* suggested that a "vote for the third term ticket is virtually a vote for the Democratic party. Remember that, you men who are aligned with the Progressives.... It would be a terrible blow to our city to have her mills shut down, or only run at greatly reduced wages."[17]

The Republicans' strategy backfired. The Democrats ridiculed the Republicans for their threats and claimed that their scare tactics were nothing more than a "last-ditch Bogey Man."[18] Meanwhile, the *Manchester Advocate*, which one week earlier had written that "the greatest complaint of the wage worker comes when corporations butt into politics ... for the purpose of controlling municipal and state affairs," directly charged Amoskeag with trying to intimidate voters. Reporter Frank H. Challis also remarked that the "interference of the Amoskeag at its best is gratuitous. Its candidate has not the ghost of a show of winning, and any responsible man knows it.... The employes [sic] of Amoskeag cannot cannot [sic] be DRIVEN TO THE POLLS WITH A LASH."[19]

The *Advocate* was right. Democrats won every House seat in the Fifth Ward, though a self-described "Republican of progressive tendencies"—the Rev. Thomas Chalmers, a member of the *Advocate*'s Board of Directors—earned a seat in the state senate with 62 percent of the ward's vote. Statewide, Democrats won all five Executive Council seats and 197 seats in the legislature. Although the Republicans had won 208 seats, the Democrats struck a deal with the Progressives—some of whom, such as Clifford L. Snow of Manchester's Third Ward, actually had been elected as Republicans—and created a coalition that, in January, elected Progressive William Britton as Speaker of the House. A Democrat served as Senate President and another, Samuel Felker, was elected Governor—the first Democrat to hold that office since 1874.[20] Following the lead of President-elect Woodrow Wilson, the Democratic Party promised to take up progressive causes in New Hampshire. They also threatened to pass legislation that jeopardized Healy's job security with the Manchester Police Department. But more important, Amoskeag's control over its work force was endangered, and it could not turn to the state for help.

After the devastating election results and the disruptions of 1912, the Amoskeag Manufacturing Company sought to reassert its influence over the city and reestablish control of its workforce. The company continued to suffer setbacks in 1913, particularly in its influence over the Chief of Police. The success of the Manufacturers League in 1912 also encouraged the New England League to consider a return to the city after a seven-year absence, setting up a confrontation pitting the minor league against the Amoskeag Manufacturing Company. To counteract these setbacks, Amoskeag expanded its benevolence programs, apparently hoping to win over the loyalty of their employees. A new newspaper, operated ostensibly by the Amoskeag Textile Club, would act as the company's trusted mouthpiece. Both to promote readership in its paper and to continue the "Americanization" of its work force, the Textile Club turned to baseball and the improvement of the Manufacturers League. In the end, Amoskeag's dedication to its baseball program resulted in the construction of one of the earliest concrete-and-steel ballparks outside of any major American city or college campus.

6

Minor Leagues

Despite a difficult year that culminated in significant electoral losses, conditions slowly improved for the textile industry, and for Amoskeag in particular. In late November, after the acquittal of Joseph Ettor, Arturo Giovannitti, and Joseph Caruso by a Massachusetts jury for their alleged roles in the Anna LoPizzo murder, the IWW's direct influence over labor issues in New England waned.[1] In 1913, Bill Haywood and other IWW leaders focused their attention on Paterson, New Jersey; the failure of that and other strikes during the year led to significant turmoil within the IWW. Many organizers dropped out of the union. William Trautmann, one of the IWW's founders who led strike efforts in Lowell and had claimed victory in Manchester when Amoskeag announced wage increases, left the IWW over strike tactics and the union's alleged misuse of funds collected for Lawrence strikers.[2] Pearl McGill, who worked on the IWW's behalf in factory cities throughout New England, left the IWW and enrolled at the Iowa State Teachers' College.[3] Meanwhile, the Socialist Party broke with the IWW, condemning its tactics, while locally the New Hampshire Free Speech Alliance waited for Governor Bass and the Executive Council to issue a decision in the group's complaint against Chief Healy and the Manchester Police Commission.

But the problems did not vanish entirely. Though weakened, the IWW survived, and IWW-inspired work stoppages materialized throughout the New England textile industry over the next few years. Some resulted in violence, arrests, and—as in the case of a June 1913 strike in Ipswich, Massachusetts—sometimes death.[4] Even at Amoskeag, 28 Greek spinners briefly walked off their jobs on January 8 to protest the firing of two employees for "staying out from work."[5] Meanwhile, Jesse Markee and others like him kept the union movement alive in Manchester, albeit on behalf of the American Federation of Labor rather than the IWW, and Amoskeag would continue to struggle for control over city and state governments after Democratic and Progressive gains in the 1912 elections. At the same time, the city's shoe factories began to yield to union demands to reduce the average worker's hours, placing added pressure on Amoskeag to do the same. But perhaps the most immediate menace to Amoskeag came from minor-league baseball, and specifically the New England League, which threatened to take away the company's monopoly over organized baseball in the city. Through the creation of a company newspaper and promotion of a proposed minor league, Amoskeag kept the New England League at bay—but only temporarily.

On November 12, 1912, magnates for the eight-team New England League met at the New American General Court in Boston. Only five cities were represented at the meeting, as the league had assumed control of the Fall River franchise because its owners could not meet their financial obligations, and two other teams had folded during the previous season. Thus, the league was reduced to fielding teams in Lawrence, Lowell, Worcester, Brockton, and Lynn, and a new location for the Fall River team had not yet been finalized. The league also hoped to place a new club in Portland, though the distance of Portland from other league cities promised to increase travel expenses for all clubs.[6] Financially, the best way by which to make the Portland franchise work would be to move the league northward—in other words, place at least one additional franchise in northern Massachusetts, southern New Hampshire, and/or Maine.

The success of the Manufacturers League and Manchester's newfound interest in baseball caught the attention of New England League officials. League owners believed that recent population growth made baseball a "paying proposition" in Manchester, while the increased presence of the shoe industry seemed to dilute Amoskeag's potential influence over the game. Therefore in early November, Massachusetts lawyer and New England League team owner Louis Pieper negotiated with Amoskeag to relocate the Fall River franchise to Manchester. However, he met with what the *Leader* termed an "obstacle." Apparently, Amoskeag's influence was much greater than Pieper and other owners had anticipated, as the corporation owned Varick Park, the one site in the city at which professional baseball might be played profitably.[7] Soon after, Frank Leonard, who had been given an option to purchase the Fall River team, arrived in Manchester to negotiate.

Varick Park, located along Valley Street between Maple and Beech Streets, might have been Manchester's oldest remaining ball grounds. At least as early as 1880, the flat Amoskeag-owned lot known informally as "the Plains" was used by schools and school-aged children for baseball and other sports. By 1891, after the development of the city's formal ball fields in North and West Manchester into house lots, the Plains became the city's most convenient grounds for baseball. That year, with the help of Amoskeag surveyors sent by Herman Straw, a group of residents created the Amoskeag Athletic Association and transformed the property into the Beech Street Grounds, with a sculpted diamond, fence, and two wooden grandstands that could accommodate 1,000 people. The association even fielded a New England League team, called the Amoskeags in honor of Straw's employer for his help in renovating the Plains.

This and a subsequent team failed, however. Therefore, in 1894, again with Amoskeag's help, local businessman Thomas Varick spent $3,000 to redevelop the site for track-and-field events, bicycle races, and baseball and football games. He had the grounds re-graded, constructed a 40-foot-wide, quarter-mile dirt track, and moved the grandstands and park entrances several yards eastward. The re-named Varick Park opened in 1894, though within a few years Varick sold his interest to another local resident, William Freeman.[3] Regardless, the park's proximity to downtown Manchester and the fact that it remained the city's only baseball field equipped with covered grandstands made it the only grounds in the city capable of supporting professional baseball.

Perhaps because of Varick Park's location, the Amoskeag Textile Club commenced negotiations with Freeman to assume complete ownership of the complex in June 1912. By mid–October Freeman and the club had come to an agreement. The ATC planned to completely transform the grounds by rearranging the field and erecting a new grandstand facing north, rather than east as the existing structures had been oriented since 1894.[9] Through Varick Park the Textile Club was committing itself to the Manufacturers League, and as Frank Leonard attempted to negotiate for the park's use, he found that the club neither wished to share the park nor compete with an outside organization for the loyalty of Manchester's baseball fans. The *Mirror* summarized Amoskeag's position: "The Manufacturers league boomed the game when it was dead in Manchester, and aroused much interest, and feels that it has the FIRST RIGHT TO ITS GROUNDS."[10]

Scheduling also posed a problem. The club told Leonard "that its first interest was naturally the Manufacturers league, and as the New England league team would want half of the Saturdays, and the Manufacturers league games take place on Saturday, there has not appeared any way by which each party can reach a mutually satisfactory understanding."[11] Leonard did offer to play double-headers (a Manufacturers League game followed by a New England League contest) on the twelve Saturdays when the proposed minor-league team was not on the road, though this did not reassure the Amoskeag Textile Club's board of governors.

Despite the ATC's position, some baseball fans wanted the New England League to return to Manchester. In mid–November, the *Mirror* published a letter written by someone identified only as "A FAN." In it, the anonymous author—who apparently represented the city's merchant and professional classes—extolled the benefits of having a minor-league baseball team in Manchester: "...for those who are trying to boost the city the chance has come, and no obstacle should be put in the way to hinder its coming." If a New England League team did not move to Manchester, the fan believed, it would be because the "club in control of Varick park does not seem to desire to have a New England league team here...." And while the "Manufacturers league is all right in its place," the author believed that it "is far from playing New England league ball, which by the way, is very little below the big league standard...."[12]

On November 21, despite the fan's pleas, the Amoskeag Textile Club officially refused the use of Varick Park to Frank Leonard. In a letter to Leonard, the club wrote that "it has been decided practically by the board [of governors], as an impossibility for them to consider the turning over of Varick Park to outside capital." Its action had been "actuated by the sentiment of the heads of the different organizations in the Manufacturers League," the board claimed. The club did offer to "lend whatever efforts possible" in helping the league to locate another suitable grounds on which to erect its own baseball park. "That is, if there is land owned by the Amoskeag which the New England leaguers would like for ball park uses, the corporation will take the question under advisement." The Amoskeag Manufacturing Company even suggested that the New England League consider constructing a stadium on the circus grounds lying immediately east of Varick Park.[13] But the *Mirror* estimated that the construction of a wooden ballpark would cost the New England League $15,000—apparently not an investment that the profit-oriented New England League could afford to make.[14] Shortly thereafter, even after Saint Anselm College coach George Cassidy suggested an athletic park might be built on the city's West Side and shared by the New England League and the city's soccer clubs, Frank Leonard withdrew his bid to place a team in Manchester.[15]

The New England League, needing to finalize its schedule, bypassed Manchester and placed new teams in New Bedford, Fall River, and Portland. The *Mirror* responded by publishing an article highlighting the "uncertainty" surrounding the health of other teams in the New England League, suggesting that Manchester was lucky not to have a club in the circuit. Meanwhile, as the Amoskeag Textile Club prepared to unveil its plans for Varick Park, it continued to receive criticism for its position on the New England League. Within two weeks, the club would respond to that criticism in the first issue of its new company newspaper.

In the wake of the November election results, some workers in Manchester saw improvements in their working conditions. For instance, in mid–November the W. H. McElwain Shoe Company reduced its workweek from 58 to 54 hours. Most of its 7,000 employees would work from 6:45 AM until 5:35 PM each weekday, with a shorter workday on Saturdays. The *Advocate* responded to the news by congratulating the company "on its disposition to better the conditions of operatives under its employ" and by stating its hope that "it will be but a short time before the rule of 48 hours per week, the principle for which the A. F. of L. has so long contended, will be put into effect by this company." But the article concluded by stating "what a grand thing it would be if the Amoskeag corporation followed in the course so beneficially inaugurated by the McElwain people.... In the language of the street: 'It's up to the Amoskeag.' Will it rise to the occasion?"[16]

The Amoskeag Manufacturing Company made no effort to reduce its employees' work hours. However, on December 2, 1912, the Amoskeag Textile Club published the first issue of the *Amoskeag Bulletin*. The *Bulletin* was an impressive newspaper of between eight and sixteen pages, with five columns per page and photographs scattered throughout, all printed on high-quality paper and costing one cent—the same price as the *Leader*. Published twice per month, the paper was edited by William B. McKay, the head of the company's printing department who also served as an officer in the Amoskeag Textile Club, president of the Manufacturers League, and member of the New Hampshire State Republican Committee.[17] Ostensibly, the *Bulletin* existed "to promote interest in the Amoskeag Textile Club, furnish the members of the club with information concerning the doings of the Board of Governors, keep the members in touch with matters of interest about the [mill] yard and endeavor to create a general good feeling among the employees of the Amoskeag Manufacturing Company."[18] Of course, as a 1939 federal report suggested, it "probably was not a free forum for discussion" between labor and management.[19] Rather, Amoskeag could use the *Bulletin* to control the flow and tenor of information about the company, bypassing the *Leader* and other city newspapers.

In the *Bulletin*'s first issue, McKay used the front page to advertise an upcoming Textile Club-sponsored talk about the Panama Canal. The paper notified employees of the availability of first-aid care for Amoskeag employees during the workday, and of free dental care for Amoskeag employees and their children (provided the child was under fourteen years of age when, presumably, he or she would enter the workforce). It also touted the advantages of carrying the Amoskeag Textile Club's membership card at all times, the availability of books in the club's reading room, and a declaration that the company had decided to fly American flags—26 in all, with several more to be added—on all of its buildings on a permanent basis.

Yet the most interesting, and seemingly out-of-place, item on the front page of the *Bulletin*'s December 2, 1912, issue was one about baseball. In the full-column article, the unnamed author—likely McKay himself—noted that Amoskeag had been unfairly targeted for denying the New England League use of Varick Park. The writer noted that the Amoskeag Textile Club's Board of Governors—and emphatically *not* the Amoskeag Manufacturing Company—had "preserv[ed] Varick Park for the use of mill and shoe factory operatives on the only half-holiday in the week." He continued:

> Considering the fact that the Amoskeag Textile Club, in a way, was the father of the Manufacturers League, having done so much to make it a success, the governors could not conscientiously do anything that would cause harm to the future of the league. It had already been decided that Varick park would be made into an athletic field that could give the young men of Manchester an opportunity to develop and at the same time furnish a means of entertainment that would keep many from seeking diversion in harmful and perhaps dangerous enjoyments.

The article's author reiterated that the club offered to help a New England League team find grounds in Manchester. However, "it seems to be an assured fact that unless the promoters were given a place to play the games without being obliged to dig into their jeans to any extent, the lukewarm enthusiasm [for baseball among Manchester's fans] would very soon turn cold.... It has been demonstrated that the Amoskeag Textile Club has the welfare of the sport-loving public at heart as well as promoting good feeling and harmony among its own members."[20]

On December 6, the *Mirror* reprinted the entire *Bulletin* article, adding that through the *Bulletin* the Amoskeag Textile Club had explained its position on minor-league baseball "in a most manly manner."[21] Even so, some among Manchester's merchants and professionals were doubtful about Amoskeag's intentions. For example, an anonymous baseball fan saw a conspiracy among the Textile Club's Board of Governors and the *Bulletin* and the *Mirror* to keep the New England League out of Manchester. The fan felt that the *Bulletin*'s front-page article about the league had been "written by some member of the Amoskeag Textile club or Manufacturers league. I would arise to remark that it sounds like trying to put a coat of whitewash on themselves and give them a clean bill of health." Even if the Amoskeag Manufacturing Company had had "nothing to do with a kibosh on the New England League proposition," the individual believed that "the Amoskeag Textile club put it on ... and no amount of bulletin or newspaper writings can change it."[22]

Regardless of how readers felt about the New England League situation, the *Bulletin* was an immediate success. Both the *Mirror* and the *Union* welcomed the new publication, and *L'Avenir National* called it an "innovation" that would promote unity between the corporation and its employees. This "new initiative," *L'Avenir*'s editors claimed, proved that the officials of "our great corporation" had only the best of intentions with regard to creating a positive working environment for its employees.[23]

Jesse Markee, however, was cynical about the *Bulletin*, which he saw as nothing more than a mouthpiece for Amoskeag's anti-union management. In fact, his newspaper targeted editor William McKay, a former union member who seemingly had turned his back on labor:

> The *Amoskeag Bulletin* is the name of a new publication making its appearance in Manchester. It is without doubt the finest specimen of typographic art of this century. The paper stock is the best obtainable and the ink, a raven black, makes a contrast beyond description. The dream fancies of Faust and Guttenberg have been realized and upon the Amoskeag Textile Club shines the whole glory. No. Some glory for ye editor. Wm. B. McKay is it. Once a member of the best and most charitable organizations on earth, and receiving the best within its gift, the International Typographical Union. While a member of the Musicians' Union was chosen president of the organization, and scooped in all the fat jobs as trap drummer. But alas! He has been promoted to the field of higher journalism.[24]

For two weeks after the inaugural issue of the *Bulletin* appeared, rumors circulated that the Amoskeag Textile Club would, indeed, accept proposals for outside use of Varick Park, but not from the class-B New England League. On December 10, the *Mirror* and *L'Avenir National* learned that a lower-level class-C league, to be known as the Northeastern Baseball League, was being formed in Binghamton, New York. Six cities reportedly had applied for membership in the league, including Bangor and Portland, Maine; Pawtucket, Rhode Island; Taunton, Massachusetts; and Manchester and Nashua, New Hampshire. The league also expressed an interest in placing teams either in Augusta or Lewiston, Maine, and Salem or Gloucester, Massachusetts. John T. Manning of Binghamton received the rights to operate the Manchester franchise.[25]

Publicly, the Amoskeag Textile Club remained silent on the issue. Instead, the club's Board of Governors unveiled its plans for the reconstruction of Varick Park. "TEXTILE FIELD IS NEW NAME; EXIT VARICK PARK" proclaimed a headline on the front page of the December 16 *Amoskeag Bulletin*. Although details remained sketchy, the Textile Club promised to replace the dilapidated Varick Park grandstand with a "substantial wooden grand-stand facing north, capable of seating about four thousand people." The "tumble-down" condition of the fences necessitated that they be taken down, and the club planned to construct new ten-foot wooden walls "built of matched boards and on top of which will be barbed wire to stop anyone from using that route as an entrance." New refreshment stands, dressing rooms, "sanitary toilet rooms," and ticket offices would be constructed beneath the grandstand, and the gully along Valley

Street was to be graded to allow access to the new facility, which, as the headline suggested, was to be renamed "Textile Field." "The Amoskeag Textile Club ... have done something that should put the club in the front rank of philanthropic institutions," bragged the *Bulletin*. "It is expected that at least ten thousand dollars will be expended in making Textile Field one of the best parks of its kind in this section of the country."[26]

A day later the *Mirror* announced the Amoskeag Textile Club's plans, closely summarizing the previous day's *Bulletin* article. The newspaper also reported on problems in the New England League, such as the fact that four league teams lacked managers, and that Frank Leonard continued to have trouble finding a place for his team to play in Portland. The *Leader* speculated that Leonard's team would end up in Portland, though the league still might consider transferring the New Bedford franchise to Manchester if conditions improved.[27]

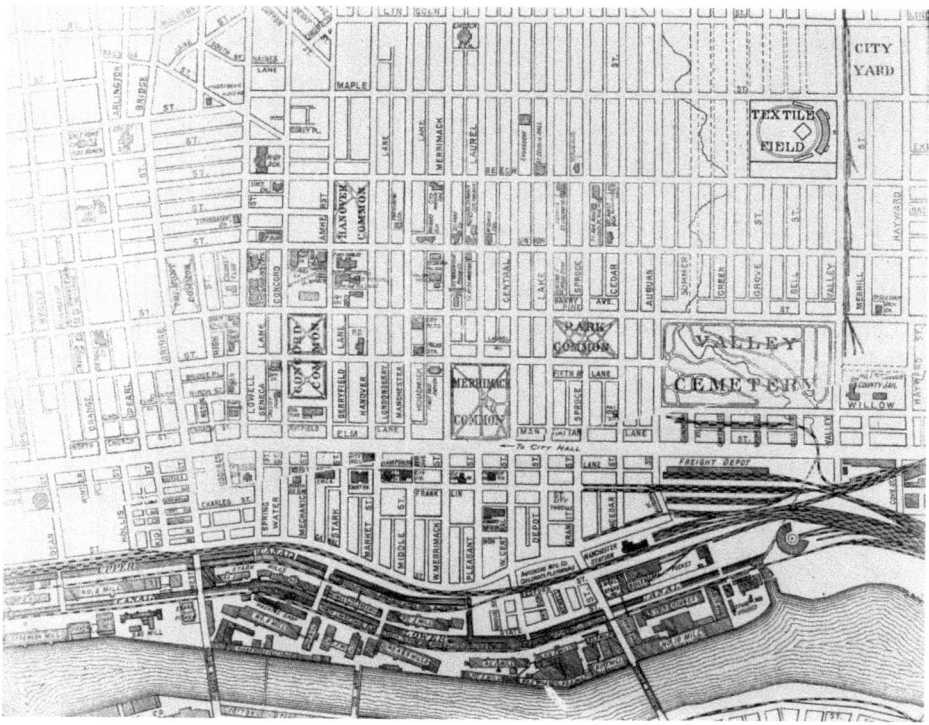

Downtown Manchester and part of the Amoskeag Millyard, circa 1915. The map, which is oriented with north to the left, shows the location and layout of Textile Field after its conversion from Varick Park (courtesy Manchester [New Hampshire] Historic Association).

Then, two days after Christmas, John Manning arrived in Manchester. By this time, the planned Northeastern League was to include teams from Manchester, Bangor, Portland, Lewiston, Taunton, Gloucester, and two other cities, with Nashua and Concord under consideration for one of the vacant spots. If Manning could not secure a field in Manchester, he would instead place his team in Biddeford, Maine. But he told the *Mirror* that he preferred the Queen City. "Manchester, with her splendid enterprise and numerous activities, is the place for a league team.... To my mind there is no one thing which advertises and gives prominence to a city more than a winning baseball team, and this is what we hope to have in Manchester."[28]

During his visit, Manning met with city business leaders, Amoskeag Textile Club president and Amoskeag Manufacturing Company superintendent William Parker Straw, and "many of the city's 'dyed-in-the-wool fans.'" His impressions of the city were so favorable, according to the *Mirror*, that he "had about made up his mind to go ahead, should he be unable to make satisfactory arrangements with the Amoskeag Textile club to divide dates at Textile field, and lease grounds, enclose them and erect a grand stand and bleachers." He also promised that Manchester would be the jewel of the Northeastern League: the league's first annual meeting would occur in the city on January 23, 1913.[29]

If Manning truly worried that he would not be able to secure use of Textile Field, he need not have. William Parker Straw, after meeting with Manning, immediately convened the Textile Club's board of governors. After hearing Manning's proposal, the board, ignoring its arguments in denying the New England League use of the grounds, voted unanimously to allow him the use of Textile Field.[30] Manning seemed genuinely surprised by the result, telling a reporter that he "had been led to believe ... that the Textile club was opposed to professional baseball, and to Manchester having a league team but instead I met with the most hearty kind of approval of my plans, and an assurance of help."[31] The *Leader* also expressed astonishment, noting that "it was generally understood that the club stood opposed to the entrance of a league baseball team into this city in opposition to the Textile league of local clubs.... [The club's] action in giving to Mr. Manning the use of Textile field comes as a decided surprise."[32]

Although Manchester newspapers now proclaimed that the city was assured a professional baseball team for 1913, some questions remained. First, no one was quite sure who would be represented in the league. The *Mirror* and *L'Avenir National* both reported that the proposed league would include Manchester, Bangor, Portland, Lewiston, Taunton, Fitchburg, and two other teams, though only two days earlier the league had included Gloucester rather than

Fitchburg. The *Leader* claimed that the league would consist of Manchester, Portland, Bangor, Gloucester, Taunton, and three other teams. More ominous, perhaps, was the fact that Manning told reporters he had signed "six players of experience, including a pitcher, catcher, and third baseman of known ability," but he refused to reveal their names.[33]

On January 1, the *Bulletin* appeared with front-page news about a new method of teaching English to immigrants—an important development, given that in 1910, nearly 10,700 of Manchester's residents above the age of ten could not speak English.[34] About two weeks earlier, the Amoskeag Textile Club had sponsored a demonstration in which Dr. Peter Roberts taught a group of fourteen Polish immigrants, ranging in age between sixteen and 25 years old, how to speak key phrases in English. As members of the board of governors looked on, Roberts introduced his class to a series of words and phrases relating to getting up in the morning. The lesson was the first of thirty to which Roberts owned the copyright, all part of a series that the Amoskeag Textile Club was considering adopting as part of its English-language curriculum. The *Bulletin* proclaimed that the time, effort, and money spent demonstrated how the club "is in sympathy with everything that tends to promote better conditions among the employees of the Amoskeag Manufacturing Company."

In the same issue, the *Bulletin* pronounced that the ATC "would do everything possible to further the interests of league baseball in Manchester. That statement is now made good and will set at rest the statements of those who have been going about with the ready hammer." The club repeated what already had been announced by John Manning: that the Northeastern League would place a franchise in Manchester at Textile Field, and that the Manufacturers League would continue to operate. It also confirmed that on Saturdays when both leagues have scheduled games for Manchester, a double-header would be arranged, with the Textile Club and the new minor-league team splitting receipts evenly.[35]

Specifics about the arrangement began to surface shortly thereafter, as did questions about the team's potential profitability. On weekdays—days, incidentally, on which most of Manchester's factory workers were not released from work until after 6:00 at night—Manning would pay visiting teams 40 percent of the non-grandstand gate receipts, and divide the remaining sixty percent evenly with the Textile Club. The grandstand receipts would be split equally between Manning's team and the club. On Saturdays and holidays, the visiting team would receive one-half of all non-grandstand gate receipts, and Manning's team and the Textile Club would split the remaining receipts, both grandstand and non-grandstand, equally. According to the *Mirror*, the team was unlikely to make a profit.[36]

Questions about the venture also arose in other New England cities. A Lowell newspaper commented, "Just how long the new league will last is a question being discussed by the New England league magnates, who are somewhat piqued because Manchester didn't warm up to Frank Leonard's advances.... By the way, why is Manchester so anxious to get into a class C league, when it had a chance to enter class B ranks?" From Portland, meanwhile, came word that "the Northeastern league has not as yet aroused enthusiasm in that city.... The circuit, as proposed, is a dead one at the outset. Manchester and Portland are the only cities [in the league] that are within reasonable distance of each other and are at the same time paying propositions."[37] A few days later, the *Bangor Commercial* announced that "the Northeastern Baseball League is dead before it was born," to which the acting president of the league replied, "I think the New England league is working overtime in trying to stop our league."[38]

On January 21, John Manning arrived in Manchester to prepare for the Northeastern League meeting, which was to be held at the New Manchester House two days later. Prior to the meeting, Manning suggested that although questions had arisen regarding the possibility of placing a team in Portland, that city would, indeed, be represented in the Northeastern League, as would Manchester, Bangor, Lewiston, Biddeford, Taunton, either Newburyport or Fitchburg, and either Concord or Nashua. The first meeting saw those present elect former Manchester Mayor E. J. Knowlton to be the league's honorary president. Later, in a seven-hour session lasting until after midnight, and in a move that reflected the league's tenuous hold on Portland, the group selected Chicago White Sox scout and former Portland Mayor George Mills to be the league's "permanent" president, secretary, and treasurer. The league discussed a constitution and bylaws, adopted a 112-game schedule and a salary cap of $1,400 per team, and voted that ten percent of the gross gate receipts be reserved to cover league administrative costs. In the end, the league voted to admit eight teams, each of which was to deposit $25.00 with the league treasurer prior to April 1. Teams would represent Manchester, Portland, Bangor, Gloucester, Lewiston, and, most surprisingly, St. John's, New Brunswick. Two additional cities were to be chosen from among Fitchburg and Salem, Massachusetts, and Concord, New Hampshire.[39]

Less than a week after the Northeastern League's meeting, the Manufacturers League began to organize for the 1913 season. Officials announced that the league would enter the season with six teams, one each representing Amoskeag, McElwain, Beacon, Stark, and Reed firms, with a sixth team to be added at a later date. Perhaps part of the reason for the league's sudden prominence in the pages of the *Mirror* was the fact that the Manufacturers League elected the *Mirror*'s Horace L. Robbins to be its official scorekeeper. The league also voted to ratify the Amoskeag Textile Club's actions regarding the Northeastern League.[40]

Due to the high cost of travel among its cities, the success of the Northeastern League seemed to rest on Portland, where Frank Leonard was negotiating to place his New England League team. Unfortunately for the new league, Leonard was successful, and by January 29 the Northeastern League appeared dead. Two days later, New England League president Tim Murnane called an emergency meeting in which that league voted to transfer the Fall River franchise to Portland under the ownership of Frank Leonard.[41] "Without doubt," suggested the *Bulletin*, "the [Northeastern League] men who were engineering the scheme were laboring in perfect faith with the belief that everything had been working in their favor, and this apparent double cross has upset their plans."[42]

While the Northeastern League failed to materialize, the Amoskeag Textile Club had, for the time being, successfully blocked the New England League from Manchester. This seems to have been Amoskeag's primary goal in supporting the Northeastern League. The ATC does not appear to have opposed the idea of a Manchester club in the failed league, probably because the league pledged to work with the club to ensure the continued success of the Manufacturers League—something that the profit-oriented (and probably more realistic) owners of the New England League would not do. Regardless, only the Manufacturers League would occupy the new Textile Field in 1913, and the Amoskeag Textile Club would retain total control over the grounds as part of its effort to Americanize and otherwise control the Amoskeag workforce through baseball.

Baseball was only one area in which Amoskeag attempted to reestablish its influence over its city and its workforce. In 1913, the company—unused to losing elections—also turned its sights on New Hampshire state government, where a Progressive-Democratic coalition threatened to reduce Amoskeag's influence even further.

7

Problems of Government

In January, as the future of the Northeastern League dimmed, the newly elected New Hampshire General Court met in Concord. In one of their more contentious orders of business, legislators cast their votes for United States senator. Despite the Progressive-Democratic coalition, members of the two parties could not agree on a candidate.[1] On the 43rd ballot, after two months in which Democrat Henry Hollis consistently outpolled his challengers, but was unable to garner a majority, Hollis finally was elected, in part because his party was able to convince a handful of Republicans to vote for him.[2]

The Amoskeag Manufacturing Company was particularly interested in the General Court's choice of United States senator. Therefore, company officials must have noticed the votes of Representative Clifford L. Snow, a Republican from Manchester's Third Ward. Given his party affiliation and the fact that his father-in-law worked as an engineer for Amoskeag, Snow might have been expected to support the company. However, Snow tended to vote with the Progressives, often in direct contradiction to the interests of Amoskeag and the pro-business wing of the Republican Party. This was particularly true in the question of United States senator. On the first several ballots, Snow voted for Robert Bass. Later, when Bass's support began to wane, he switched his support to another Progressive, William J. Britton, then to Democrats Calvin Page of Portsmouth and George Carpenter of Wolfeboro, before eventually settling on Hollis.

To Amoskeag, and to Republicans in general, voting for a Democrat who opposed the protective tariff on imported cotton textiles, among other goods, was unforgivable. But to vote for Hollis in particular was to vote for a candidate who claimed openly that Amoskeag was "a foe to the wage earner in this state" and "a detriment to New Hampshire."[3] Perhaps as a result, or perhaps for reasons of his own doing, Snow would pay for his actions. Even as Amoskeag began promoting the 1913 Manufacturers League season, and during a legislative session in which Amoskeag's authority would erode further, Representative Snow would become the first state legislator ever forcibly removed from office.

Twenty-nine-year-old Clifford L. Snow arrived at the New Hampshire State House on Wednesday, January 1, 1913, for the first day of the new legislative session. A house- and sign-painter by trade, Snow grew up in Goffstown until, at the age of fourteen, he moved to the neighboring city of Manchester. By 1910 he lived with his wife and in-laws in an apartment on Pine Street, just a few blocks from tenement buildings owned by the Amoskeag Manufacturing Company, the company that employed his father-in-law, Charles Savory. His wife of almost seven years, Caddie, worked as a stitcher in a local shoe factory. Snow began his political career in 1908, winning a seat on the Board of Selectmen for Ward Three. In 1912 he ran as a progressive Republican for a seat in the legislature, winning easily.[4]

The legislature began the new session with a roll call. Snow, signaling his intent to be a progressive leader in the House, moved that the clerk appoint two members to fetch Governor Bass to preside over the swearing in of the body. The clerk chose Snow and Raymond Stevens of Landaff to call for the governor, who entered the chamber to complete his constitutional duties. The legislature spent the remainder of the day and part of the next electing a Speaker of the House, eventually settling on William Britton on the sixth ballot.

On January 14, after nearly two weeks of organizing for the coming year, members of the General Court finally held an election for United States senator. In the House, Henry Hollis received 198 votes, and Republican Henry Quinby tallied 108. But with thirteen candidates receiving votes, no one received a majority. On the next ballot, Hollis received 196 votes to Quinby's 96. In both cases, Robert Bass received enough votes that, if his totals were added to Hollis's, the Democrat would have won. But Progressives, including those nominally of the Democratic and Republican parties, found no grounds for compromise. The election would continue for two months.

Henry Hollis's eventual election to the United States Senate seemed inevitable. But as *Concord Monitor* editor George Moses joked, the Amoskeag Manufacturing Company "would cheerfully commit burglary, arson and murder" to keep Hollis out of Washington.[5] Amoskeag had made its position clear during the election: its managers strongly opposed Hollis's likely vote to reduce or eliminate the tariff. The reason was obvious to anyone who followed economic trends in the United States, for at the time, the New England textile industry already was losing ground—and profits—to firms in the South.[6]

Many of those receiving votes during the House elections for United States senator appear to have been prominent Manchester-area politicians who might have supported Amoskeag, including *Union* publisher Rosecrans Pillsbury and Manchester benefactor and business leader Frank Carpenter, both Republicans. Yet lawyer Gordon Woodbury's sudden appearance as a candidate is notable as well. Woodbury was a 49-year-old Democrat from Bedford who had attended Phillips Exeter Academy and Harvard University, held a law degree from Columbia University, and had owned the *Manchester Union* from 1896 to 1905 before becoming an editorial writer for the *Boston Herald*. He was also known to be an "anti–Hollis Democrat." Woodbury's name did not appear until the third ballot, when Bedford representative Perham Parker, a Republican, cast his vote for the Democrat. Subsequently, Woodbury began to receive votes from Democrats such as Nazaire Boulanger of Manchester. In elections thereafter, Woodbury never received a significant number of votes—generally between three and eight out of about 400 cast. But as the weeks dragged on, some took notice when he did not formally withdraw his name from consideration despite the fact that his candidacy took votes away from a fellow Democrat.[7]

The legislature finally resolved its stalemate on March 13 when, by a 189–182 vote, Henry Hollis was named on a majority of the ballots cast. Jesse Markee's *Manchester Advocate* responded positively, suggesting that the election of Hollis represented "a second revolution in the State of New Hampshire" within the past year, the first having been the overthrow of the Republican establishment in the November elections. Regarding Hollis's election, the *Advocate* also noted that "a feeling of perfect satisfaction" is "strongly manifest among shoe workers in all the factories of the town." But while the newspaper suggested that Amoskeag employees felt the same way, they would only express that opinion "after a glance assures them that the enemy will not overhear the expression"—highlighting their attitude toward, but also the power of, their employer.[8]

Clifford Snow was among those who crossed party lines and voted for Hollis. Two weeks earlier, rumors began to circulate that some legislators' votes had been compromised by bribes and offers of political favor. When asked by the *Advocate*, one unnamed Manchester Democrat who opposed Hollis's election refused to deny that he had *not* been approached with a bribe, saying only, "I will tell you about it after they elect a United States Senator." In response to these rumors, the legislature appointed a committee consisting of Democrat Albert Demerritt of Durham, Republican Ezra Smith of Peterborough, and Holderness Republican Harold Webster, the last of whom typically voted with the Progressives.[9] The committee held four hearings between March 17 and April 7 and produced two reports. The legislature took up both on April 10.

Throughout the winter and early spring, even as it debated the choice for senator and investigated its members for wrongdoing, the General Court was able to consider legislation. Perhaps not surprisingly, in February the House followed Governor Felker's recommendation and voted to ratify what would become the Seventeenth Amendment, allowing for the popular election of United States senators. Yet representatives worked on other legislation as well. For example, in one instance that promised to help Amoskeag's workers as well as the Manufacturers League, Clifford Snow joined several other Manchester representatives in supporting a bill to legalize Sunday baseball in New Hampshire. Up to that time Sunday baseball remained illegal in several eastern states, including New Hampshire. Even at the major-league level, the Boston Red Sox were prohibited from playing baseball in Massachusetts on Sundays, as were the Boston Braves—a team that was so desperate for fans that it had scheduled a handful of Sunday contests at Hoboken, New Jersey and Rocky Point, Rhode Island a decade earlier.[10]

After a push from Manchester representative Hobart Pillsbury, the bill to legalize Sunday baseball came before the legislature on February 27. Had it been enacted, cities and towns would have had the right to permit Sunday baseball as long as games began after 1:00 in the afternoon and were completed before dark, and did not take place within 1,000 feet of a church. One Manchester representative spoke in favor of the bill, saying that his city "was a manufacturing city where the people worked from sunup until dark in the mills and ... they should be allowed to enjoy some recreation on the only day available to them for such purpose." Despite the Manchester delegation's support, the bill was defeated by a vote of 174 to 108.[11]

At the same time, baseball fans in Manchester slowly realized that they would be without professional baseball again in the coming year. Occasionally, the *Leader*, *Mirror*, or the *Union* might suggest that the New England League still wished to place one of its clubs in Manchester. The *Mirror*, in particular, used those occasions to remind Manchester baseball fans that neither the Manufacturers League nor the Amoskeag Textile Club opposed a New England League team for Manchester, "for they welcomed the coming of John Manning and the Northeastern League."[12]

Perhaps to deflect criticism, the Amoskeag Textile Club attempted to generate excitement for the Manufacturers League through the city's newspapers. In February, *L'Avenir National* reported that Amoskeag would hire Fred Brice, athletic director for Manchester High School, as its coach, which the *Bulletin* confirmed three days later.[13] The *Bulletin* also corroborated a *Mirror* report that Amoskeag pitcher Willard Taber was mulling over an offer to join the Cleveland Naps of the American League, though *L'Avenir National* later reported that Taber would remain in Manchester.[14] Perhaps not coincidentally, a few weeks after he rejected Cleveland's overture, Taber was promoted to the position of General Inspector in the No. 11 cloth room, later said by one of his supervisors to be the pitcher's best job in his three years with the company. Taber remained in this position, despite the fact that his supervisor did not feel that the pitcher was very good at it, until he was reassigned in December 1914.[15]

Additionally, in mid–February Amoskeag announced that one of its new employees, Emil Pernod, likely would join its baseball team as a catcher.[16] Like Taber, Pernod hailed from Columbus, Ohio, and according to *L'Avenir National* had played for a minor-league club in the American Association. Amoskeag employment records show that the 24-year-old Pernod was hired on February 3—only eleven days before the *L'Avenir* report—as an inspector in the cloth room, a position similar to the one to which Taber would be promoted. Clearly, he had been hired by Amoskeag to play baseball in the Manufacturers League. He worked as a cloth inspector until June 10 when, according to his file, he was "employed as room man."[17]

By hiring Brice and Pernod and promoting Taber, Amoskeag implied that the Manufacturers League had professional-caliber talent, and that the city did not need a minor-league team. News from other Manufacturers League teams supported this implication. The Hoyt Shoe Company announced that it recruited Phenomenal Smith to manage its team, while the Stark Mills hired Arthur Gibbs, a pitcher from the Connecticut State League.[18] The *Mirror* even ran columns announcing roster moves among the Manufacturers League teams, and speculating about which club would win the league championship and which players were best at their positions.[19]

As its January term progressed, the legislature continued to take up Progressive initiatives, many of which threatened Amoskeag's power and profitability. One of these was a bill to reduce the workweek for mill operatives from 58 to 54 hours. After it was amended in the senate to allow for a 55-hour workweek, the bill passed both chambers and was signed into law by Governor Felker. The new legislation would take effect on January 1, 1914, giving the Amoskeag Manufacturing Company and other industries several months to plan for the change.[20] For his part, Thomas Chalmers understood how Amoskeag might oppose the legislation. "Undoubtedly this great corporation, and others like it, was much disturbed over the determination of the ... legislature to pass such a law," he wrote. "It was natural that they should oppose it.... [But] the local good will which the Amoskeag enjoys in Manchester today more than balances the added cost of administration resulting from this enactment." In other words, if Amoskeag were to support the law, not reduce wages, and otherwise maintain its positive relationship with its workforce, it would benefit from a healthier, happier workforce.[21]

More immediately ominous was a plan to reform city police commissions in the state. Throughout the fall, Governor Bass and the Executive Council took their time in considering the New Hampshire Free Speech Alliance's complaint against Chief Michael Healy. Bass wrote to Boston Mayor John "Honey Fitz" Fitzgerald about the police situation in his city, particularly relating to oversight of the Police Chief and the handling of public meetings and strikes. He also brought Healy and members of the Free Speech Alliance back to Concord in December, allowing Healy and Alliance attorney Mederic Guilbeault to go on record accusing each other of lying. George Warren, lawyer for the Manchester Police Commission, reiterated that the owners of the Polish, Stark, and Jolliet Halls—not Chief Healy—prevented the Cigarmakers' Union from renting the buildings to "speakers from Lawrence connected with the IWW at a time when riots were practically existing in the city of Lawrence."

In his arguments to the Governor and Executive Council, Warren tried to clarify Chief Healy's role in the affair, notably invoking the name of Big Bill Haywood several times as he did so:

> [T]he evidence is that neither the proprietor of the Polish Hall or of Stark Hall refused the use of those halls for any other reason except that they had been deceived by the parties who came to them for the purpose of hiring them, and this is especially true in regard to the hall of the Jolliet club. It was not hired for the purpose of having Big Bill Hayward [sic] make a speech there, and when Chief Healy accidentally saw some "dodgers" that had been thrown out the day before, announcing that Big Bill Hayward was going to speak there that night, he called up the president of that club and asked him if he knew about it. It seems that the president did not know it, and he conferred with the chief and he took it up with the directors, and he did the wise thing not only for the Jolliet club but for the people of Manchester in refusing the use of that hall at that time for the purpose of allowing Big Bill Hayward to speak.[22]

Newspapers such as the *Mirror* carried neither Guilbeault's response nor his arguments against the Police Commission. Regardless, after the conclusion of the proceedings, the Governor and Executive Council issued a ruling: that the Manchester Police Commission, "through its officers and agents, used undue influence in abridging freedom of speech" in denying IWW operatives to speak in Manchester. While granting that "said influence was exerted at a time of industrial unrest, when an unbiased judgment may have been that the best interests of the city demanded such action," the Governor and Executive Council did nothing to punish Michael Healy. Instead, though their terms of office ended within a few weeks, they promised to revisit the issue "if at any time there be further denial directly or indirectly, of the right of free speech to any law-abiding citizen by the police department of the city of Manchester."[23]

Once in office, the newly elected Progressive-Democratic coalition apparently disagreed with the former Governor and Executive Council's inaction, and instead proposed to change how police commissioners received their appointments. Prior to 1913, commissioners were appointed locally and served

IWW co-founder William D. "Big Bill" Haywood (in dark suit, coat, and bowler, behind child) leading Lowell strikers in 1912. Haywood, the best known and most feared of the IWW's leaders, traveled throughout New England to garner support for the Lawrence strikers. Police Chief Michael Healy later claimed to have kept Haywood from speaking in Manchester (Bain Collection, Prints & Photographs Division, Library of Congress, LC-B2-2392-2).

six-year terms. Under the new law, each city's commission was to be appointed by the Governor, with the advice and approval of the Executive Council. Commissioners had to be residents of the city or town of the commission on which they served for at least five years prior to their three-year appointment, and no more than two commissioners in each city could represent the same political party. Each commission could remove any officer for just cause, and commissioners had the power to make all rules for the governing of the police force. Moreover, the governor had the authority to remove commissioners at any time with the Executive Council's approval.[24]

The bill was aimed at Michael Healy, for it effectively meant that the New Hampshire governor, rather than local city governments (and, by extension, powerful corporations such as the Amoskeag Manufacturing Company), would have control over the hiring and firing of the Manchester Chief of Police. Yet Chief Healy found a surprising ally in Frank Knox's *Manchester Leader*. The

Leader published a series of editorials in which its editor claimed that the "sole aim" of the "so-called police commission bill" was "to 'get' Chief Healy." Knox, who had arrived in Manchester seven months after the first Free Speech incident, was impressed with Healy's record of securing peace, order, and the protection of property in the city. He asserted that the Manchester police chief's enemies simply wanted to remove him because he had "played politics."[25]

On May 23, once the governor had signed the police commission bill into law, the *Leader* asserted that the bill's supporters generally came from "two classes active in the anti–Healy movement":

> One is the lawless, disorderly element who resent the rigorous enforcement of the laws governing prostitution and the selling of intoxicants, although this does not include the better class of retail liquor dealers. And the other class comprises some of the active politicians in the Democratic party who charge Healy in times past, with using the police department for political ends.

The former group, claimed the *Leader,* wanted to make Manchester a lawless city, a haven for corruption and disorder, and would be neutralized by the will of the majority. The latter, on the other hand, probably was right in its assertion that Healy had been political. That fact did not justify the police commission bill, according to the *Leader,* for potentially it made the police commission itself—and, therefore, the police chiefs of several New Hampshire cities— political pawns of the governor.

Finally, the *Leader* defended Healy, who, Knox and his editorial staff believed, should be reappointed to the position of Chief of Police:

> We give Police Chief Healy credit for being not only an efficient and effective police official, which his bitterest enemies freely admit, but being as well a man of, at least, average intelligence and perceptions. As such he doubtless recognizes that the present day public temper will not brook interference by the police in politics. If this is true and we believe it is, would not the public interest best be served by retaining a police chief who has admittedly made Manchester one of the most orderly cities in the country, in which crime seldom goes undetected and unpublished?[26]

The *Leader* continued its defense of Healy into the summer, at one point even printing a wordless editorial entitled "Some Reasons Why Chief Healy Should Be Fired."[27] The newspaper's efforts became so farcical that at one point, the *Manchester Advocate* suggested that "politics, situations, business and numerous other things" clouded the *Leader's* efforts. "Healy, individually and as an officer, considering efficiency, is perfectly satisfactory," wrote Jesse Markee. But, he added, "people do not want ... tyranny." Rather, workers needed assurances that the "police commission ... will be guided by prescribed law and not by personal and corporation privilege, [and that its members] will at all times respect the 1st and 8th Amendments to the Constitution of the United States."[28]

7. Problems of Government

Despite Clifford Snow's support for Sunday baseball, his vote for Senator Hollis had endeared him neither to pro-business Republicans nor to the Progressives who supported Robert Bass throughout the ordeal. Still, the public was surprised when, on April 10, it learned the results of the Special Committee on Investigation on the Senatorial Question's inquiry. On the one hand, the committee's three members issued a report in which they found "no evidence that any offer of money or any promise of any other improper consideration whatever has been made to any member of this Legislature to influence his vote for or against any candidate for United States senator." However, Republican Ezra Smith and Republican-Progressive Harold Webster issued a second report, one that their Democratic colleague refused to sign, in which they found Snow guilty of "conduct discreditable to himself and highly disgraceful to this House, and constituting a stigma upon the reputation and dignity and honor of this House." For his actions, they recommended that Snow be expelled from the chamber.

The Smith-Webster report accused Snow of five improper acts. At the beginning of January, Snow allegedly told the secretary of the New Hampshire Republican Party that, for $100 each, he and nine Democrats would vote for Franklin Worcester for senator instead of Henry Hollis. Two weeks later, he was said to have approached Governor's Council candidate Elmer Tilton and offered to "obtain votes" for him, provided Tilton "'do the right thing' by said Snow." At the start of February he met with Gordon Woodbury at Woodbury's office to discuss his candidacy for the Senate, allegedly offering his vote and those of three other legislators in return for $1,000. At about the same time he supposedly approached Woodbury's agent in Manchester, again offering his vote and those of two others in return for $200. And finally, on February 17, while on a trip to the town of Franklin, Snow "visited a so-called 'road house.'"[29] Later, the committee added a new allegation: that Snow had worked for Franklin Worcester in December, and was paid $100 to canvas votes for him with the promise of an appointment to the position of License Board Inspector.[30]

Additional and sometimes contradictory details emerged over the next several days. A Republican representative from Manchester's Third Ward, John S. Wheeler, claimed that Snow had approached him on a train and, "exhibiting a large roll of bills," offered to put Wheeler "in the way of making $800 or $900 at the legislature." Meanwhile, the Reverend Chalmers revealed that the General Court had hired private detectives to investigate rumors of bribery. One of the detectives, Fred Stearns, said that he had found nothing linking Snow to those rumors.

Snow had his own story, a written version of which he released to the *Nashua Telegraph*. Woodbury, he claimed, had called him the "best man in the

New Hampshire legislature" as recently as March 6, and they "went to the barroom at the Eagle hotel together" that morning. But that afternoon, Snow voted for Hollis rather than for Woodbury. "Mr. Woodbury has not spoken to me since," he claimed. He also posited a theory to explain Woodbury's testimony against him before the legislative committee: "Mr. Woodbury ... was constantly after me to vote for him and sent others to urge me to do so. They have not got anything on me, and as I have already said, it is a clear case of 'sorehead.' Mr. Woodbury tried to get me to use my influence with the Progressives to bring them over to him."[31]

After some question about procedure—no member of the state General Court ever had been expelled—legislators determined that only a majority vote was needed to pass a motion of expulsion. Reports circulated in the *Mirror* that the Democrats would come to Snow's rescue, and some did defend him at the expulsion hearing on April 17.[32] Most notably, Walpole representative Charles J. O'Neil stated that there was "no foundation in fact" for the resolution to expel Snow, and he questioned the character of the witnesses who testified against the Manchester representative. These included Gordon Woodbury who, noted O'Neil, had refused to withdraw his name from consideration in the senatorial election even as the General Court could not muster a majority in the election of Senator Hollis.[33] The Walpole senator suggested that "a Manchester corporation" was behind Woodbury's candidacy, and that Woodbury's actions in remaining in the race were "a desperate effort [by that corporation] to defeat in some manner, the regular candidate of the Democratic party." O'Neil felt that "Mr. Snow's word was as good as Mr. Woodbury's," and that Snow should not be expelled.[34]

Although no concrete evidence exists to suggest that the Amoskeag Manufacturing Company was behind the drive to expel Snow, the "Manchester corporation" to which O'Neil referred as having backed Woodbury undoubtedly was Amoskeag. Exactly how Woodbury's candidacy would have benefitted Amoskeag is unclear. If O'Neil is to be believed, possibly the corporation's managers felt that Woodbury was less likely to support pro-tariff legislation than Hollis. Maybe Amoskeag hoped to create enough chaos that the choice of a senator would be delayed, benefitting the company through the absence of one Democratic vote in the United States Senate. Perhaps the Amoskeag Manufacturing Company hoped to divide Democrats until a consensus candidate—one who supported Amoskeag—could be found. Or, given that Snow was accused of selling his vote but had voted for Henry Hollis, Amoskeag may have wished to cast some doubt on the legitimacy of Hollis's election.[35] What is clear is that Woodbury did have political aspirations; in 1916, he unsuccessfully ran to represent New Hampshire's First Congressional District in the

United States House of Representatives.³⁶ Regardless of whether or not Amoskeag played a role in Woodbury's candidacy for the Senate in 1913, the fact that the Walpole representative should allude to the corporation's alleged interference in the senatorial election suggests just how much the November election results continued to worry Amoskeag's management—and just how little some politicians trusted Amoskeag.

In the end, O'Neil's defense could not save Snow. On the motion of fellow Ward Three Republican Hobart Pillsbury (who, ironically, would go to jail for embezzlement sixteen years later after two terms as New Hampshire Secretary of State), the legislature voted in favor of expulsion, 177 to 119. Of Manchester's 54 representatives who were present for the debate, 32 voted with the majority.

Snow's removal from office was symbolic, as it indicated that Progressives, who often ran on an anti-corruption platform, could be just as corrupt as any Democrat or Republican. It signified an important setback in the state's progressive movement. Snow himself would return to Manchester, and by 1920 had abandoned his painting business and worked in a local shoe factory with his second wife Ellen.³⁷ But as Snow's removal was finalized, regardless of whether or not Manchester residents cared about his ignominious and brief time in the House or saw its significance, they had something better to which to look forward: the construction of Textile Field.

8

Textile Field

On March 1, a month after the Northeastern League's demise and two days after the legislature appointed a committee to investigate rumors surrounding Clifford Snow, the Manufacturers League released its schedule for the 1913 season. Only five teams would compete for the league championship; the board of governors could not entice any of the city's smaller manufacturers to join the organization. Two games were scheduled on Saturdays, meaning each team would have one out of every five Saturdays off. The lack of a sixth team also required the use of only two baseball grounds: Textile Field, which was to be utilized even as the grandstand was being constructed; and the Rock Rimmon grounds, which would now be accessible by street car.

The most important baseball news of the late winter and early spring, however, was that the Amoskeag Textile Club's plans for the former Varick Park had changed. "When the Amoskeag Manufacturing Company starts to do things you can generally make up your mind that it will be done right," stated a March 1 *Bulletin* column entitled "Textile Field Gossip." In the article, the Textile Club announced that the grandstand, which was to have been built of wood, now would be constructed primarily of concrete and steel, so that "any doubt as to the stability of the big stand is now brushed aside." Then, to assure readers of Amoskeag's benevolent, employee-friendly intent, the article continued that the company wished "to safeguard the lives of those who may be in the stand when it is crowded and the decision to substitute [fireproof materials] ... is looked upon as a fine thing."[1]

Although the column was relegated to the second page of the *Bulletin*, the announcement was significant: Manchester was to be home to one of the few concrete-and-steel grandstands in the United States. Instead of a minor-league team in either the New England League or the Northeastern League, the Amoskeag Textile Club itself would provide fans with high-caliber baseball. It promised to build, in effect, a scaled-down major-league stadium, and to provide professional-level baseball talent in the form of the Manufacturers League. Although the local league failed to live up to the promise, Amoskeag nonetheless attempted to elevate its status by luring the reigning World Series champions to the city for an exhibition game against Manufacturers League players.

That reinforced concrete and steel would be used in stadium construction in a city the size of Manchester was highly unusual in 1913. Concrete and steel had been the construction materials of choice among most major-league teams only since 1909, and the practice of erecting grandstands using permanent, fireproof materials was almost unheard of outside of a major city. Among the sixteen major-league teams, eleven played in concrete-and-steel stadiums built or expanded between 1909 and 1912, with a twelfth, the Brooklyn Dodgers, set to open Ebbets Field in 1913. (This number includes the New York Yankees, which shared the Polo Grounds as a tenant of the New York Giants It does not include the Philadelphia Phillies, whose home stadium was constructed in 1895 and served as a prototype of sorts to later concrete-and-steel stadiums.) In

The Textile Field grandstand under construction, 1913 (courtesy Manchester [New Hampshire] Historic Association).

Boston, where the Red Sox had dedicated the new Fenway Park less than a year earlier, the city's other team, the Braves, still made its home in an older ballpark constructed of wood.[2]

The construction of concrete-and-steel ballparks after 1909 resulted from a number of factors. The first of these was that in the Progressive Era, landowners and government officials at all levels were being pressured to consider the safety of patrons at public events. Too many fires at movie theaters and hotels or collapsed grandstands at sporting events had convinced the public that owners of public venues should be forced to consider public safety, and if they would not do so, government should become involved through regulation.[3] Chief Healy's argument that the 1912 gathering of Lawrence strike sympathizers in a wooden shop could not occur without a permit had drawn on that sentiment. Furthermore, Manchester itself had seen its share of fires—201 were reported to the police in the year ending June 30, 1912.[4] Thus, the *Bulletin*'s statement that Amoskeag wished "to safeguard the lives of those who may be in the stand when it is crowded" by constructing a ballpark with fireproof materials likely is genuine.

The construction materials used in the project also had symbolic meaning. Most minor-league owners—and until recently, even major-league clubs—did not have the resources to construct permanent grandstands for their teams. In fact, the lack of stability within professional baseball meant that investment in such a venture was impractical. When the Philadelphia Athletics and Pittsburgh Pirates unveiled Shibe Park and Forbes Field, respectively, in 1909, the new ballparks were viewed widely as signaling those teams' commitment to their communities.[5] Similarly, the new Textile Field represented the Amoskeag Textile Club's (and by extension, the Amoskeag Manufacturing Company's) commitment to Manchester and its intent to make the Manufacturers League a permanent fixture in the city.

Whether or not a fireproof grandstand would have been proposed for Manchester without pressure from the New England League or the failure of the Northeastern League is debatable. The lack of a professional baseball team in Manchester certainly had exposed the Textile Club to criticism. For the Manufacturers League to fill the void, it would have to be seen as a professional-caliber league. The Amoskeag Manufacturing Company, by designing a baseball stadium more impressive than those of some major-league baseball clubs, may have been attempting to elevate its fledgling baseball league to that status.

Work on the new baseball stadium commenced by April 1. Within two days the demolition and excavation work had been completed, and "a force of 25 men, engineers, electricians, and common laborers" worked day and night on construction. "The grandstand will be one of the finest structures of its kind in New England," reported the *Mirror*, "with a seating capacity of 3,500 people."[6]

The structure was to be 50 feet deep and 300 feet long, with six entrances that promised to "do away with the heretofore unavoidable mauling the spectators were subjected to" while leaving old Varick Park. Automobiles would be permitted to enter the grounds via Maple Street, and plans were made for them to park in the outfield and at the east end of the field. Dressing rooms, lockers, toilet rooms beneath the grandstand ramps, a steel truss roof, and eleven fire hydrants around the field ensured that once finished, Textile Field would in every way be a safe, modern, and convenient facility in which fans could enjoy athletic contests.[7]

By April 15, concrete foundations had been poured at the site, and the first four carloads of bricks had been unloaded along Valley Street. Meanwhile, the Amoskeag Textile Club attempted to drum up interest in baseball by planning a trip to Boston. "Everybody's going to Boston on May 3rd to see what the Red Sox will do to that Washington team," proclaimed the *Bulletin*. More than 300 club members attended the game at Fenway Park, only to see the Red Sox lose. They were not entirely disappointed, though, for Washington's heralded pitcher, Walter Johnson, pitched in relief.[8]

As construction progressed on Textile Field, the Manufacturers League teams tuned up for the regular season. For the Fast Day holiday, the Amoskeag baseball team arranged for a double-header against Portland of the New England League. Amoskeag lost both games in the still-incomplete stadium before 5,500 spectators. During its trip to Manchester, Portland also defeated Phenomenal Smith's Beacons, 9–5. But the Beacons lost more than just the game. When the Portland club departed Manchester on the morning of April 26, it left having signed two of the Beacons' best players, Chucky McCarthy and Eddie Flanagan. Perhaps as a result, the Beacons lost an early May exhibition game to Saint Anselm College, 13–4.[9]

Even as it was being built, Textile Field made an impression on local residents. On May 6, Frank Knox's *Manchester Leader* suggested that Manchester residents "make a trip to the Textile Club Athletic field and look over the operations in progress there, which, when concluded, will give to this city one of the best equipped athletic fields in the country." The editorial continued:

> It will also serve as an illustration of intelligent, resultful co-operation on the part of a huge industrial corporation with its employes [sic] in promoting interest in wholesome, out-of-door recreation. During its remarkable history, the Amoskeag Corporation has done many things which have characterized the far-seeing quality of its management, in its treatment of its employes, but nothing ever attempted, we venture, will approach in popularity its rehabilitation of the old Varick Park....
> Constructive social workers long ago discovered the most effective method of combating evil influences in any community, among any class, to be the provisicn of an acceptable and popular substitute for the evil whose elimination was desired. We regard it as no

exaggeration to say that such an institution as the Textile Club Athletic field will do more to render harmless the evil influences of every sort which are inevitable in any city, than any single institution which could be named, unless we except the Y. M. C. A. whose appeal is along somewhat similar lines.[10]

The *Leader*'s pro–Amoskeag stance may seem surprising considering the militantly progressive politics espoused by Frank Knox the previous fall. While Knox called for an end to government corruption and supported the improvement of conditions for factory workers statewide, never had he nor New Hampshire progressives in general supported viewpoints that promoted the disruption of social order. But to be fair, by connecting corporate benevolence in the form of an expanded and updated stadium with the elimination of "evil" influences, the *Leader* was not abandoning its progressive stance. Many people of the era argued that uplifting places could combat negative influences. Parks and playgrounds could ward off juvenile delinquency, for instance, while libraries and monuments might help educate and edify the people, particularly in urban places in which immigrants might be cut off from the countryside.[11]

Even so, to herald the role of Amoskeag in the construction of Textile Field, and to favor upholding the social order in a city that Amoskeag still controlled in many ways, probably was not what Robert Bass had anticipated when he arranged the funding of the *Leader*. With Bass seemingly irrelevant in state politics and the Progressives upsetting the balance of power, maybe Knox hoped to reconcile Progressives with the Republican Party. Or, perhaps he was concerned by the fact that the *Leader*'s average daily circulation had fallen to 12,428 in the week ending May 3—less than half its peak the previous October. The editor also may have veered his newspaper to the right in response to an attempted advertising boycott of the *Leader* by the city's business community. Just as possible, though, Knox might have been attempting to convince Rosecrans Pillsbury, the owner of the Republican *Manchester Union*, to agree to merge their struggling newspapers, with Knox assuming the roles of editor and publisher. Regardless, by lauding Amoskeag management for being "wisely generous" with its employees and the community at large in the construction of Textile Field, Knox had signaled that the Manchester establishment—and Amoskeag in particular—need not fear the *Manchester Leader*.[12]

On May 10, despite a "violent and cold wind," the Manufacturers League opened its second season. About 1,500 people arrived at Textile Field, and some were admitted into the not-yet-completed grandstand to watch the battle between Amoskeag and the Beacons. Shortly before 3:00, league treasurer Hilton Slayton escorted the Beacons to the center-field flagpole, where they again hoisted the 1912 Manufacturers League pennant to fly above the park. Then, William Parker Straw walked onto to the Textile Field diamond and took the ball offered to him by umpire Barney McLaughlin. Straw took the mound and threw the ball to Amoskeag catcher Jim O'Rourke, past John McCarthy, who had taken his place in the batter's box for the Beacons. "Stri-i-i-ke-One!" yelled McLaughlin. Straw relinquished the mound to Amoskeag pitcher Jack Parker, who did not fare as well, for Amoskeag lost to Phenomenal Smith's Beacons, 7–2.[13]

Another 700 fans arrived at the Amoskeag Recreation Grounds at Rock Rimmon for the game between McElwain and the Reeds. There, Superintendent Herbert A. Trull of the W. H. McElwain Company threw out the first pitch, though newspapers do not record whether or not his was a strike. Playing conditions were difficult at the Rock Rimmon grounds, because nothing there protected players and spectators from the cold wind and blowing dust. Despite this problem, newspapers reported that this game was the more exciting of the two, as McElwain defeated the Reeds, 4–3.[14]

The first few weeks of the season were competitive. By Memorial Day, Amoskeag's record stood at three wins against one loss, putting the team a half-game ahead of the Beacons and the Starks (both 2–1), and a game and a half ahead of McElwain (1–2). Only the Reeds (0–3) had failed to win a game. Attendance at the contests had been respectable as well, with a total of 4,500 taking in the Memorial Day games. The state of the Textile Field playing surface was not particularly good, but no one seemed to mind, for on Memorial Day the new grandstand opened to the public.[15]

Of course, the grandstand and continued success of the Manufacturers League only made Manchester more desirable to New England League officials. While the city league continued to insist that its product was virtually professional—it even suggested that it might sign on to the National Agreement, making it a class-D professional minor league—some newspapers supported the opinion that Manchester should be home to a class-B New England League club. On May 19, the *Leader* reported that either the Fall River or New Bedford team could be moved to Manchester during the season. "But all hopes go glimmering when one realized that the only available site is Textile park, and there is little chance of the Manufacturers league welcoming such an invasion by allowing the use of their grounds." Still, the Amoskeag Textile Club did want to show off its new baseball grounds, so it permitted the New England League to plan an official game for Textile Field in late July.[16]

The Textile Club was justifiably proud of its new grandstand. A 1915 article from an out-of-state newspaper described it:

> It is located about a mile from the center of the city, where electric car service makes it most accessible to the public. It comprises six acres of smoothly rolled ground, inclosed [sic] by substantial fencing, and is equipped with a quarter-mile running track 15 feet wide,

encircling a diamond and gridiron, and illuminated at night with 28 arc lights for [non-baseball] night events. A 100-yard straightaway track extends along the grandstand front, and both tracks are of the finest cinder construction. The grandstand, accommodating 3000 people, is of the most modern fireproof construction, and with 16 boxes, bleachers and temporary provisions, 11,000 spectators can be cared for. Convenient clubrooms under both ends of the grandstand are equipped with baths, lockers and other features.[17]

While the arched openings in the grandstand's facade along Hanover Street are vaguely reminiscent of those of Chicago's Comiskey Park, which had opened in 1910, Boston's Fenway Park seems to have been the most direct baseball-related influence on Textile Field. In fact, a published 1912 World Series seating plan for Fenway Park made its way into the Mechanical Department's work-order files before plans for the new Textile Field grandstand were unveiled. The structure itself was built to resemble most of the industrial architecture already existing in Manchester. The Amoskeag Millyard and many of the buildings belonging to the city's other industries—with the exception of the McElwain Company's new factories on the east bank of the Merrimack River—conformed to the Amoskeag Manufacturing Company's architectural standards.[18] Thus, most industrial buildings were constructed of the same dark-red brick, featured similar arched windows, were surrounded by similar distinctive stone pylons connected by iron fences, and sometimes even featured streetlights at the base of which were printed the interlocking letters "A-M-Co." Under the direction of Amoskeag engineer Perry Dow, managers at the Amoskeag Manufacturing Company had designed the Textile Field grandstand with many of these characteristics as well. In other words, they created a structure that could remind spectators of the benevolence, power, and ubiquitous presence of the corporation in their lives.

With such an impressive ballpark at their disposal, the club's officers believed that a suitable dedication was in order, preferably something that emphasized how Amoskeag was able to provide baseball of sufficient quality to compensate for the lack of a true minor league in Manchester. With that in mind, on June 15 the *Amoskeag Bulletin* proclaimed that once the final improvements were made to Textile Field, the Amoskeag Textile Club would hold a grand opening for the grounds. The day might even feature a game between a local team and the Boston Red Sox. "This goes to show that the committee intends to have nothing but the best there is," announced the *Bulletin*, "and if negotiations fail along this line the matter will be taken up with other major league clubs."[19]

As June came to a close and plans for a Red Sox game in Manchester failed to materialize, the Manchester Police Department announced the arrest of Albert Smith and Alma Dionne of Bridge Street. The 24-year-old Dionne, described as "a young girl" by the *Union*, was charged with prostitution and, after retracting her original plea of not guilty, sentenced by Judge Harry Loveren to ninety days in the House of Correction. Smith, meanwhile, was arrested "for being a pimp, but it was discovered by the prosecutors that there is no law to prohibit this." After considering the possibility of charging Smith under the federal Mann Act, which made illegal the transport of women across state lines for prostitution and other "immoral purposes," the Manchester police settled on charges of illegal bookmaking. Apparently, Smith had sold tickets in a baseball pool to a number of people, including disgraced former New Hampshire Representative Clifford Snow.[20]

On the very day that the *Union* reported on the Dionne and Smith case, Frank Knox stunned the city with an announcement that appeared only on the *Union*'s editorial page: the *Leader* and the *Union* had merged. Knox himself would head the new Union-Leader Corporation, which eventually would publish the *Leader* each morning and the *Union* on an evening schedule, Monday through Saturday. Knox, or perhaps a proxy writing on his behalf, promised that the older, formerly Republican newspaper "politically will be independent. Its news columns will in a partisan sense know no politics, and its editorial columns will be free from partisan personalities. It will be the organ of no man, or set of men. As an institution it will belong to New Hampshire, and will attempt, to the full extent of its power and ability, to serve solely the highest interests of the state."[21]

Despite the *Union*'s statements about editorial independence, the *Union* and the *Leader* slowly became indistinguishable—and purely Republican. As recently as May, the *Leader* had covered a dinner for Progressive Party leaders hosted by Robert Bass in nearby Hooksett. But Knox believed that because of its history, the Democratic Party—whose platform had borrowed many of its planks from Progressives in 1912—would revert to conservatism because of "its historic support of the theory of states' rights." This view was in direct opposition to the progressive movement, which relied on "the establishment of a strong centralized national power" to enact its reforms. Ultimately, he felt, one of the remaining parties—Progressives or Republicans—would die out, leading the survivor to promote progressive reforms.

Soon, Knox came to believe that the Republicans, and not the Progressives, would emerge as the dominant alternative to the conservatism of the Democratic Party. When that happened, the *Union* and *Leader* emerged as a unified Republican voice, no doubt aided by the fact that while Bass still held shares in the new Union-Leader Corporation, Republican and former *Union* publisher Rosecrans Pillsbury held an even greater stake and, therefore, wielded considerably more power over the newspapers.[22]

As the content of the two newspapers increasingly overlapped, with developing news stories that were broken by one newspaper expanded in the next, observers worried about the effect the merger would have on employees. Jesse Markee wrote that the deal "has seriously concerned many of the journeymen printers of the town this week," particularly "those who have dependents here" and who might find themselves without a job once the merger was completed.[23] A year later, Typographical Local 152 reported that most of the printers who had lost work eventually found new jobs, and that the Union-Leader Corporation had constructed a new state-of-the-art building in which to house its expanded operations.[24]

Knox did retain some of the *Union*'s staff, including sports reporter Jack Finn. Finn, a former baseball player, was so well known in Manchester that his columns were among the few in any local newspaper in New Hampshire to include a byline. Knox also let some of the *Union*'s editorial staff go, replacing them with new names to oversee the city desk, the women's page, and other sections. But for all intents and purposes, the *Union* and the *Leader* were now one newspaper—a Republican one that seemingly would not threaten Amoskeag's power.

On the day of the *Union* and *Leader* merger, the *Amoskeag Bulletin* reminded readers of the positive impact that the Textile Club had on Amoskeag's workers by highlighting a recent article in Manchester's *other* English-language daily, the *Manchester Mirror*. The Manufacturers League, which, according to the *Bulletin*, "is possible only through the Amoskeag," was particularly successful, especially when one considers the ATC's "erection of the mammoth grandstand in Textile field and other alterations under way [which] will convert the former Varick park into one of the greatest playing fields in the country for a city the size of Manchester."[25]

Even so, the Manufacturers League was not without its problems. In May, Amoskeag's highly touted catcher Emil Pernod resigned as the team's captain and considered leaving the club altogether after creating a "hostile attitude" among his teammates.[26] Willard Taber injured himself in preseason workouts, and two months into the season had shown nothing of the form that had garnered him the attention of the Cleveland Naps in February.[27]

Players for the Stark team created problems for the whole league, and in particular for its umpires. In early June, the Starks protested the results of its game against the Beacons, complaining that an umpire had ruled one of the Beacons out at second base on an attempted steal, but then reversed his decision, ultimately costing the Starks the game.[28] A month later, the *Mirror* reported that the only reason umpire Jim McLaughlin "did not eject the whole Stark team from the field was because the spectators had paid their money to see a ball game, and he did not care to break it up."[29]

Newspapers buzzed about allegations that "both Jim and Mike McLaughlin are incompetent umpires, and that such men as 'Betsy' Collins and Barney McLaughlin should be added to the staff of the Manufacturers league." On July 12, the *Mirror* complained that the Amoskeag-Reed game was a "wretched exhibition of the national pastime," made worse by the fact that "umpiring was poor: it was worse than that; it was, if the term be permissible, rotten."[30] A few days later, umpire Mike McLaughlin resigned because "his functions had become nothing but disagreeable."[31]

Clearly, if the league did not put a stop to the problems that were plaguing it, the embarrassment would reflect poorly on the Amoskeag Textile Club and its parent corporation. Worse, the problems threatened to undermine the very tenets of the baseball creed that Amoskeag wanted to promote. Therefore, on the evening of July 16, William McKay called league officials and managers to the Amoskeag Employment Office for a meeting. There, the Manufacturers League president, beating his fists against the table for effect, "verbally scourged the managers of the teams in the circuit, and in the heat of his argument commanded them, and later when he became calm, requested them to make it their business to have the players understand that a repetition of the 'crabbing' which has been holding the field ... will not be tolerated in the future." Managers pledged that only the team captain would be permitted to question umpires' decisions. The group also absolved Jim McLaughlin of any wrongdoing, though the *Mirror* reported that the umpire "will be given a little lay-off, during which time he may think over a few poor decisions he made in the Stark-Beacon game." Manchester police officer Arthur Conlon took McLaughlin's place. The organization also voted to adopt a new umpiring system in which two men would umpire each game, one stationed behind home plate and the other to work the baselines.[32]

During the course of the meeting, some members of the group raised concerns about the condition of Textile Field, where workers continued to fill the outfield with crushed stone and sand and constructed wooden bleachers in foul territory. That problem was to be expected. More problematic, however, was the fact that some spectators parked their automobiles and carriages along the perimeter of the playing surface. "Textile field, as everyone will agree, is one of the greatest of its kind in the country and there is perhaps no other park in the country where autos are allowed to monopolize the space on either side of the foul lines," reported the *Mirror*. "To make the field thoroughly up to date it is believed that autos should not be allowed in the grounds." As a result, the group asked ATC President William Parker Straw to have a section of the circus grounds east of the ballpark designated for parking, and to hire a police officer to watch the vehicles during games. Straw consented, and on July 19 the club placed placards around Textile Field announcing a parking ban.[33]

On Wednesday, July 24, five days after the parking ban went into effect, the Amoskeag baseball team hosted the Lowells of the New England League. Lowell won the contest, 14–7, revealing that the Manufacturers League had far to go to match the quality and skill of the New England League. Between 1,000 and 1,200 fans watched from the Textile Field stands, and while that number fell far short of the grandstand's capacity of approximately 3,500, the *Mirror* noted that "attendance was all that could be expected for a weekday." After all, the Amoskeag Textile Club had scheduled the game for a time when most of the city's blue-collar employees were at work—meaning the crowd was made up of the city's professionals and merchants.[34]

Lowell manager Jimmy Gray and several of his players were impressed with the new park, and Gray even suggested that a New England League team eventually would relocate to the city. The *Mirror* opposed this plan, stating that "the present condition of the New England league, wobbly, uncertain to smash at any moment, bespeaks anything but a bright future for it, and it is doubtful if the Amoskeag Textile club ... would consent to allow a New England league team to come here." The newspaper predicted that if the league constructed its own stadium in the city and competed directly with the Manufacturers League, the New England League team would fail. The league, asserted the newspaper, was "testing this city out to the fullest extent, but it will hardly do them any good, it is said, since it is all up to the Amoskeag Textile club."[35] This comment only served to highlight Amoskeag's attempts at control.

As the end of July approached, another series of games loomed—this time official games involving two New England League teams, again scheduled for Textile Field. The exhibition featuring the Boston Red Sox, originally promised for June or July, still had not been finalized. And although the *Leader* no longer seemed a threat to Amoskeag, William McKay had imposed his authority over the Manufacturers League, and Textile Field appeared to be a rousing success, Amoskeag's control over Manchester still was anything but certain.

In due course, Manchester baseball fans would be able to witness professional baseball in a new more-or-less fireproof stadium. In the meantime, however, regular citizens had other concerns, as demonstrated by events originating in the city's Eighth Ward.

9

The Rise of the Eighth Ward

Although the Amoskeag Textile Club took great pride in and expected much to come from its plans for Textile Field, interest in the project may not have been as great as the club's leaders believed. In fact, while the new Textile Field grandstand was expected to benefit the Amoskeag Manufacturing Company and some of the shoe companies that had seen labor unrest in 1912, far more pressing problems than a lack of a permanent professional-grade grandstand faced many of the city's residential districts. This was particularly true of sections in which the Amoskeag Manufacturing Company held no social or economic interests, sections which—perhaps not coincidentally—tended to be ignored by city government.

Manchester's underserved Eighth Ward is a case in point. This area, in which Amoskeag owned just one plot of land, was beginning to see growth after the construction of a small shoe factory in the late nineteenth century and the routing of a state highway through the ward along Second Street. The potential for even more growth existed thanks to the W. H. McElwain Shoe Company. Located adjacent to the ward on the east bank of the Merrimack River near its confluence with the Piscataquog River, the factory was in the process of expanding and modernizing its operations in Manchester. In late 1912, McElwain opened a new wing in its central plant, creating 500 new jobs in the process. "The West Side, especially Ward 8" reported the *Mirror*, "sees in the opening of the new plant great growth for it in the next few years. With the new bridge across the Merrimack it opens an enormous tract on the West Side which is expected to be covered in homes in the near future."

Despite their interest in McElwain's expansion, Eighth Ward residents could be forgiven if they viewed this report with some skepticism. Most obviously, no bridge yet existed across the Merrimack south of Granite Street. That meant anyone wishing to travel between the Eighth Ward and the factory complex directly across the river had to cover a considerable distance along a route that took them through the Amoskeag Millyard. Making matters worse, public demand regularly overwhelmed the city's streetcar network in southwestern Manchester, something that a new, direct connection between South Manchester and the Eighth Ward would help to alleviate. And while McElwain promised to aid in the construction of the proposed bridge, newly elected alderman Gustav Wenzel had already attempted, without success, to convince the city to construct the bridge during a previous term in office.[1]

In fact, the Eighth Ward rarely received much attention from city government. Residents complained amongst themselves about the condition of the streets, including the state highway, the crime resulting from absence of police in the ward, and the lack of enforcement of either speed or zoning laws. The ward's only public park, Wolfe Park, regularly flooded. As the only section of the city without convenient access to a playground, children spent summers playing in the streets and along the banks of the Merrimack and Piscataquog Rivers, endangering their lives. And most concerning, fire coverage was inadequate even as the city reneged on a promise to construct a fire station there. Surely, these issues were far more important to the residents of the Eighth Ward than a baseball stadium being constructed across the river by a corporation that had little connection to the ward.

Manchester's inattention to the Eighth Ward resulted from three factors: the Amoskeag Manufacturing Company's patterns of land ownership in the city, the company's control over City Hall, and the inability of the ward's residents to cooperate across ethnic lines. Through its control of city government, Amoskeag advanced and protected its own interests. Because the company owned virtually no land in the Eighth Ward, the city paid little attention to the neighborhoods in the southwestern part of the city. And as the ward's three largest ethnic groups—Germans, Irish, and French-Canadians—showed little interest in unity across ethnic lines, elected officials felt no grassroots pressure to alter their attitude toward the ward.

That situation promised to change. In November 1912, Manchester voters overwhelmingly elected Democrat Charles Hayes to be the city's new mayor; in fact, he won every district of the city except the Ninth Ward, a predominantly French-Canadian ward that supported Quebec native Victor Roy in the election.[2] After taking office in January, Hayes consistently attended public meetings and proved adept at listening to complaints, rarely taking a position before understanding where the public stood on an issue. Perhaps heartened by this development, but also grasping how McElwain's expansion might benefit the Eighth Ward, residents of southwestern Manchester decided the time had come to unify and demand improvements to their section of the city. And as was the case a year earlier in the Lawrence strike, children played an important role in that effort.

In general, working-class residents of Manchester supported the changes in local, state, and national government that came after the 1912 elections. Even so, changes in local government proved difficult to initiate. The Board of Mayor and Aldermen typically included Amoskeag employees or sympathizers on it, regardless of party. In fact, a "machine" of sorts, one that backed Amoskeag and various special interests, ultimately managed the city. Jesse Markee's *Advocate* questioned the political situation often, such as when, in early 1913, a proposed change to the city charter meant that a political party would have to receive 20 percent of the vote for its candidates to appear on the next election's ballot. This move was widely seen as an attempt to reduce the influence of the city's emergent Socialist Party, many of whose members disapproved of Chief Healy's handling of the free speech movement a year earlier. In response, the *Advocate* took a principled position when it accused the "standpat gang that has infested the city hall for many years" of "not losing any sleep over consistency[,] but when a matter comes up for discussion that is of special interest to one of their number, they line up for action and little consideration is given the welfare of the city, justice, or the rights of men."[3] Other than the *Advocate*, though, no media outlet questioned the status quo. In fact, they openly supported it.

Manchester citizens hoped to shake up that status quo in 1913. On March 10, city officials met to choose commissioners and assessors. "Usually," reported the *Advocate*, "these meetings are poorly attended by those who should take an active interest in the city's welfare," with only the "'perpetuals,' who rely solely on city positions for their existence" in the audience. This year's meeting was different. "There were quite a few present who were not looking for a city job, and they made their presence known. They convinced the Manchester delegation that the people were talking, and not the job hunters." This, according to the *Advocate*, was proof that "the common people are becoming dreadfully tired of boss rule in Manchester."[4]

Boss rule or not, under Amoskeag's watchful eye the city of Manchester had created an impressive network of parks and playgrounds. The city's five playgrounds were developed as part of a national progressive movement aimed at "saving" urban children from poverty and crime while also teaching them American cultural values. Playgrounds, supporters argued, took children off the streets and out of watering holes where their unsupervised, unstructured play could get them into trouble as victims of accidents or as perpetrators of crimes. Criminal offenses could be innocuous at first—playing baseball in the streets, for example, was an activity that also exposed children to the dangers of sporadic but fast-moving automobiles. From street games, children might graduate to more serious activities, including gambling, robbery, or prostitution.[5]

Managers at the Amoskeag Manufacturing Company appear to have agreed with those who believed playgrounds could tame the aggressions of poor and working-class children. In the spring of 1911, the company developed the site of the former Concord and Montreal Railroad depot into a children's playground. Located near the corner of Granite and Canal Streets between the Amoskeag millyard and the Sullivan 7–20–4 Cigar Factory, the 1.2-acre tract of land was "fitted with modern fixtures, shelter shed, toilet building, baseball ground, running track, pond for wading, swings, appliances for athletics and

The Amoskeag Manufacturing Company children's playground opened in 1911 between Canal Street (which separates the playground from the Sullivan 7-20-4 Cigar Factory to the right) and the railroad tracks that ran along Amoskeag's upper canal. The playground, which included a swimming pond, a small baseball diamond, a swingset, a roofed pavilion, and large flagpole flying an American flag, was part of a national movement that promoted safe play for children (courtesy Manchester [New Hampshire] Historic Association).

other attractions for youth." In July, a few months after the playground opened, a *Union* reporter visited the park with a photographer. Believing it had already "taken its place as one of the institutions for the improvement of child life in Manchester," the reporter noted that the "playground has been good for both boys and girls. Of course the boys would have found places to play, but many of them would have gone to the river and the record of the summer shows the dangers there in the hot weather. Here they have had the fun of getting into the water, and have been safe."[6]

The Amoskeag Playground, the Barry Playground on the city's South Side (also on Amoskeag-owned land), the new playground associated with the development of the Rock Rimmon park, and other neighborhood playgrounds probably did help to keep some of the city's children out of the dirty, dangerous waters of the Merrimack River. In a time when parents typically worked 58 hours per week in the city's textile and shoe factories, playgrounds also satisfied the city's social and moral leaders by keeping children safely off the streets. But city playgrounds were not accessible to everyone. In fact, the Eighth Ward claimed to be the only ward in the city without easy access to a satisfactory playground.

Perhaps sensing the growing reform movement in the city, residents of the Eighth Ward saw an opportunity to improve their section of the city after years of neglect. Manchester's German clubs, particularly the Manchester *Turn Verein* (or "Turner Club"), began the movement by focusing on obtaining a playground for the ward's children. But they soon realized that their efforts would be more effective if the ward's non–Germans joined the effort. Therefore, at the beginning of May, the club approached the Ward Eight Democratic Club, which called for a public meeting to discuss the matter.

In response to the call, more than 30 prominent citizens met at the ward's Democratic Club headquarters. While they "unanimously decided that it was time for the English-speaking residents to take a hand, out of the recognition of the mutuality of interests involved," in the words of the *Mirror*, the group nonetheless engaged in "several heated discussions" to open the meeting. One person demanded to know why Wolfe Park could not be used as a playground, to which Democratic Party activist Charles McLaughlin, who chaired the meeting, replied that aside from its inaccessibility, "it might be [used] if it were not under water most of the time." Those in attendance also veered off topic, complaining about the ward's roads and local fire coverage. Eventually, the group united behind two actions. First, they would petition the city to "sprinkle or oil" the streets, particularly Second Street and South Main Street, the ward's principle thoroughfares. Second, and more important, they agreed to support a children's march to City Hall to demand a playground.[7]

On May 5, Eighth Ward leaders prepared teachers and students for their march. William Duval and Charles McLaughlin called on the Sacred Heart of Jesus and St. Raphael's Schools, respectively. Local politician Herman Rodelsperger appeared at the ward's German-language school. Clarence McKean visited the Varney and Main Street schools, while John Donnelly took care of the Parker School and spoke with the Parents' Association, Advance Club, and West Side teachers.[8]

Meanwhile, Gustav Wenzel met with Amoskeag Manufacturing Company Agent Herman Straw. Since Amoskeag had erected or allowed the construction of at least three of the city's playgrounds on company-owned land, Wenzel—acting on behalf of the group that met at the Democratic Club—hoped to convince Straw to allow the ward to develop a playground on an Amoskeag-owned piece of property along Granite Street. Although located near the ward's northeast corner (despite the fact that newspapers commonly claimed it to be centrally located), it was the only parcel of Amoskeag-owned land remaining in the Eighth Ward. Straw promised to take the matter under advisement.[9]

On the afternoon of May 6, about 600 schoolchildren gathered in their schoolyards before making their way to Granite Street in Piscataquog Village. At precisely 4:30, led by a fife and drum corps, the students marched to the Granite Street bridge and over the Merrimack River, through the southern part of the Amoskeag Millyard, passing the Amoskeag company playground, and veering onto Depot Street before turning left onto Elm Street. Accompanied by more than 200 adults, most of whom followed behind, and carrying American flags and placards reading "We Want Playgrounds on the West Side," they continued on to City Hall—about a mile in total—where Mayor Hayes greeted them on Market Street.

At 5:00, with several police officers in the area to protect the children from traffic, Charles McKean stepped forward to introduce Mayor Hayes to the assembly. Charles Hall, a student at the Varney School, then stepped forward and presented the mayor with a petition, followed in succession by five other students. All told, between 1,100 and 1,300 West Side students signed the petitions requesting a playground for the Eighth Ward. Mayor Hayes praised the work of the public and parochial schools of the city, and congratulated the children for their activism relating to the playground movement. He then expressed his support for a playground and promised to present the petition to the Board of Mayor and Aldermen that evening. He also stated his hope that the children would use the grounds to develop themselves "into fine athletes." He continued, "If you take as much interest in your studies as you do in this movement, you will make excellent men and women in the future." With that, and after receiving three cheers from the crowd, the mayor disappeared into his office, and the children organized for their return march to Piscataquog Village.[10]

The media's response to the children's march was to accentuate the charm of the event. But the *Union*, which sent a photographer to cover the event, also noted that the "West Side playground movement is one of the most important that has been introduced in this section of the city for some time." Unbeknownst to many of the city's residents, this march was only the start. In fact, within two days citizens would meet again at Ward Eight Democratic Club headquarters. Not only would they continue to push for a playground; now, they were determined to obtain a new fire station for southwestern Manchester.[11]

For about a decade, the residents of the Eighth Ward had complained about fire coverage in the southern part of Manchester's West Side. At the time, the entire section was served by two horse-drawn pieces of fire apparatus housed at a station on North Main Street, near Piscataquog Village just south of the ward's northern boundary, with a second station located farther north. Although the southern location probably was satisfactory for the village, the entire area south of Piscataquog Village—exactly the area that stood to benefit from the expansion of the McElwain factory, provided a bridge was built—lacked coverage. In 1912 the city did appropriate $19,000 to construct a station at the corner of South Main and Woodbury Streets. Those plans were abandoned in April 1913 when a city-hired contractor concluded that the site was too wet for construction.[12] When the contractor halted the project, so too did the city, deciding instead to install a mechanized "Flying Squadron" fire truck at the North Main Street station. This action did little to placate Eighth Ward residents.

With that in mind, and already having proven that the people of the Eighth Ward could unite for a common cause, the Democratic Club called a mass meeting to discuss both fire coverage and the playground issue. In response, a large group of angry citizens gathered at the club's headquarters on the evening of May 9. "It was evident from the manner in which the session opened," reported the *Mirror*, "that, for once at least, West Manchester was about to come into its own, so to speak."

German immigrant and former alderman Adolph Wagner was among those who spoke at the meeting. "As you all know," he told the crowd, "this section of the city has been practically ignored for years. The blame of this condition falls on all of us, and the simple explanation of the whole situation is that we have always appeared in humble supplication instead of demanding what we know is due us." He noted that West Manchester—including McGregorville and Amoskeag Village, neither of which was within the Eighth Ward's boundaries—was home to about a third of the city's population, "and yet we pay more taxes and get less than any other section. It is simply because we have never forced our demands in the right way." He continued:

> We have to pay high rates of insurance on account of the lack of adequate fire protection in the section in dispute, yet two gentlemen of the lands and buildings committee assume to tell us that we do not need any additional protection. When you stop to realize that the only fire protection on the entire West Side consists of the horse-drawn apparatus in the Fulton and Fire King engine houses, it is simply outrageous.... For years there has been a demand for more protection south of the 'Squog river. Now we have finally been given the necessary appropriation for the construction of the fire house that we have been agitating and if we haven't enough stamina to fight for the retention of what has been given us how can we ever expect to get anything on our own inertia?[13]

Four nights later, another large crowd, along with invited guests Mayor Charles Hayes and Fire Chief Thomas Lane, met to continue their discussion. The conversation was no less heated than it had been at the previous meeting. Wagner again took the floor, describing how West Manchester had become "a dumping ground for the refuse of the rest of the municipality," and that it was "high time for the citizens to rise in their dignity and fight for their rights." According to the *Mirror*, he "said the treatment accorded to that section of the city was a disgrace, and that West Manchester was the worst example of municipal abuse that the state afforded." His remarks reportedly "brought down the house with applause."[14]

After Wagner, other residents took turns addressing the crowd, all of them in support of restoring the appropriation to build a fire station south of the Piscataquog River. Property owner Grant Gagnon asked why East Manchester had four times the fire protection of West Manchester. Another resident, James Leach, questioned why the city revoked the appropriation for a fire station when the previous administration, in granting it in the first place, essentially admitted that the Eighth Ward needed additional fire coverage. State representative Arthur Moquin complained, "For years this section of the city of Manchester has been shamefully neglected. We are suffering for sewers, sidewalks and adequate illumination of our public streets. It is high time that the taxpayers of this side received more just and honest treatment at the hands of the city government."

Charles McLaughlin, who presided over the meeting, gave Chief Lane and Mayor Hayes a chance to respond to the crowd. Lane told those assembled that he agreed with them, and that each year his annual report to the city included mention of the need for a new West Side fire station. Hayes, under whom the project had stalled, was less forthcoming, blaming the previous administration for the problems with the contractor and the city's Lands and Buildings Committee for attempting to cancel the project. But to some in the crowd, he appeared to support the district's cause when he stated, somewhat ambiguously, "I believe that you know what you need and what you want, and that you are entitled to your just proportion of the municipal expenditures.... I can only say that I stand ready to do all in my power to see that you get your just proportion of that which is due you."[15]

Before the meeting adjourned, the citizens of the Eighth Ward passed a series of resolutions supporting the construction of a fire station south of the Piscataquog River, and appointed a three-person committee to meet with the Lands and Buildings Committee to discuss them. The group also created a formal, nonpartisan community organization to advocate for all West Side neighborhoods and residents, not just those of the Eighth Ward. Eventually known as the West Manchester Improvement Association, it was, Adolph Wagner believed, "the only manner in which we can hope to command recognition."[16] Had the Amoskeag Manufacturing Company owned more land or held other interests in the Eighth Ward, the mayor and committee members might have given that recognition more readily. But in truth, concrete actions from local government officials came only after public pressure and, often, significant adverse publicity.

With the formation of the community association, progress on the fire station was rapid. Some controversy ensued when Alderman Gustav Wenzel, possibly owing to his desire to find a new location for the proposed fire house, neglected to present a resolution to the Board of Mayor and Aldermen calling for the city to obtain a $3,500 loan to begin the project. But the project went forward, and by August 12 the municipality had purchased a parcel of land at the corner of South Main and McDuffee Streets for $800. Construction on a brick fire station commenced soon after.[17]

Despite Mayor Hayes's support, residents of the Eighth Ward seemingly had to rely on the Amoskeag Manufacturing Company to provide them with a playground—meaning this initiative took far more effort than the fire station. The city's omnipresent corporate benefactor had gained wide praise for supplying most of the city's children with open spaces and playgrounds. However, Amoskeag managers would not accede to the West Side Improvement Society's request that the company donate its Granite Street lot to the city, as Gustav Wenzel had asked Herman Straw to consider earlier in the month. Instead, Straw's son, William Parker Straw, informed the group that Amoskeag might be willing to part with a parcel of land known as Whittemore Flatts, also known as the Valley Grounds, a popular baseball and recreation grounds located just outside the Eighth Ward. These negotiations suggest that Amoskeag held far more control over the use of lands for public benefit than did the actual local government.

On the evening of May 16, the Improvement Society met in the Democratic Club's headquarters to discuss the playground situation. Opinions about Amoskeag's offer were decidedly mixed. Some residents sided with Councilman John Shea, who saw no reason why Amoskeag might find the Granite Street lot so valuable. He argued that the Granite Street lot was better situated for a playground than Whittemore Flatts, as it was at least within the Eighth Ward. Besides, he suggested, accepting the Whittemore Flatts parcel would only add another playground to the Ninth Ward without adding one to the Eighth, while also weakening the Eighth Ward's ability to obtain a playground of its own.[18]

Adolph Wagner disagreed with Shea. "We can demand that the city buy us land for public playgrounds," he said, "but we cannot say to a corporation that they must give us such a piece of ground or we won't take any."[19] Charles McLaughlin added that the playground problem was a matter that originated not with Amoskeag, but with the attitude of city government toward companies like Amoskeag:

> Of course, we all know that the city should have purchased its park system in the first place, and then our children would not now be dependent on corporate generosity for a place in which to play. Any city of 80,000 inhabitants should be in a position to purchase its own playgrounds and parks and to command special considerations, and it is only due to the exceeding generosity of past administrations in the wholesale dispensation of tax exemption to every corporate charlatan that came to town that we are not able to do so.[20]

Selectman John Barry, meanwhile, presented another idea. The Amoskeag Manufacturing Company was rumored to be considering a land swap with the city. In return for a deed to the city's former Poor Farm, which Amoskeag hoped to make into a retirement home for some of its longtime employees, the company would provide the city with deeds to a number of properties around the city, including those to selected parks and playgrounds that Amoskeag presently leased to the city. Barry told the crowd that since "the other parks, namely, Varick park and the North End park, would not help the West Side situation in any way and that they were not equipped as playgrounds in the first place," the city might be able to include Amoskeag's Granite Street land in its negotiations.[21]

Over the next few weeks, Wagner, McLaughlin, and other representatives of the Improvement Society and the city's German clubs met with city officials and Amoskeag managers to find a solution to the playground issue. McLaughlin suggested to Mayor Hayes that the city obtain a ten-year lease for use of Amoskeag's Granite Street lot, as the only other suitable locations in the ward—including the Charles Kimball Walker lot on South Main Street—were unavailable at that time. Adolph Wagner agreed, reminding the mayor of the children's march earlier that month and adding that without a park, children would "of necessity get into the streets" to play.[22] Mayor Hayes promised "speedy action" to secure a playground site, and the city did approach Amoskeag with the committee's idea to lease Amoskeag's Granite Street lot.[23] Yet the company continued to wield tight control over its land and refused to deal with the city regarding the Eighth Ward. Thus, Amoskeag retained its power over the impotent mayor and city government in general. The matter remained unresolved for almost four years.

In the end, Eighth Ward residents did get both their fire station and their permanent playground. The latter would have to wait until 1917, when the city purchased land along South Main Street from the heirs of the late Charles Kimball Walker, former superintendent of the Manchester Water Works Department. Originally called Walker Park, the site was renamed in 1918 for Henry J. Sweeney, the first Manchester resident killed in World War I.[24] Both the fire station and the playground represented victories for the people of the West Side, as they proved that by unifying across ethnic and neighborhood lines, citizens could overcome the Amoskeag Manufacturing Company's indifference toward them and directly influence city government themselves.

The possibility of a bridge over the Merrimack River, meanwhile, dragged into 1914. In private, Amoskeag officials focused on defeating the bridge, as it would do nothing to help the company. In fact, its construction might only strengthen the McElwain factory's position in the city, much to Amoskeag's detriment. Publicly, though, they remained much more interested in bringing the Boston Red Sox to Manchester to help dedicate Textile Field.

10

Manchester and the Red Sox

Since the establishment of the National Association in 1871, Manchester fans had always shown more than a passing interest in major-league baseball. As a result, during the nineteenth century the city saw its share of exhibition games featuring various National Association and National League teams. The first of these came in July 1875, when Albert Spalding and the Boston Red Stockings—which, by 1913, had taken the name "Braves"—defeated the Manchester Atlantics, 22–5. Amazingly, fans at the time were only disappointed that the Red Stockings did not appear to be trying harder.

Over the next decade and a half, Manchester teams continued to arrange games with major-league clubs. Boston's National Leaguers made two more visits to Manchester in 1877, splitting their games with the local team. In fact, Manchester's performance in those games had been so impressive that Cap Anson, having spoken to a number of Boston players, traveled to the city with his Chicago White Stockings. In two games over two days, Manchester won one game, while Chicago won the other by a 1–0 score.[1]

Between 1876 and 1889, most local baseball games featuring major-league clubs were held on the West Side at the so-called 'Squog Grounds. Located on Amoskeag-owned land along Douglas and Conant Streets at the edge of the Eighth Ward, the ballpark—known officially as the West End Grounds—featured a wooden grandstand and fences, clubhouse facilities, and after 1884, a bicycle track. The ballpark was abandoned in the early 1880s and nearly turned into a residential neighborhood to accommodate the influx of new immigrants to the area, but a group of residents appealed to Amoskeag's Herman Straw for help. Showing initiative that was largely absent during the Eighth Ward's playground movement in 1913, Straw ordered the city to halt its plans to expand Barr Street through the site, and sent Herman Horne of the City Engineer's Office to lay out the new grounds. The lot remained the city's premier baseball grounds for another four years, even hosting an exhibition game featuring the Boston Beaneaters and the team's star outfielder, Mike "King" Kelly, in 1888.[2]

But the 'Squog Grounds had closed by the early 1890s, and Amoskeag sold off the property for development as a residential neighborhood. Meanwhile, interest in the Boston National League club waned, even as the team continued winning championships into the late 1890s. From 1903 to 1913 the team failed to post a single winning record, and in four of those seasons—from 1909 to 1912—the team lost 100 games every year. Predictably, the Boston club steadily lost fans.

Making matters worse, when the American League team that later became known as the Red Sox began operations in 1901, the club signed some of the National League team's best talent, plus nationally known players such as Cy Young. The club also charged half what the Braves did for a ticket—only 25 cents. As a result, the Red Sox outdrew the Braves by about a two-to-one margin.[3] Fans were rewarded with the first World Series championship in 1903, followed by another American League championship a year later. The team's success continued to hold fan interest into 1913, and Manchester baseball supporters looked forward to any opportunity to see the Red Sox.

Manchester's first chance to see the Boston Americans came on October 2, 1901. That afternoon, after its first season in the American League, the team arrived at Varick Park to take on Phenomenal Smith's New England League club. Despite the clouds that threatened the day's game, the team—known to readers of the *Manchester Union* as the "Bean-eaters," though officially lacking a nickname—entered Varick Park in memorable style.[4] "Immediately," reported the *Union*, "the men jumped out of the barouches, another jiffy a half dozen balls were flying through the air, and ten overgrown boys were doing funny things with the leather." Led by captain and third-baseman Jimmy Collins, the Boston aggregate, dressed in season-worn grey uniforms trimmed in blue, with "BOSTON" inscribed in block letters across the chest, provided an added bonus to the fans seated in the wooden grandstand when Cy Young was announced as Boston's pitcher.[5]

In addition to the 600, 700, or 1,000 fans in attendance—four different newspapers reported three different numbers—eleven players representing the city of Manchester watched the American Leaguers' pregame exhibition.[6] Boston's trip to Manchester was arranged by William Freeman, the manager of Varick Park, and for the occasion Phenomenal Smith had assembled a formidable team of New England League all-stars to face them in this one game.[7] They were good ballplayers, but as a reporter for the *Boston Globe* noted, the local club still was nothing more than an "aggregation of players ... who played under the name of the Manchesters," wearing the green-trimmed white uniforms of the team that Smith had managed during the summer of 1901.[8]

The game that ensued did not inspire accolades from the newspaper reporters in attendance. The *Union* complained that "the Collins men were not playing ball with the interest that might be expected in one of the championship games," and suggested that Boston's pregame exhibition might "have been a discouraging sight" for Manchester players.[9] The *Mirror* was blunt in its criticism, its correspondent suggesting that "the contest … wasn't half so interesting as last Saturday's [local] Ryefield's-Shamrock game."[10] Manchester outhit Boston, but six Manchester errors led to five unearned runs in the fourth inning. Boston won the game, 6–1.

Twelve years later, much had changed. The Red Sox were more popular in Manchester than ever, but Textile Field looked nothing like it had in 1901, when it was known as Varick Park. Curious about the new stadium, Boston pitcher "Smoky Joe" Wood drove to Manchester for a July 30 game between

Joe Wood, the popular pitcher for the Boston Red Sox, at Fenway Park, 1912 (Bain Collection, Prints and Photographs Division, Library of Congress, LC-B2-2441-6).

the Lawrence and New Bedford clubs of the New England League. His interest was in more than just the stadium; his brother, Pete, was likely to pitch that day. "Smoky Joe," beloved throughout New England for his dominant pitching performance in 1912, had spent most of the 1913 season recovering from ankle, thumb, and arm injuries, and had not played for the Red Sox since early in the month.[11] The Red Sox clearly missed the team's star pitcher; at the time of Wood's visit, Boston was mired in fifth place, having won exactly half of its 92 games that season.

Upon Wood's arrival at Textile Field, where crushed stone still was being added to the outfield and wooden bleachers were being erected, the pitcher parked his automobile along the east side of the diamond—encouraged to do so by local fans despite the new on-field parking ban—then took his seat in the new grandstand. Pete Wood did not pitch until the ninth inning, but newspaper accounts suggest that the Red Sox star enjoyed the game. After the contest, a "gang of admiring youthful rooters" followed Joe Wood as he crossed the diamond, then watched as he got into his car and departed.[12]

While Joe Wood's appearance at the New Bedford-Lawrence game was a highlight to the fans who attended, the game itself—as well as the next day's contest between the same two teams—would prove far more important to baseball in Manchester. *Union-Leader* sports editor Jack Finn noted as much on the morning of the first game, writing that "[w]hether or not we are to have a league club in this city next season, will in large part, be decided by the manner in which the fans turn out today and tomorrow to witness the championship games...."[13] The games did not disappoint the fans—1,500 of whom attended the July 30 game, 1,000 the following day, despite the fact that the contests were scheduled for consecutive Wednesday and Thursday afternoons when Amoskeag employees still were at work.[14] Lawrence and New Bedford split their series, and fans delighted in watching Manufacturers League alumnus Billy Levesque win the second game for New Bedford with a two-run, tenth-inning single. Most damaging to Amoskeag and the Manufacturers League, however, had to be Finn's assessment of the second game: "Unlike other games which have been played recently in Manchester there was a snap and ginger all along the line. There wasn't any delay at the start, no crabbing of the ump, and the play went freshly and smoothly. It was a new experience for Manchester and the fans appreciated it."[15]

Obviously, Finn's words were aimed at the Manufacturers League. Yet the Amoskeag Textile Club already had set events in motion to win over Manchester's baseball fans in favor of the local amateur league. In June, the club had assembled a three-man committee to plan the opening of Textile Field. One member, Amoskeag superintendent Perry H. Dow, who had supervised the

Varick Park overhaul, traveled to Boston to meet with Red Sox president James McAleer in hopes of arranging an exhibition game with the reigning World Series champions.[16] Dow negotiated with the American League club throughout the month, providing occasional updates to Manchester's media through the *Amoskeag Bulletin*. Finally, on August 1, the Amoskeag Textile Club announced that the Red Sox would indeed appear in Manchester on September 8, in a game against a team of all-stars representing the Manufacturers League.[17]

The timing of Amoskeag's announcement was impeccable. Articles about the pending Red Sox exhibition in Manchester appeared in the very newspapers—generally on the very same pages—that proclaimed the New Bedford-Lawrence series a decided success and speculated on when the New England League would place a team in Manchester. Further countering those proclamations, the *Amoskeag Bulletin* also carried a front-page editorial in its August 1 edition asking whether the local reporters "who are paid for furnishing 'food for fans' are really in earnest, and honestly and truly believe" their assertions:

> Because the Amoskeag Textile Club has seen fit to build an athletic field which will long stand out as a monument to the club's progressiveness and desire to do good, is no valid reason why the plant should be turned over to an almost-defunct league....
>
> It is very poor dope ... in taking attendance at Wednesday's game as a proof that Manchester is crazy for a New England league team. Why shouldn't they draw a good crowd on such a day? With practically all the stores in the city closed and the only professional league game of the season as an attraction there should have been at least 3000 people at Textile Field to warrant the outburst that emanated from some writers....
>
> There is great interest in baseball in Manchester. The interest has been created during the last two years by the Manufacturers league. The success of the local league has been made possible by the reason that it only cost a dime to see a game and the feeling of rivalry existing in the different mills and factories has been kept at a high pitch.[18]

Just as the *Manchester Leader* had used the Boston Red Sox to boost sales and its political positions the previous October, the Amoskeag Textile Club used the team to promote the Manufacturers League. To counter charges that Manufacturers League games seldom started on time and were marred by poor play, poor umpiring, and poor sportsmanship, the company boasted that the selection of an all-star team to play against the Red Sox would cause "all of the players ... [to] hustle all the more," and that sportsmanship would be one of the qualities that coaches would consider in choosing players for the team.[19] In subsequent issues, the *Bulletin* exclaimed that the Boston Braves would loan the All-Stars two seldom-used players, pitcher Paul Strand and catcher Walt Tragresser, and in a headline joked that the "Red Sox May Not Win" as a result.[20]

Meanwhile, the *Bulletin* publicly opposed the New England League's advances on Manchester. "The people of Manchester do not want a New

England league team in this city," proclaimed the Textile Club publication, and it promised that the Manufacturers League would provide sufficient professional-caliber entertainment—particularly if plans to expand the league to other cities in the Merrimack Valley came to fruition. Ultimately, the *Bulletin* insinuated that the New England League would have competed with Amoskeag in the latter's goal to create loyal employees who primarily identified with the company:

> The Amoskeag Textile Club was founded, primarily, to promote a feeling of fellowship and loyalty—loyalty to each other and to the great concern whose name it bears. It has taken steps to broaden its work in many directions, one being the movement which resulted in the Manufacturers league. The extensive improvements in Textile Field are the outcome of this step.
> The Textile Club has put itself under this financial burden simply and solely that its baseball team and those other teams associated with it in this league may have the best that can be had in athletic grounds. It has asked nobody to share the burden. What it has to offer, it offers freely and it takes as its reward, the appreciation of every player and every loyal supporter of the Manufacturers league.[21]

Amoskeag's claim to put baseball above profit appears true; after all, the company (through the Amoskeag Textile Club) already had spent $30,000 on a stadium with no hope of recouping that cost in ticket sales. In fact, unstated in the *Bulletin*'s comment is the fact that Amoskeag's true cost savings would come later in the form of labor peace with a non-unionized, loyal workforce, along with whatever economic benefits might come with a positive public image.

While the Textile Club opposed the New England League in print, club officials continued making arrangements for the Red Sox game. By early September, preparations were complete. John Carney, who took over the Amoskeag Textile Club team in August, would manage the All-Stars, and traveled to Boston to secure the services of an umpire for the game.[22] At Perry Dow's invitation, James McAleer traveled to Boston to see Textile Field, and apparently took time to meet with friends including Carney and Phenomenal Smith.[23] Dedication day, meanwhile, was scheduled to begin with a series of events involving the Red Sox, followed by a "soccer football" game between the Amoskeag Textile Club and the Manchester Light Blues, and a spectacular fireworks show at nightfall. Afternoon admission was set at 25 and 50 cents, and 10 and 15 cents for the evening.[24] Providing even more legitimacy to Amoskeag's efforts came the announcement that the Red Sox would bring the Boston Royal Rooters—including Boston Mayor John "Honey Fitz" Fitzgerald, saloonkeeper Michael "Nuf Ced" McGreevy, actor Hap Ward, and *Boston Globe* sportswriter (and New England League president) Tim Murnane.[25]

Local media blanketed Manchester with advertisements more than a week before the big day. "Boston Red Sox, Champions du Monde," read the French-language advertisement in *L'Avenir National*, "vs. les Meillers Jouers de la Ligue des Manufacturiers. L'equipe de la Ligue Locale Sera Assiste d'une Batterie du Boston National."[26] ("Boston Red Sox, World Champions, vs. the Best Players in the Manufacturers League. The local Team will be Assisted by a Battery on Loan from the Boston Nationals.")

"The regular lineup of the Red Sox is guaranteed," proclaimed another advertisement, this one in the *Amoskeag Bulletin*. The Amoskeag Manufacturing Company was so interested in making Dedication Day a success that officials allowed employees to leave work early. Even Manchester's public schools, which planned to open their academic years that very morning, announced that they would excuse students from the afternoon session, provided they presented a note from their parents.[27]

Finally, on September 8, the Red Sox arrived in Manchester. Automobiles carrying members of the Red Sox entered the city between 11:00 and 11:30.

Dedication Day at Textile Field, September 8, 1913, featuring the Boston Red Sox and the Manufacturers League All-Stars (courtesy Manchester [New Hampshire] Historic Association).

Amoskeag Textile Club officials escorted the team to the Derryfield Club, an elite club on Mechanic Street—coincidentally, only a few hundred feet from the spot at which Red Sox fan and Manchester Police Chief Michael Healy ordered his officers to arrest six Free Speech Alliance protestors eighteen months earlier. The players spent "considerable time in lounging about the rooms" after lunch, smoking, relaxing, and talking with Amoskeag and Manchester officials.

A little before 1:30 that afternoon, the team emerged from the club wearing their grey flannel uniforms, the words "RED SOX" across the chest in scarlet block letters. To great fanfare, players walked a short distance to the YMCA building, where members of the five Manufacturers League teams and representatives of the Boston Royal Rooters met them. "Honey Fitz" Fitzgerald spoke about the occasion, and—as he was wont to do, usually without provocation[28]—led his fellow Rooters in a rendition of "Sweet Adeline."

At 1:40, between 20 and 30 automobiles decorated in red Amoskeag Textile Club pennants carried players from all six teams, as well as former New Hampshire governor Charles Floyd, Manchester mayor Charles Hayes, and other honored guests, in a parade to Textile Field.

The crowd waiting inside the ballpark was estimated at more than 7,000 people; the *Manchester Mirror* noted that "every available inch of space in the grand stand and the bleachers was occupied, and thousands of others were strewn along the foul lines, some even going so far as to seek seating accommodations in the center garden." The field, which still lacked grass, had been leveled and was declared "smooth as could be desired." On the center-field flagpole, beneath the Stars and Stripes, flew the Amoskeag Textile Club's bright red flag, monogrammed in black with the club's seal. Approximately 600 additional pennants were suspended throughout the park from the grandstand, from electrical wires, and from light posts—the last of which held a total of 40 arc lights of 200 candlepower, supposedly enough to "make the arena as light as day for evening pastimes." As the vehicles entered the complex, players were met with a deafening mixture of applause, the sound of 21 aerial maroon bombs exploding in air (audible for a distance of eight miles), and the music of the Megaphone Quartet of Boston accompanied by the Amoskeag Textile Club Band.

Once the teams disembarked from their vehicles, players began to loosen up. When the Red Sox took the field for pregame practice, they were met with a warm round of applause. Shortly before 3:00, members of both teams posed together in front of the new grandstand for photographs, after which the teams took positions on benches outside their respective dugouts. A relay race between teams from Amoskeag and McElwain commenced the afternoon's athletic activities, with Red Sox manager Bill Carrigan and outfielder Tris Speaker serving as judges. As soon as the relay ended, the official announcer of the Red Sox revealed that day's batteries: for Manchester, Paul Strand and Walt Tragresser; for the Red Sox, Joe Wood and Les Nunamaker. According to the *Bulletin*, the announcement that Wood was to pitch caused prolonged, "deafening" cheers from the crowd. "'Smoky Joe' is without doubt one of the greatest pitchers who ever pulled on a padded glove," it claimed. "He has been heralded far and wide as the equal to the best and many and memorable are the victories to his credit over such slab artists as Walter Johnson, Vean Gregg and others of paralleled prominence."[29] That the man who had won three games in the previous autumn's World Series was pitching in Manchester highlighted the importance of the new field and its owners, the Amoskeag Manufacturing Company.

The announcement of Wood was surprising given his injuries. Yet his appearance in Manchester may have had something to do with team politics. The 1912 and 1913 Red Sox were a team deeply divided by religion and loyalty. Wood and Tris Speaker led one faction of allegedly anti–Catholic players, while another clique consisted of Catholics and was led by Bill Carrigan, Harry Hooper, and Duffy Lewis. Wood and Speaker were supporters of former manager Jake Stahl, whom McAleer had fired in July for his team's poor performance and amidst rumors that Stahl would take McAleer's place as team president. McAleer replaced Stahl with the team's catcher, Carrigan. In his biography of Hooper, writer Paul Zingg speculates that "Wood's own desire to discount any tension between the pro–Stahl group and Carrigan may have contributed to the arm problems that would ever after plague his pitching career. His premature return to the mound [after Stahl's firing] was as much a gesture of support for the new manager as it was a signal that the team was not going to forfeit the entire season while it worked to get its house in order."[30] There is no way to know for certain, but conceivably, Perry Dow, recognizing Wood's celebrity status in Manchester, might have asked McAleer to play him in Manchester; McAleer had forwarded the request to Carrigan; and Wood, wanting to avoid controversy, was too professional to say no.

Universally, the media proclaimed the ensuing game to be one of the best ever witnessed in Manchester. The Red Sox played many of the team's stars for most of the game, including Speaker, Hooper, Larry Gardner, and Steve Yerkes, though Carrigan removed Wood in favor of rookie Dutch Leonard after three innings. Boston scored three times in the game: Hooper scored an unearned run in the first inning; Wood tripled in the third, then scored on Hooper's sacrifice fly; and Leonard scored from second on a Hooper single in the eighth. Manchester scored but once, when Frank Lyons—who had three hits on the day, all against Leonard—crossed the plate in the ninth inning on Sam Harris's triple.

After the game, a number of players from both teams retired to the YMCA on Mechanic Street to use the pool. Later, they joined other honored guests, including Strand, Tragresser, and members of the Royal Rooters for dinner at the Derryfield Club, after which many of them returned to Textile Field to watch as the Amoskeag Textile Club defeated the Manchester Light Blues, 1–0, in a soccer game under the arc lights. The *Mirror* correspondent thought the soccer game a "novelty," but was surprised at the knowledge of the sport—which was widely popular in Europe—shown by the 7,000 people in attendance. A spectacular fireworks display capped off the evening.

The Amoskeag Manufacturing Company accomplished much in its dedication of Textile Field. James McAleer claimed that "outside of the big league ball parks, there is not a more up-to-date or better equipped playing field in the country." Coaches and administrators from Dartmouth College and Saint Anselm College, as well as "scores of other college and athletic officials," also were suitably impressed, some even suggesting that they would work with the Amoskeag Textile Club to schedule baseball and football contests in Manchester. Meanwhile, the All-Stars themselves received praise from those on hand: Braves pitcher Paul Strand was particularly effusive in his comments about his Manchester teammates, while the Red Sox paid Amoskeag the ultimate compliment by offering Frank Lyons—the man who laid the first brick at Textile Field in April—a tryout with the major-league team.[31]

As for Amoskeag's hope of unifying its foreign-born employees and the city's immigrant population as a whole, the popularity of the soccer contest—despite the *Mirror* reporter's lack of understanding of the game—suggests that other sports might have been just as effective, though perhaps not in as acceptable a way as a supposedly "American" and "Americanizing" game such as baseball was believed to have been. Furthermore, the fact that the *Mirror* reporter ended his column on the day's events with praise for the Manchester Police Department for "watchfulness personified," its officers "ready to curb any disturbance or quell any excitement," suggests at least one person's distrust of the multiethnic crowd. Still, the same reporter wrote that "all classes of people united to make the day a gala one."[32]

Obviously, officials with the Amoskeag Manufacturing Company still hoped to keep the New England League out of Manchester. By having invited the league to play a number of exhibition and league games at Textile Field in 1913, however, Amoskeag seems only to have strengthened the resolve of league officials to find a way to wrest control of the baseball grounds from the Manufacturers League. As the most modern baseball park in New England outside of Boston, Textile Field would have been the jewel of the New England League. The desperation of league officials to place a team in the stadium, Amoskeag's continued protection of its own baseball league, and new and continuing challenges to the company's control over Manchester, resulted in a conflict that ultimately would cause all of organized professional baseball, including the Red Sox, to boycott Manchester.

11

"Textile Field hath been Assailed!"

Textile Field's significance to the baseball world probably was not lost on directors of the New England League, many of whom—including league President Tim Murnane, who attended the Dedication Day exercises—had seen the park and the large crowds it attracted. Both the minor-league games in July and the Red Sox exhibition were so successful, in fact, that the New England League redoubled its efforts to place a team in Manchester, but only if that team could play at Textile Field. Meanwhile, the Amoskeag Textile Club remained steadfast in its desire to control baseball in the city.

Against a backdrop in which the Amoskeag Manufacturing Company attempted to reassert its own dominance over Manchester, the Textile Club and the New England League arrived at an impasse. But the New England League had a weapon with which to interrupt the ATC's baseball plans in 1914: the National Association, to which most major and minor leagues belonged and through which it could instigate a boycott of Textile Field by all of professional baseball. As a result, not only would the Amoskeag club be unable to schedule exhibition games against New England League teams; but now, not even the Red Sox would be able to play in the city. Coincidentally, two former ballplayers familiar to Manchester, Fred Lake and John Carney, found themselves at the center of the controversy.

The Manufacturers League ended its 1913 season on September 27 with an exhibition series between the first-place Beacons and the second-place Starks. Although the Starks won both games of the series, the Beacons technically won the season's championship, and as the Stark players cheered, the Beacons received the pennant from William McKay. While some members of the Amoskeag Textile Club made arrangements to travel to the Polo Grounds to watch a World Series game between the New York Giants and the Philadelphia Athletics, a *Mirror* reporter wrote after the Beacon-Stark series that "it's getting too near football time and the public has had pretty nearly enough of baseball for 1913."[1]

Even so, the Amoskeag Textile Club began its preparations for the 1914 baseball season nearly as soon as the 1913 World Series ended. In November, the club named John Carney to direct the Textile Club's athletic association. Carney took over as manager of the Amoskeag baseball team in early August after the sudden resignation of Fred Brice, under whom the heavily favored Amoskeag club had performed poorly. Carney was well known in New Hampshire baseball circles. In 1886 he played first base for the independent Manchester Maroons at the 'Squog Grounds in West Manchester, where female fans gave him the nickname "Handsome John." In the late 1880s and early 1890s, he played first base for major-league clubs in Washington, Buffalo, Milwaukee, and Cincinnati. He also spent most of the 1890s and early 1900s in the minor leagues, and by 1902 had surfaced in Concord as an owner of the New England League franchise there. By 1908 he was managing the Trenton club in the Tri-State League, where he found his club threatened when an independent league, also with a team in Trenton, attempted to sign his players away from him. Carney responded to that threat by transferring some of his team's road games back to Trenton and by offering free attractions at his ballpark while the team was away, thereby providing constant competition for the local independent club. Subsequently, Carney returned home to his farm in Litchfield, New Hampshire, and successfully coached the Phillips Exeter baseball team before taking over as Amoskeag's baseball coach.[2]

Upon officially joining the Amoskeag work force in November, Carney organized a promotional campaign for Textile Field. The Textile Club printed 20-page brochures, to be distributed to athletic departments at major colleges around New England, "setting forth the advantages of Manchester as an athletic center and showing photographs of Textile Field resplendent in its Dedication Day crowd." He also negotiated with Dartmouth College to bring a football game to Manchester and contacted several major-league baseball clubs in the hopes of luring them to Manchester for exhibition games in 1914.[3]

At about the same time, the New England League formulated its plans for the 1914 season. On December 5, league officials met at the Copley Plaza Hotel in Boston. Hoping to break the Amoskeag Textile Club's hold over Textile Field, the group turned to Fred Lake, the one-time catcher who had been part of the conspiracy to throw the 1899 New England League season in Manchester's favor. League officials granted the New Bedford franchise to Lake and authorized him to transfer the club to Manchester or, if negotiations there failed, to Fitchburg, Massachusetts. Over the next week the new owner spoke with William Parker Straw about use of Textile Field. According to the *Amoskeag*

11. "Textile Field hath been Assailed!"

Fred Lake, probably in 1910 when he managed the Boston Doves (later the Braves). The one-time Manchester manager who allegedly conspired with Phenomenal Smith to throw the New England League's 1899 season in Manchester's favor, Lake returned to the city in 1914 with the hope of transferring his team to Textile Field (National Baseball Hall of Fame Library, Cooperstown, New York).

Bulletin, he went so far as to suggest that he would construct his own ballpark, but when Straw proposed to "go with him and secure suitable grounds," Lake did not accept the offer. The new owner also met with officials from Fitchburg who, according to *L'Avenir National,* were more likely than the Textile Club to grant use of their grounds on terms Lake would accept.[4]

New England League owners wanted to place a team in Manchester rather than Fitchburg. They authorized Lake to negotiate with Straw even though by that time, Straw already had rebuffed the league in its attempts to secure Textile Field. On December 5, the day of the New England League's Copley Plaza meeting, the Amoskeag Textile Club president wrote to Amoskeag Treasurer Frederic C. Dumaine in Boston to apprise him of the situation:

> I have been over very carefully the proposition made to us by Mr. Dunbar [New England League official Frank E. Dunbar] of letting Textile Field to a New England League team, and in connection with this have looked pretty carefully into the New England League itself. I find that financially it is in very poor condition, there being at least three and possibly four franchises for sale. The New Bedford team which was very poorly supported last year is the one that the league wishes to transfer to Manchester.
>
> We ourselves through Mr. John Carney ... [are] arranging to use the Field Wednesdays and Saturdays, and I cannot but feel that a New England team would work to the disadvantage of our local organisations [sic]. I have therefore written a letter ... to Mr. Dunbar, with whom I have previously had several telephone conversations, saying that we considered it unwise to lease Textile Field. I trust that you will think the decision a wise one.[5]

Despite the rejection, the New England League remained desperate to place a team in Textile Field, and Frederick Lovett Lake appeared to be just the person to accomplish that goal. The Cornwallis, Nova Scotia native had played parts of five seasons with major-league clubs in Boston, Louisville, and Pittsburgh, during which time he compiled a .232 batting average over 48 games. He also spent time in the minor leagues, particularly among the New England League's Merrimack Valley clubs. There, he captained Manchester in 1899 and Lowell in the early 1900s—in fact, in one 1901 game, Lake stole home for the winning run against Phenomenal Smith's Manchester club. Whether or not anyone in Manchester recalled the 47-year-old former catcher's connections to the city is not known, but he was remembered for managing the Red Sox in 1908 and 1909 and the Boston Doves (later renamed the Braves) in 1910—teams with which he had found little success.[6]

As the New England League sought a return to Manchester, the Amoskeag Manufacturing Company worked at restoring its control over the city. For instance, in December, having learned from the mistakes of the 1912 Lawrence strike, the company finally announced that it would not reduce employee wages in response to the state-mandated reduction in workweek hours from 58 to 55. As a result, the company did not see the violence or work stoppages that had plagued the American Woolen Company in Lawrence two years earlier, and Amoskeag could publicly congratulate itself for its "fine action" and its "loyalty to employees." Moreover, it could inject politics into its benevolence—after all, the company claimed, its action came despite an ongoing "depression" in the textile industry allegedly resulting from "the reduction in tariff rates" by Democrats in Washington.[7]

11. "Textile Field hath been Assailed!"

Meanwhile, Amoskeag's short-term control over the city's police department seemingly was solidified. In December, the city's new police commission—consisting of a Progressive and two Democrats, all appointed by the Governor and Executive Council—at last chose Michael Healy to continue as Manchester's Chief of Police. The decision took the commission several weeks to finalize, bringing the *Mirror* to accuse the Democratic Party of "incompetency" and partisanship in its handling of the situation. In fact, at one point during the summer rumors circulated that Healy "had been marked for slaughter"—that Governor Felker personally approached one candidate and offered to make him Manchester's Chief of Police, and that several others had already turned down the position.

But with his job now secure, Healy went to work to impose his sense of justice over the city's criminal system. According to historian Melissa Klapper, with no recreational space available at home, immigrants found that venues of commercial entertainment became "major instruments of Americanization." Perhaps not coincidentally, Healy's efforts concentrated on the regulation of pool halls, threats to raid gambling parlors, and on ensuring that the city's plays and films conformed to his concepts of morality and decency. He also became vocal in his opposition to Prohibition, which was not surprising considering the importance of the so-called Healy Method to the police departments' coffers. He did, however, claim to support Prohibition if alcohol distribution could be stopped entirely—something he believed impossible. Equally predictable given its unflinching support of Healy, the *Union-Leader* backed the police chief. So, too, did the *Mirror*, which called his efforts to protect Manchester's youth from films such as *The Traffic in Souls* and plays including *House of Bondage* "the right sort of censorship."[8]

The police remained busy in 1914. Phenomenal Smith continued to work the night shift, and twice in a one-week period in March he had to bring unconscious prisoners—both incarcerated for public drunkenness—to the hospital. Another officer, while passing the Amoskeag Employment Bureau office at the corner of Canal and Stark Streets, heard escaping steam and, with the help of the Amoskeag night watchman, found a "steam valve blowing off with 12 lbs steam on the indicator and no water in the boiler." The policeman put out the fire in the boiler, likely saving the company's employment records and the building itself from damage.

Other matters occupied the police as well. Besides drunkenness, the most common complaints included robbery and theft (particularly of clothes and shoes), fires, and injuries. Baseball continued to be a minor problem. On at least three occasions officers responded to complaints about boys creating a nuisance by "playing ball," and on another, police were called to investigate the theft of a catcher's mitt from the Textile Field ticket office. The department continued to fixate on the Greek community in its descriptions of victims and perpetrators, even though numerous French Canadian and Irish surnames still appeared in the blotters.

Perhaps the saddest moment regarding the city's Greeks came in June, when Smith responded to a call at Amoskeag's wool washing room and found "Demetrios Sakarikos, 31 years of age, a Greek, who had been killed by a machine which he was cleaning." Sakarikos's shirt sleeve became caught, dragging the employee into the machine, which crushed his head and upper body. Workers took nearly 40 minutes to remove Skarikos's remains from the machinery. Media treated the accident as a sad event, but one to be expected in an industrial plant, even one with the safety protocols that the Amoskeag Manufacturing Company claimed to have in place. Certainly, local newspapers did not blame Amoskeag for the death.[9]

With the announcement that Healy would continue to serve as the city's police chief, the Manufacturers League organized for the 1914 season. Initially,

John Carney (back row, center) with his Amoskeag Textile Club baseball team at Textile Field, 1914 (courtesy Manchester [New Hampshire] Historic Association).

the league seemingly was poised to expand its operations beyond city limits to include teams from Derry, Suncook, Nashua, and Concord, but the plan did not appear financially feasible and the Board of Directors dismissed the idea. Although the group would need multiple meetings to organize for the 1914 season, on January 7 the league did elect William McKay as its president. More notably, the group elected a new secretary: the *Union-Leader*'s Jack Finn. This act, combined with the decision to pay the league's officers a salary of $100 for the season, ensured that the best-known sports columnist in Manchester and occasional critic of the Manufacturers League would support the league in 1914.[10]

By the end of January, the league had finalized its organization. Again it consisted of five clubs, one each representing the Amoskeag, McElwain, Stark, Reed, and Hoyt companies. Teams had until April 6—rather than March 1, as in the previous season—to finalize their rosters, thereby allowing managers more time to "get a line on the talent available by seeing the men in real workouts." Each Saturday, four teams would play in Manchester, while a fifth team would travel to Suncook to play against a nine representing the mills in that community. If the experiment with Suncook proved successful, league officials promised to make Suncook a part of the Manufacturers League in 1915.[11]

With the league in place, John Carney continued his work of scheduling exhibition games for the Amoskeag club. In February, he indicated that he had reached agreements with representatives of the Red Sox, Chicago Cubs, and Philadelphia Athletics to bring those teams to Manchester. The Red Sox were scheduled to come to town on August 17 and the Athletics on September 2, Carney announced, but a date for the Cubs had not yet been determined. Providence of the International League would play Amoskeag on August 6, and Toronto would come to play on a date to be determined, while Lawrence of the New England League was scheduled for April 18. He also arranged for the Holy Cross and Carlisle Indian Training School football teams to meet at Textile Field on November 7 and was negotiating with other professional and semi-pro baseball and college football teams from around the Northeast to make appearances at Textile Field over the next nine months. "There will be no end to good things athletically for Manchester this summer," predicted the *Mirror*.[12] Unfortunately for the Amoskeag Textile Club, this prediction proved premature, for Carney's announcements gave the New England League a weapon in its fight to place a team in Manchester.

Early in 1914, the New England League approved the transfer of its New Bedford, Fall River, and Brockton, Massachusetts clubs to Fitchburg and Haverhill, Massachusetts, and Lewiston, Maine, respectively. These moves seemingly ended any question of the New England League placing a club in Manchester. As the *Union-Leader* reported, Fred Lake had "made an attempt to get into

Manchester [in December] ... but was unsuccessful in his efforts to secure grounds," leading him to place his club in Fitchburg.[13]

Carney stood by the Amoskeag Textile Club's public assertion that Textile Field was to be reserved primarily for use by the club and the Manufacturers League. In fact, his overzealousness in protecting the club's interests put Carney at odds with Manchester High School, which claimed that he had "imposed prohibitive conditions on the school teams" and that, as a result, the high school might have to drop baseball and football. After intense pressure from the school, the *Union-Leader,* and the *Mirror,* unnamed officials of the Amoskeag Manufacturing Company stepped in to negotiate a face-saving settlement with the high school, and peace was restored.[14]

Unlike the high school, the New England League continued to be locked out of Textile Field except to play its annual exhibition games against Amoskeag and other Manufacturers League teams. Even though Lake claimed that arrangements at Fitchburg were to his satisfaction, the league was not ready to give up. On March 4, at the Copley Plaza Hotel, New England League officials voted to boycott the city of Manchester, cancelling all of its exhibition and league games already planned for Textile Field. The given reason for this boycott was retaliation against the Amoskeag Manufacturing Company for its refusal to allow Fred Lake to place his team at the ballpark. The boycott did not include Lowell's planned game against Saint Anselm College, perhaps because—despite coach Phenomenal Smith's familiarity with John Carney—the college had been unable to secure use of Textile Field. The Amoskeag Textile Club would not budge, forcing the college to make alternate arrangements for playing the New England League team. As a result, the game was planned for a field behind the school's academic buildings in Goffstown, where the college athletic council planned to erect temporary bleachers.[15]

The Amoskeag Textile Club responded to the New England League's boycott with anger. On March 7 John Carney issued a statement, which was published in full in both the *Mirror* and the *Bulletin.* In it, the Textile Club director called the "attempted boycott" a "'spite move'" and claimed that the New England League had no moral basis for imposing the ban. "Far from opposing Fred Lake when he wanted to place a team here," he stated, "President W. Parker Straw of the club offered to assist Mr. Lake in finding grounds, and was to so arrange the schedule of games as to have no conflicting dates with him when big attractions were to be had."[16]

The *Bulletin,* meanwhile, recorded the textile club's dismay in two articles in its March 16 issue. In one, the club expressed its disappointment in the New England League, stating that the "exhibition of child's temper, the churlishness of their action in voting to have nothing to do with the Textile Club, an amateur organization, or which any team who plays with them, means more than the canceling of a few games. It means the lowering of the standard of the man in all the ranks of professional baseball." The ATC also claimed that it could not have leased the stadium to a league team "in justice to the Manufacturers league," and that it would not have done so even had they foreseen the New England League's boycott.

The *Bulletin* also published a provocative, sarcastic front-page article. Entitled "And It Has Come To Pass" and subtitled "Poor Textile Field," the article claimed that "Textile Field hath been assailed!" and that it "hath been decreed unfit for players of the baseball game." In its sarcasm, the article may have revealed the true motivations of the Amoskeag Manufacturing Company, even if the words were couched as an attempt to console Textile Field itself rather than the workers they were intended to sway:

> If thou couldst return to thy former happiness! Oh, for the days of Varick Park! Nobody didst want thee then. Thine unsafe stand and sickly fence held no attraction for him or he. Ah, indeed, those were the happy days! Thou couldst rot, for all the notice thou didst get would fail to fill a nut.
> But hark! Do not grieve, dear heart. Thou art our child and the paternal spirit within our breast bursts forth and bids thee stop thy lamentations. Thou still have us! Thy foster parent is still upon the job. Do not grieve, say we, for some day it will be our turn at bat....
> We have builded for a purpose. Couldst we forsake that purpose for another of doubtful consequence? Verily, we could not![17]

If anybody noticed the *Bulletin*'s reference to paternalism and benevolence, the city's newspapers made no mention. Even so, this passage does suggest Amoskeag's desire to retain its workers' loyalty through baseball, and the threat to Amoskeag's control that the New England League represented.

Jack Finn and the *Union-Leader* supported the Amoskeag Textile Club's position. Finn wrote, "We're all strong for professional baseball but can't see a logical reason why the New England league should expect the fine new park, erected at the expense of the Textile club, to be turned over to them. It is personal property and the owners have a right to use it as they see fit." The sports editor also lambasted the New England League for punishing Manchester fans, none of whom had anything to do with the boycott, and predicted that the club would be even less likely than before to permit a league team to use the stadium in the future.[18]

The New England League, meanwhile, continued to pressure the Amoskeag Textile Club. As a signatory to the National Agreement, the organization compelled other professional baseball leagues to honor its boycott of Manchester. As a result, newspapers in some New England League cities reported that nearly all of the major and minor league clubs that had promised to play exhibition games in Manchester in 1914—including the Red Sox and Cubs—had cancelled. Only one exception remained: the Philadelphia Athletics. Even with that team, however, nothing was certain, and the *Union-Leader* reported that the owner of the New England League's Worcester franchise, Jesse Burkett, was close to convincing Philadelphia owner-manager Connie Mack to cancel his planned trip to Manchester.[19]

Despite the setback, the Amoskeag Textile Club claimed that the 1914 season would not be a total loss. John Carney was able to keep upcoming dates with independent clubs, including the Boston Athletic Club Pilgrims, the Chinese University baseball team from Honolulu, and the Brooklyn Royal Giants, an African-American team based in New York which one historian has called "one of the best ballclubs in the East during the first decade of the century."[20] But the possibility that the Amoskeag Manufacturing Company could provide major-league-caliber baseball to the people of Manchester was now in question.

Regardless of these problems, officials of the Manufacturers League prepared for the upcoming season. The *Mirror* reported that the league's managers "have been very busy signing players from Maine to the Mason-Dixon line and as far west as Ohio." McElwain recruited John Kelly, a pitcher from Kansas City who was newsworthy for being "deaf and dumb." John Carney signed well-known Yale star "Buster" Brown and pitcher Jack Fraser, the latter of whom was touted, incorrectly, as having played for the Philadelphia Athletics. Amoskeag provided both with relatively easy jobs in the corporation. The Stark club brought back Billy Levesque, who had played for New Bedford in the previous year's New England League games at Textile Field, and signed a pitcher named Eaton who previously had pitched for professional and independent teams.[21] By April 6, the day on which all players had to be employed by and working in the city's manufacturers, all four teams had signed several out-of-towners to bolster their squads.

Not everyone favored the way by which league rosters were being filled. Both Jack Finn and the *Bulletin* had to defend the practice of hiring outside talent by suggesting that the fans demanded it; as Finn claimed, "they are the ones who support the game."[22] Amoskeag went further, claiming that if the league "can induce a number of young men of the caliber necessary to make good ball players, who are willing to enter the employment of a factory and work six days for the privilege of playing ball one-half day in each week, then the league should be commended." Regardless, the league was making progress, hoping to demonstrate that the city would not need the New England League or teams from any other league for professional-caliber baseball. In fact, officials were so sure that they even promised that they would not take the New England League to court to force it to lift the boycott.[23]

In these recruiting activities, the New England League saw another opportunity by which to pressure the Amoskeag Textile Club into giving Fred Lake access to Textile Field. On April 21, the *Leader* reported that the minor league had filed charges with the National Baseball Association, "alleging that teams in the Manufacturers league were to play men who were ignoring contracts made with teams protected by organized ball"—in other words, the league was violating organized baseball's reserve clause.

The Manufacturers League was not actually bound by the National Agreement; technically it was not even a professional league. However, 1914 saw the Federal League declare itself a new major league not bound to the National Agreement. At all levels of professional baseball, owners feared that their teams would be raided as the "Feds" attempted to fill their own rosters. This was particularly problematic for American and National League teams, as the National Agreement allowed them to enforce a "reserve clause" that bound players to a team even after the expiration of their contract.[24] The Federal League, not to mention the Manufacturers League, had not signed on to the National Agreement and potentially could sign these players, allowing them break the "reserve fence." In filing its charges, the New England League probably hoped to prey on these fears, thereby putting more pressure on Amoskeag to allow Fred Lake to use Textile Field.

In the end, the Amoskeag Textile Club's Board of Governors voted to respect the reserve clause. "If players under contract are to play in the Manufacturers league," reported the *Union-Leader*, "they must procure the sanction of the professional club managers." Yet the Textile Club's compliance with the reserve fence was self-serving. "While it is impossible for the Manufacturers league to get the protection of the National Association, the directors of the association feel that they cannot afford to have the league pointed out as a party not in harmony with the National association agreement of professional leagues."[25] In other words, the Amoskeag Textile Club had no interest in being associated with the Federal League at that time, though that would change in 1915. Rather, the club still hoped to reconcile with professional baseball, perhaps in the hope of attracting major-league and high-level minor-league clubs for exhibitions once the problems with the New England League were resolved.

The Manufacturers League eventually sent a list of its players to the New England League president and received no reply. "[It] looks as though the whole scheme was to give the Manufacturers league a black eye with the public," wrote league secretary Jack Finn in his *Union-Leader* column, "due to the fact that the Amoskeag Textile club would not turn over its fine new ball plant to the New England League."[26] Yet the professional-baseball boycott of

Manchester did have an effect, and the New England League would eventually gain a foothold in Manchester before the end of the baseball season.

Even so, the Amoskeag Manufacturing Company's problems with the New England League were not its most pressing, even if they were among its most public. Rather, the company found it had other issues to deal with regarding its eroding control in Manchester, among them the *Manchester Advocate* and the W. H. McElwain Shoe Company.

12

Amoskeag's Local Challenges

Obviously, Amoskeag's troubles with the New England League threatened the public-relations centerpiece of its welfare-work programs. The Amoskeag Textile Club and the Manufacturers League could continue to use Textile Field for baseball, of course, and the ATC would still be able to invite regionally and nationally known barnstorming clubs for exhibitions in Manchester. But the national boycott of Manchester meant local residents would be unable to see New England League games, as they had in 1913, or the promised contests between Amoskeag and the Chicago Cubs, Philadelphia Athletics, or Boston Red Sox.

Organized baseball's boycott, though, was just one of the Amoskeag Manufacturing Company's challenges in 1914. As poverty continued to be a problem in Manchester, Amoskeag saw more opposition to its employment practices—some originating with the *Manchester Advocate,* others with textile employees themselves. At the same time, the W. H. McElwain Shoe Company, which also saw its employment practices criticized, began to threaten Amoskeag's control over the city. With residents of the Eighth Ward and, seemingly, city government behind it, the city's second-largest employer continued to push for a bridge over the Merrimack River to connect its central plant to the city's West Side. Amoskeag would have to keep McElwain in its place—but to do so meant exposing the company's blatant control over city government.

On March 13, 1914, between 150 and 200 weavers walked out of Amoskeag's No. 11 Mill in a dispute over working conditions. They claimed that recent changes in the goods they produced—ironically, the mill had begun manufacturing American flags in early December—should be accompanied by a higher wage scale. They also expressed dissatisfaction with a recent order for them to place their lunch baskets in their lockers rather than hanging them on their looms, as they alleged that the lockers were infested with water bugs.

Superintendent William Parker Straw met with a committee of eight people appointed to address the workers' grievances, and while he agreed to look into improving conditions regarding the lockers, Straw refused to make any changes to the wage scale. Employees returned to work after a day-and-a-half strike, but not before Straw admonished the committee about "the folly of a walkout for such trivial causes, which could be carried to authorities of the corporation for dignified adjustment."[1]

Even if they rarely occurred at Amoskeag, short-lived strikes such as this one were increasingly common in Manchester. The previous August, for instance, the F.M. Hoyt Shoe Company, located three blocks south of Textile Field, saw about 200 employees walk off their jobs. That work stoppage, which lasted less than a day, was precipitated by what the *Advocate* termed an "obnoxious foreman" who, though in his position only temporarily, "began the revolutionizing of shop conditions to the extent that his dismissal was the only thing for consideration by those under him." After the workers retreated to their union hall, Hoyt's business agent met with a union representative. The strikers eventually returned to work, and the following day Charles Marrow of Hoyt's Boston office arrived to fire the foreman. The company also fined two employees ten dollars each for their roles in the strike.[2]

A section of the McElwain Central Plant in Manchester, 2016 (Scott Roper).

12. Amoskeag's Local Challenges

One important difference between the two strikes was the role of the local shoemaker's union in the Hoyt case. Hoyt employees complained about working conditions directly to their union representative, who was able to arrange for an acceptable outcome with Hoyt management through arbitration. With no union, Amoskeag employees had neither a central representative with the authority to bargain on their behalf, nor an accepted process by which to submit complaints to Amoskeag's management. Worse, but tellingly, William Parker Straw had treated workers as children and dismissed their complaints about wages, workplace conditions, and storage of midday meals as "trivial."

Perhaps because of this attitude, about a week after the brief Amoskeag walkout, a number of Amoskeag textile workers met to discuss organizing a union. "There is evidence of a number of large organizations in the textile industry in Manchester in the near future, judging from the enthusiasm and an equally important feature—the absence of dread of the employer," wrote an *Advocate* reporter. "It has been predicted in Manchester that a trades union would have to be 1,000 strong before the workers could muster sufficient courage to enroll. Recent events have proven quite to the contrary." The reporter added that while Amoskeag management's opinions on the matter were not known, it "is generally believed that between two evils (as perhaps they view it)—the I.W.W. and the A.F. of L.—they choose the least evil. One or the other is inevitable."[3] Ultimately nothing came of the meeting, but to those who hoped to improve working and living conditions for Amoskeag employees, the situation seemed much more promising than it had before 1912.

Amoskeag employees were not the only workers in Manchester without strong union representation. In fact, the recent expansion of the city's largest shoe company, the W. H. McElwain Company, was partly designed to reduce the company's presence in Massachusetts, where shoe-worker unions were much stronger than in New Hampshire.[4] Unfortunately, the lack of union representation may have played a role in a 1913 incident when a McElwain shoe worker, identified in the newspapers only as "a Greek," attacked his foreman, James Redmond. According to the *Union*, Redmond had fired the immigrant because he had "disregarded one or more of the factory rules," and the discharge was necessary so "that discipline and order be maintained." The *Union* continued:

> As the time wore on, the Greek became more and more convinced in his own mind that he had been wronged and so strong did the desire for revenge grow upon him, that the intent of getting even with the boss.
>
> When Mr. Redmond, who, by the way, would say but little of the affair, made his appearance, the Greek set upon him and had not Mr. Redmond been a man who knew well how

to take care of himself in an emergency of the kind, there is no doubt that he would have fared badly at the hands of the infuriated assailant. As it was he succeeded in warding off the vicious blows and then the usual knife was brought into play, with the result that Mr. Redmond received a slight scratch which was of little moment, but bled profusely. The Greek received more than he gave and beat a hasty retreat.[5]

In one respect, the Redmond incident was atypical of the local stories that newspapers typically covered: it apparently did not involve alcohol. Just one day before the McElwain incident, the *Union* reported that "the dock at the Wednesday morning session of the municipal court was occupied mostly by drunks."[6] That same day, the body of Albert Johnson, a 29-year-old Swedish immigrant, was found in front of the Stark Hotel, his throat cut "from ear to ear." That morning at 5:30 Johnson had told his roommate that he was "going to get some air." The *Mirror* suggested that Johnson had an alcohol problem, as he had been estranged from his wife because of his alleged "excessive intoxication." While they ruled the death a suicide, police were stunned at how close Johnson came to severing his own head with a razor blade.

The *Mirror* also reported on an incident at the Manchester Police Department where a 17-year-old girl complained to an officer that her parents had been "beastly drunk all day and that for the entire day the six other children beside herself, ranging in age down to a nursing infant of two months, had been without food." The girl's father had taken ten dollars from her—which she earned at a local mill—and shut her out of the family's home on Hanover Street. The police arrested the parents, John and Mary Milne, along with five other adults in a sting at a Pine Street house, and charged them all with drunkenness. Shortly after, "a tot five years old entered the station, leading a smaller brother, and asked for some of her father's money to buy milk for the infant." The police provided the children with supper, and then released their parents after the Milnes promised to care for their children.[7]

No one seems to have connected these incidents to Chief Michael Healy or his "Healy Method." That these problems existed in a city in which alcohol sales remained technically illegal should have raised concern among the city's moralists. But the monthly fines levied by the courts on the city's liquor outlets supported the Manchester Police Department's activities, and through them Healy claimed to have reduced the number of Manchester saloons to fewer than 100, down from 500 in the 1890s.[8] Perhaps as a result, Frank Knox's *Leader* (and, subsequently, the *Union*) continued to support Healy into 1914 and beyond, and even Jesse Markee's *Manchester Advocate* professed no ill toward the chief.

One reason Markee ignored even the possibility that alcohol abuse might relate to the Healy Method is that he—and the American Federation of

Labor—viewed alcoholism and violence as resulting from low wages and unemployment. To the *Advocate*'s publisher, these issues related directly to foreign immigration. About the Redmond incident, Markee wrote that the "American Federation of Labor many years ago undertook to impress upon the minds of American manufacturers the importance of upholding the standards of the American workmen. With that was pledged arbitration." But, he added, corporate leaders decided that instead of investing in workers already in the United States, they would import less expensive laborers from abroad. Unfortunately, foreign workers knew nothing of American law, Markee alleged, echoing mainstream editorials that had appeared in local dailies during the Bread and Roses Strike. As a result, he felt that managers "are beginning to realize that they cannot succeed in forcing the worker below the American standard" of living, and that perhaps soon, companies will eschew foreign immigrants in favor of more expensive unionized workers.[9]

By 1914, Markee's opinions had not changed. That March, in an editorial entitled, "Was He Lured to His Death?," the publisher revealed that the United States received 200,000 immigrants each month, and that many of those "are induced to leave their native homes through the alluring influences of advertising posted in foreign seaports by a combination of American corporations and the steamship companies." He then related the story of 32-year-old Polish immigrant Anthony Konopka, whose body recently had been found floating in one of the canals that ran through the Amoskeag millyard. Markee alleged that Konopka had been misled by American companies into leaving Poland to search for work in the United States, where he hoped to "establish a better home for himself and family." Markee continued:

> After scouring other parts of this country in the vain search for work he came to Manchester with the same discouraging results. The strain was too great for his mental power. He threw himself in the canal. A multitude of people witnessed the recovery of the body, but few realized the tragic story of his death. He was to them a stranger and a tramp. The newspapers said he was probably insane.

Markee concluded by suggesting that the "first step by the American government in solving the immigration question would be to apprehend and place a good severe penalty of servitude upon those who violate the immigration laws."[10]

Unquestionably, Amoskeag agents did play a role in recruiting immigrants to work in the mills, particularly from Quebec. But in connecting this story to Manchester, Markee probably exaggerated the role of the city's corporations and underestimated the part that ethnic communities played in bringing recent immigrants to the city. In their 1939 study of the Amoskeag Manufacturing Company, for example, Daniel Creamer and Charles Coulter found that many of the city's turn-of-the-century Polish migrants came "usually upon the invitation of a friend or relative. The local steamship agent was frequently the intermediary and financier. That is, the agent would provide the prospective immigrant with a steamship ticket upon advance payment of half of the fare by the Manchester resident and upon the latter's giving his guarantee that the immigrant would pay the balance to the agent before he discharged any other financial obligations." Additionally, Polish workers "regarded a 60-hour week in the Amoskeag mills and a biweekly pay of $7.00 to $11.00 a considerable improvement in his economic status," as a result of which 2,000 foreign-born Poles resided in Manchester by 1920.[11]

The city's Greek community would not have related to Markee's depiction either, though considering the small number of strikebreakers who arrived in the city in 1903, their experiences probably were more mixed than those of the city's Polish immigrants. Greeks seeking work at Amoskeag first arrived in the 1890s, followed by a larger group hoping to escape military service with the onset of a brief war between Greece and the Ottoman Empire in 1897. The establishment of a Greek Orthodox church in 1905, as well as continued employment opportunities in Amoskeag and the city's shoe factories, made Manchester an enticing destination for Greek immigrants. About 200 migrants left for Greece to participate in the Balkan War in 1912, but when they returned to Manchester they brought family and friends with them. Additionally, many Manchester Greeks claimed that their migration to the city had been "spontaneous and unguided":

> It was pointed out, for instance, that a Manchester Greek would go to New York to meet a steamer bringing his wife or other relatives. On the same boat would be many Greeks who had very little money and no knowledge of the English language and who were very much bewildered by the vastness of the country. It was only logical that they would be more than willing to follow this man who knew their native tongue and who told them of the many employment opportunities that Manchester could offer.[12]

Regardless, the *Advocate* continued to attack Amoskeag and other Manchester corporations for encouraging foreign immigration and the poverty and other problems that came with it. But the newspaper also began to question Amoskeag's apparent solution to those problems: welfare-work programs. It did not criticize the company directly, however. Rather, the newspaper reprinted articles from other sources that called into question the true purpose of welfare work in general. An article reproduced from the *Portland Press* in Maine described how employers hoped to control employee loyalties through welfare work, and that such programs were being introduced in lieu of increasing wages. Another that appeared originally in *The Atlantic Monthly* commended "every employer who undertakes, at his own expense, to improve his employes' [sic] work." But the author also reminded readers that welfare work "is not a substitute for wages," nor will it ward off unions in the long run.[13]

As the *Advocate* assailed immigration policies and welfare-work programs, the Amoskeag Manufacturing Company found that its authority over Manchester was being questioned in other ways as well. The most significant challenge came from the newly empowered citizens of the Eighth Ward. Now, however, they were joined in their fight by the W.H. McElwain Company.

As he had promised to do when he was elected in 1912, and aided by a petition signed by Eighth Ward residents, Alderman Gustav Wenzel proposed the construction of a new $185,000 bridge south of the Amoskeag Millyard to connect McElwain's central plant to the West Side. McElwain offered $20,000 to the city to help defray some of the expense. Experts believed that the bridge would encourage residential and economic growth in the Eighth Ward while also improving efficiency—and, presumably, profits—for McElwain. It would also provide a direct path between work and home for about 700 McElwain employees.

The *Mirror* supported the bridge, as did the *Union-Leader* and the *Advocate*, and all three newspapers claimed that popular opinion favored it by a wide margin. Meanwhile, a city alderman collected opinions from voters in an affluent section of the northern part of the city, finding widespread support for the project, and the Manchester Publicity Association, on behalf of its business members, expressed its desire for the bridge. At the same time the Union-Leader Corporation hired high-school boys to canvass voters throughout the city. They found that for every person who opposed construction of the bridge, thirty backed it.

But in Manchester, the only opinion that counted was that of the Amoskeag Manufacturing Company—and Amoskeag opposed the construction. Managers never explained why the company would oppose a new bridge south of the millyard. Perhaps they feared what the debt load would do to the city's budget or, as the city's largest taxpayer, to its property taxes. Or maybe they opposed the expansion of the city's Eighth Ward; the company held no financial stake there, and the expansion of the ward would have been to the political and economic benefit of McElwain, not Amoskeag. Regardless, just as the City Council seemed ready to approve the resolution, according to Frank Knox's *Manchester Leader*, Amoskeag "initiated a quiet but active campaign against the bridge." The newspaper continued:

> This influence displayed itself by the prompt change in the attitude of every member of the council, except Councilman Conery, who had been supporting the bridge project, who was, because of employment, or otherwise, under the influence of this great concern. There has never been any denial of the reason assigned for their change of front from most of the

men who changed their attitude over night, except the privately proffered excuse that they couldn't quarrel with their own bread and butter.

At this point, according to the *Leader*, McElwain officials and other champions of the bridge again canvassed the city, this time with post cards and petitions, once more finding that a majority wished to see the project through. Some of the councilmen changed their minds again, so that by June, the project was just two votes shy of the two-thirds necessary to pass a resolution calling for its construction.[14] At this point one of the councilmen who had opposed the project offered a compromise, whereby bonds would be dated May 1, 1915, rather than in 1914, effectively delaying construction for a year.

Frank Knox, believing that a fight between the city's two largest corporations for control over city government was not in Manchester's best interests, pushed McElwain and Amoskeag to accept the compromise. McElwain did so immediately, but Amoskeag managers promised only to take the matter under advisement. Eventually, Amoskeag's local managers agreed to withdraw their opposition, but asked for a week's delay so that they might explain the situation to both upper managers in Boston and to Manchester councilmen voting on Amoskeag's behalf. However, when Amoskeag's local managers conferred with the company's Boston-based treasurer, Frederic Dumaine, they "evidently encountered an unexpected obstacle to their plans," according to the *Leader*, and were instructed to oppose the bridge. As a result, the city would have to wait nearly a decade before the construction of the first Queen City Bridge.[15]

As the bridge controversy indicates, the Amoskeag Manufacturing Company retained its hold over city government. Still, the company did not emerge from the fight unfazed; in fact, the public's confidence in the company and its benevolence programs may have been shaken by the knowledge that decisions made on the city's behalf originated in Boston, not in Manchester with the Straw family. The *Leader*'s overt questioning of Amoskeag's motives likewise indicated that the company no longer held the power it once exerted over local media. Meanwhile, the W.H. McElwain Company—a partner in the Manufacturers League—demonstrated that it was willing to oppose Manchester's largest and most important corporation when its needs clashed with Amoskeag's. In fact, perhaps Manchester could no longer be considered a one-industry city.

At the same time, Amoskeag and McElwain did have one common concern: the possibility that their immigrant, non-union workers might set out to unionize. Therefore, as Amoskeag looked for ways to overcome organized baseball's boycott of Manchester, the two companies turned to another method for Americanizing the city's workforce: the American flag.

13

Rally Around the Flag

As tensions between Amoskeag and McElwain increased over the bridge issue, both companies continued to focus attention on their workers. Immigration to the city continued even while unionization efforts grew, making the Americanization of local workers a primary goal of the city's two largest employers. Yet contrary to the tenets of the baseball creed, poor sportsmanship had infected the local Manufacturers League, threatening the effectiveness of that program.

Even so, conventional knowledge held that baseball *should* have worked to Americanize workers. As a result, the Amoskeag Textile Club was not yet ready to abandon its baseball program. Nor was it ready to acquiesce to the New England League, a league that William Parker Straw had found to be financially unstable and dominated by a handful of owners who would not defer to local corporations or the Textile Club. Yet administrators must have known that, given the New England League's status as a minor league under the National Agreement, continuing to fight the region's purveyors of the National Pastime would not reflect well on Amoskeag—particularly when professional baseball's boycott meant major-league teams could not come to Manchester.

The largest cotton-textile manufacturing company in the world could not continue to play the victim in its war over Textile Field. Therefore, the Amoskeag Textile Club eventually yielded to the boycott. But it did so on its own terms, and in the process found a way to punish Fred Lake and the New England League for the embargo—seemingly proving the point that Manchester would not support New England League baseball. And while baseball remained important in the city throughout the embargo, Amoskeag officials began to realize that the game alone would not Americanize the city's foreign-born. Therefore in 1914, to supplement the ATC's other initiatives, the company utilized a more direct method, one that literally rallied workers around the American flag.

As the Manufacturing League's season approached, the Amoskeag Textile Club continued to make improvements to its two baseball parks. The Recreation Grounds at Rock Rimmon Park saw the construction of a new wire fence, "so high that climbing over is impossible, and so far distant from the baseball diamond that the only way to watch the ball tossers in action is to pay a visit to the box office." The field was leveled and re-sodded, and the club erected new wooden bleachers along the first and third base line. It may not have been Textile Field, but the improvements did mean the park could seat about 1,000 fans, about as many as Varick Park had before its transformation in 1913.[1]

Textile Field also saw improvements. Although Jack Finn complained that "the grounds will not be complete until the diamond is sodded"—apparently, the rolled-dirt diamond created too much dust, made the game uncomfortable for the fans, and made fielding difficult for players—the Textile Club decided not to make the infield a priority. Instead, officials announced that later that season, workers would build a mammoth scoreboard in the outfield, as impressive as the scoreboards at the new parks in the American and National Leagues.[2]

On May 9, 1914, while waiting for the new scoreboard to be installed, the Manufacturers League began its season with a parade of 30 automobiles, not unlike the parade enjoyed by the Red Sox and All-Stars the previous September. All of the league players climbed aboard cars and trucks and, accompanied by two bands, lined up in the Amoskeag Millyard near Granite Street. Ahead of them were trucks carrying the factory fan clubs: the McElwain Rooters, which claimed a membership of 600; and the Amoskeag and Stark fans, "mostly of the female variety" and making a lot of noise. Then, following a large white goat wearing a blanket which read "Beacon's goat," the procession headed eastward to Elm Street and north to Bridge Street, where it turned around. At Lake Avenue, the Amoskeag and Stark groups turned off and headed toward Textile Field with one of the bands, while the remaining participants turned westward onto Granite Street and proceeded to the Rock Rimmon grounds.[3]

According to the *Bulletin*, 3,700 people attended the two opening-day games. About 2,500 fans saw Amoskeag defeat Stark, 3–1, at Textile Field, and another 1,200 were reported to have witnessed Beacon's 3–1 victory over McElwain at Rock Rimmon. By the *Bulletin*'s account, however, the day's glory belonged to the Amoskeag Manufacturing Company, whose "generous spirit" was responsible for the construction of the "magnificent ball park in Textile Field and the numerous changes and improvements at the Recreation Ground." Even better, continued the paper, "[t]hat no rent is charged to the league, makes a big asset for the players who come in for a division of the receipts at the end of the season."[4] Whether anyone noticed that the *Bulletin*, which heretofore had denied Amoskeag's role in keeping the New England League out of Textile

13. Rally Around the Flag

Field, suddenly gave credit to the corporation—and not the Textile Club—for allowing the Manufacturers League to use the park for free, is not recorded.

Textile Field, meanwhile, received its scoreboard in June. It was no mere scoreboard, however; as promised, it truly did rival those at major-league ballparks. Measuring 70 feet long by 30 feet high, the slate-covered board was designed by Amoskeag electrical engineer Frank L. Clarke, a fact that allowed the company to avoid using existing patented technology. The scoreboard, which was used for the first time on June 10, consisted of two sections. The left side provided information about the game at Textile Field: balls, strikes, outs, and the number of the player at bat. (Numbers on the scoreboard corresponded with information printed in scorecards. Players did not wear numbers on their uniforms.) Changes to the numbers in this section were controlled from the press box behind home plate; pressing a button sent an electronic pulse to the scoreboard, which automatically turned a disc onto which numbers were painted.

The right side of the scoreboard was controlled manually. It was connected to the press box—and to the outside world—by telephone, and permitted the manual scoreboard operator to receive the scores of "big games" and record them on the board. This board included separate areas on which to record baseball and football scores. Notably, the scoreboard allowed fans to keep track of a second game by inning—either the concurrent Manufacturers League game at the Recreation Grounds or a major-league game in Boston. This gave the Manufacturers League an even more professional aura to it, at least for fans at Textile Field.[5]

On the evening of June 15, 1914, just five days after the scoreboard's debut, the Manchester Police Department received a complaint of boys playing baseball on Parker Street.[6] Police records do not suggest what the department might have done to discourage the boys' play, if anything; after all, at the time, the Amoskeag Textile Club was attempting to use the game to instill loyalty among its workers to Amoskeag and the United States. Still, the *Amoskeag Bulletin* was on record as opposing street ball:

> Baseball is second nature to the American boy but baseball cannot be played in the street. In order to play the game, outposts are established against the approach of the policeman. When their ball game is interrupted they take to quieter forms of play, for play they must. So they play at assault, larceny, burglary, and craps. These, too, are illegal but, in their young minds, there is no moral distinction between these games and baseball. They simply know that the police are their natural enemy.[7]

Obviously, this fact underscored the need for American cities to develop parks. While Manchester boasted of many parks, all of which had been donated by the Amoskeag Manufacturing Company, the city also had banned the playing of baseball on those grounds since the nineteenth century. Instead, children and adults wishing to play baseball were relegated to diamonds scattered occasionally throughout the city, such as the informal one at the Eighth Ward's Whittemore Grounds, or to watching the semi-professionals at Textile Field. Given these conditions, baseball alone would not suffice in the Americanization of Manchester's immigrants.

Therefore, organizations other than Amoskeag sought alternative means to the same end. The most significant efforts involved the planning of the state's Flag Day ceremonies, scheduled for Manchester on Monday, June 15. Flag Day had never been an important day in Manchester; then again, even though some states had set aside June 14 as a day on which to honor the Stars and Stripes since the 1890s, the first federally sanctioned day of commemoration would not come until 1916. Even so, the city's Flag Day Committee promised that on June 15, 1914, Manchester would be the home of the most impressive display of patriotism in the United States.

Perhaps the significance of Flag Day in Manchester best can be understood by considering the importance of the American flag both as an anti-union symbol and as a statement of assimilation. During the Bread and Roses strike of 1912, the flag had been an important counterpoint to the red flag of the IWW. In his autobiography, Bill Haywood wrote of a parade called by Lawrence's mill owners, "which included some of the priests and ministers, the business men, and most of the public school children, although their parents were strikers." Across one of the city's main streets, the group strung a banner reading, "For God and Country! The stars and stripes forever! The red flag never!" Haywood claimed that consequently, "a mad wave of patriotism came over the business element, and for a time they all wore little American flags in their buttonholes to the great satisfaction of the flag-manufacturers."[8]

As an assimilation statement, the flag was similar to the baseball creed. Involvement in Manchester's Flag Day celebration was supposed to demonstrate one's patriotism—to "**prove conclusively** that the **American Flag** is the emblem of **all the people** of New Hampshire," in the words of the *Leader*—not just people born there.[9] Daily editorials in the *Manchester Mirror*, which offered free flags to regular readers, echoed that sentiment. In one, the newspaper suggested that holding the event in Manchester was appropriate, for "it is a city made up of peoples from all countries and all climes." Ignoring the problems of 1912, the editorial continued:

> They have been law abiding and law loving. This demonstration has not therefore been caused by any great industrial upheaval or any shocking sociological event.
>
> It was born amid patriotism and has grown to unexpected and undreamed-of proportions, because of loyalty and desire to honor and perpetuate the stars and stripes. Race,

creed and sect have been forgotten, and the natural differences of everyday life have been cast aside, and all Manchester and all New Hampshire is now standing shoulder to shoulder, with hearts beating in unison to bring about an inspiring demonstration.[10]

As plans progressed, the scope of the celebration became more apparent. After a sunrise salute to the flag, several divisions of the National Guard would lead a parade down Elm Street. Organizations from all over the state would take part in the parade as well—approximately 25,000 people, according to some estimates. The city's Greek community promised to send 1,000 "sturdy sons of Greece," including 200 veterans of the Balkan War, to march in the parade, and about 5,000 members of the city's German and French societies also were expected to participate. The Flag Day Committee also received assurances that both of New Hampshire's senators, both members of the House of Representatives, the governors of New Hampshire, Massachusetts, and Rhode Island, and President Woodrow Wilson himself would be on hand for the events.[11]

On May 24, the W. H. McElwain Company was Manchester's first industry to announce that it would close on Flag Day so that its employees, many of whom were participating in the parade, could attend the day's events. Other companies remained silent on the issue, preferring to follow the lead of the Amoskeag Manufacturing Company. Two weeks later Amoskeag did finally proclaim that it, too, would declare a holiday for its workers on June 15, at which point Manchester Publicity Association president Arthur Jenks announced that "practically all of the big industrial plants of Manchester will close down on Flag Day."[12]

Apparently the day was as festive as had been advertised. At the behest of the Flag Day Committee, many downtown businesses remained open and displayed the Stars and Stripes in their windows. The parade itself was a success, having been viewed by an estimated 100,000 (in a city of roughly 70,000 people). "To the newly arrived emigrant," the *Mirror* exclaimed, "what an impression it must have made, and how the stirring scene presented by the almost endless column of flag-carriers must have appealed to his fancy."[13] One incident did disappoint some in attendance, however: the absence of President Wilson. The *Leader* seems not to have cared, its editorial staff already having stated that "we honor the flag, not the President" even before learning of Wilson's cancellation.[14] The *Mirror*, however, attempted to make a political incident of Wilson's absence, stating that "Manchester Has Been Flim-Flammed" and claiming that Senator Henry Hollis had withheld knowledge that the president would not come to Manchester.[15]

As for Amoskeag's participation, the fact that the company delayed its decision to declare a holiday for its workers on June 15 did not mean its managers had no interest in promoting ethnic unity through the flag. In fact, the company had seemed to capitalize on the beliefs embodied in the 1914 Flag

Day celebrations on at least two prior occasions, once when it announced the decision to fly flags from most of its buildings in late 1912, and again a year later when it began to produce American flags in the No. 11 Mill. The company even flew a large flag in the company playground along Canal Street.

Amoskeag's most blatant and highly publicized attempt to use the American flag to support ethnic unity came in the aftermath of Flag Day in 1914. On June 29, the company unveiled what it billed as the "Largest American Flag Ever Made." Measuring 95 feet long and 50 feet high, weighing 200 pounds, and ostensibly advertising the company's foray into the production of American flags, the banner was the product of the very employees who had caused a work stoppage in March. A photograph, taken by Harlan A. Marshall of the Amoskeag Textile Club's "Camera section," shows the flag hanging from the No. 11 Mill, covering nearly four stories of windows and dwarfing the mill employees standing at its

The Amoskeag Manufacturing Company "Great Flag," hanging from Mill No. 11 on June 29, 1914. Billed as the "largest flag ever made," the flag served three purposes: to advertise the company's foray into manufacturing American flags; to further the Americanization aims of the city's Flag Day celebrations; and to suggest the loyalty of the employees who worked in Mill No. 11—some of whom had briefly walked off their jobs a few months earlier (courtesy Manchester [New Hampshire] Historic Association).

base. The photograph adorned the front page of the July 15 issue of the *Bulletin*, and an 8x10 version was made available to the public for 35 cents each.[16] Sales of the photograph (as well as the American flags produced in the mill) helped Amoskeag tie together patriotism with the interests of the company.

If the flag supposedly could unite all ethnic groups as Americans, it would have a more difficult time doing so in the case of race. The Amoskeag baseball club welcomed the team from the Chinese University of Hawaii to Textile Field in late June, but only 800 fans witnessed Amoskeag's victory that day. The Chinese University students, most of them American-born, wore blue uniforms trimmed in red and white, which seems to have helped win over the sparse crowd. Even so, Jack Finn referred to them as "Orientals," "Chinese," "Chinamen," and "Mongolians" in his articles—all preferable, perhaps, to the *Bulletin*'s "Chinks." When the famous Brooklyn Giants independent team arrived in early July, the so-called "darkies" (also called "husky darkies," "negroes," and "colored boys" in local newspapers) handily defeated Amoskeag before only 300 fans.[17]

Just as Amoskeag found little success in promoting games against well-known independent clubs, Fred Lake had difficulty with his club in the New England League. Fitchburg was among the worst teams in the league; by July it was firmly ensconced in last place with a 24–52 record, which Lake attributed to a weak pitching staff. Still, the owner-manager claimed that he had no debt in Fitchburg, that the team "has drawn fairly well" and had benefited from the "good will of the fans" there.[18] Despite his claims, Lake must have been disenchanted with the situation in Fitchburg, for shortly after Amoskeag's early July series against the Brooklyn Giants concluded, Lake, John Carney, and William McKay again began negotiating over the New England League's possible use of Textile Field.[19]

On the morning of July 28, a rumor began circulating that the Fitchburg club would be transferred to Manchester, effective the following day. A *L'Avenir National* reporter contacted Carney, who confirmed the rumor that afternoon—apparently with enough time for the newspaper to solicit from Lake an advertisement for the next day's game before it published its evening edition. The *Leader* carried a front-page report indicating that Lake had contacted Carney three weeks earlier, but that "the deal for the transfer was put through yesterday and closed today after many conferences."[20] The *Mirror*, on the other hand, insinuated that the Textile Club, not Lake, had instigated the move, having "felt keenly the criticism that was directed at them for their alleged refusal to allow a New England team here."

Moreover, John Carney told the *Mirror* that the boycott was over. The Red Sox, Chicago White Sox, and Philadelphia Athletics all had indicated that they would come to Manchester in the coming two months: the Red Sox on

August 17, Athletics on September 2, and White Sox "as soon as they can fix the date." Carney told a *Mirror* reporter that the professionals all would play the Amoskeag Textile Club baseball team, which, the newspaper predicted, "ought to save a few dollars by being able to see them here instead of having to go to Boston or New York."[21]

Despite the good news, some worried about the effects of this sudden move on the city's new minor-league team. "The transfer," reported Frank Knox's *Leader*, "coming as it does in the middle of the season and practically without warning, does not give opportunity for any campaign designed to arouse local enthusiasm and support, such as might have been carried on in the spring...." Still, the newspaper promised to help the team succeed by carrying "detailed" reports of the team's road games. "The Leader is arranging for the installation of the necessary equipment to make possible constant communication between the press box at the Textile club playing field and The Leader office, and scores of all games by innings will appear on the Union-Leader Bulletin board."[22]

That evening's Fitchburg-Portland game originally had been scheduled to take place in Fitchburg, but was moved to Portland ahead of final negotiations for use of Textile Field. Thus, the newly relocated team's first two games in Manchester were called for 3:00 on July 29 and 30—in other words, on a Wednesday and Thursday afternoon when Amoskeag employees still were at work. (The July 29 game was postponed, and the club actually debuted with a double-header on July 30.) That was not expected to be a problem, however, for both the *Mirror* and the *Leader* reported, incorrectly, that Amoskeag had moved the Manufacturers League games out of Textile Field, allowing Lake's team to use the ball grounds on Saturday afternoons when the mills were closed.[23]

If Fred Lake had been under the assumption that he could have Textile Field to himself on Saturdays, he was wrong. In fact, on July 30, *L'Avenir National* reported that Lake had met with the directors of the Manufacturers League the previous evening, and suggested that the parties share Textile Field on Saturdays when his team was scheduled to play in Manchester. He offered to arrange double-headers, with a Manufacturers League contest to follow the New England League game. He also offered to give 20 percent of the gate receipts to the local league.

Despite the boycott, the Textile Club still owned Textile Field, and was less concerned with profits than were the owners of the New England League. Thus, operating from a position of power, the Manufacturers League rejected Lake's proposal. Instead, henceforth on Saturdays, the city league would hold single-admission double-headers at Textile Field. Representatives claimed that the

13. Rally Around the Flag

Recreation Grounds "had not been a paying proposition," though considering the time, effort, and money that the Amoskeag Manufacturing Company had expended on the West Side field, this decision—which also eliminated a portion of each week's revenues—could best be described as retribution for the New England League's recent boycott. The Amoskeag Textile Club did suggest that Lake consider using the Recreation Grounds himself, but the minor-league owner and manager declined the offer.[24] Having to play all of its Saturday games on the road at a time when Sunday baseball was not yet legal, Manchester's new team was doomed from the start. This may have been the ATC's goal: to show without doubt that the New England League could not succeed in Manchester so that it could retain its control over Textile Field unabated.

Fred Lake did make an effort to generate excitement for his team, announcing that the Boston Red Sox would play his club at Textile Field. The date, August 17, was when the Red Sox originally were to have played John Carney's Amoskeag team, but the game had been cancelled as a result of the boycott. Bill Carrigan reportedly promised that "all of his stars, Speaker, Hooper, Lewis, Henriksen, Gardner, Leonard, and others" would accompany the club to Manchester. However, fans who attended the game found that the "Boston team presented a greatly changed lineup from the one doing daily battle" in the American League; only three regulars played for the Red Sox that day. So unknown was the club's pitcher—he had been with the Red Sox since early July, but seldom had pitched—that the *Union-Leader* reporter who attended the game referred to him as "George Ruth" instead of by his preferred nickname, "Babe." One day after the game, Babe Ruth would clear waivers and be sent to Providence of the International League. Regardless, the rookie did pitch a complete game, and the Red Sox defeated Fred Lake's team, 4–2.[25]

More than anything, reporters noted the game's remarkable speed. "It was one of the fastest, if not the fastest, ever played here," reported the *Leader*. *L'Avenir National*'s opening comment was almost identical, claiming that it was "la plus rapide encore jouee au Textile Field"—the fastest ever played at Textile Field. The one-hour, 15-minute contest drew approximately 2,500 fans, which was not bad for a Monday afternoon when Amoskeag employees were at work. But it was a far cry from the 7,000 who reportedly witnessed the previous year's game between the Red Sox and the Manufacturers League All-Stars. It also did not compare favorably with the 3,500 who had turned out five days earlier to see the Red Sox in Lawrence, Massachusetts.[26] On these terms, the game was not an unqualified success.

The *Amoskeag Bulletin* devoted no space to the game. However, the Textile Club was able to manufacture its own headlines. Again demonstrating impeccable timing, on August 15—just two days before Red Sox players arrived for their game in Manchester—the *Bulletin* announced that the reigning World Series champions, the Philadelphia Athletics, would be in Manchester to play the Manufacturers League All-Stars on September 2.[27]

In the aftermath of the New England League boycott of Manchester, questions remain. Why, for example, did the Amoskeag Manufacturing Company risk alienating all of professional baseball over use of Textile Field? What was so important about baseball in Manchester that the Amoskeag Textile Club felt compelled to present the Manufacturers League as equivalent to professional leagues? And why did it do so much to sabotage Fred Lake's efforts to make his team a financial success?

One possible answer may be found in the July 5, 1914, issue of the *New Bedford Sunday Standard*. In that morning's trade and business section, the newspaper published a lengthy article about Amoskeag's benevolence activities. Entitled "The Finest Answer to I.W.W.ism," the story began with a glimpse of the Flag Day celebrations, "of the line of 25,000 marchers, English born, Scotch born, Irish born, French born, Jewish born, Greek born, Polish born, Scandinavian born, representing in fact, most of the countries of Europe, but all loyally wearing or waving or carrying the Stars and Stripes to show the pride they felt in their American citizenship." Witnessing this display of patriotism, a spectator is supposed to have asked, "but where were the I. W. W.'s with their red flag and their motto, 'No God, No Country?'"

For the author of the article, Amoskeag had successfully defended the city against the radical Wobblies:

> There was only one explanation why that man asked himself that question, and that was that he was a stranger to Manchester and to its leading industrial corporation, the Amoskeag mills. Had he known of the manner in which this, the biggest cotton manufacturing corporation in the world, handles its labor problems, of the way in which the operatives work and live, of the ways in which the mill corporation seeks to help them better their economic condition and to enjoy life, he would not have wondered that I. W. W.-ism has not gained a foothold nor that even old line unionism has failed to take root in this community.

The *Standard* article amounted to a lengthy listing of Amoskeag's welfare program: a children's playground, children's vegetable gardens, company houses, tree-lined streets, the cooperative home building plan, a company hospital, first-aid stations, electric automobiles to help transport the sick, and dental services. Ranked third, just behind the playground and gardens, was Textile Field and the baseball program:

> It is the baseball field provided by the Amoskeag Manufacturing company for the baseball lovers among its employes [sic]. The corporation has put the field in condition, has erected the grandstand, and in every way co-operated with the young men in its employ to make the Amoskeag team a winner. It permits the members of the team to leave the mill after-

noons in the summer to practice, and the players do not even lose their wages.... The [Amoskeag Textile] club gives each player a membership in the Young Men's Christian association, so that he can keep in the best physical trim. On days when big games are being played, the corporation even gives the use of its big electric trucks to carry the girl friends of the players to the field.[28]

Two years after the Lawrence strike, representatives of the New England textile industry still feared the Industrial Workers of the World. Despite its recent problems, the union not only seemed to threaten the social order; it also endangered profits in a region that could not compete with the textile industries of the South. Amoskeag promoted its benevolence program as having warded off the IWW and unions in general. Yet as Amoskeag's activities over the previous two years had shown, the foundation of those programs was corporate power—control over the city and its residents—and the company had had difficulty in maintaining that control.

Admittedly, the merged *Union-Leader* was not nearly as damaging to Amoskeag as the original *Leader* had promised to be, and despite the Queen City Bridge issue, it usually supported the company. Even the *Advocate* supported Amoskeag's continued existence, though preferably in a weakened state in which unionized workers held far more power than they did at present. In doing so, editor Jesse Markee always attempted to remain nonpartisan. But in August 1914, the *Advocate*'s politics began to shift when Markee, without explanation, announced that he would step down as editor of the *Advocate* in favor of Harold Greene. Greene, a young Harvard graduate, quickly aligned his newspaper with the politics of the Democratic Party.[29] Markee promised to stay on for a time to ease the transition, but soon had returned to the *Mirror* full-time, where he remained until leaving the city in 1918. Meanwhile, the *Advocate*'s new political leanings caused some of Manchester's more progressive residents to worry, most notably *Advocate* board member Thomas Chalmers, who believed Manchester was losing a valuable resource for promoting understanding between labor and capital. According to Chalmers:

> The Manchester Advocate had started on its career previous to the Lawrence strike. And in the days when the excitement of that strike was threatening to engulf Manchester, it served the laboring population of this city by standing squarely against the I.W.W. It worked for the maintenance of industrial peace.
>
> A more radical publication might have made great capital out of that ferment. Shortly after that time I became a member of its board of directors. I have been particularly interested in its effort to voice the better sentiment of the working people of Manchester and to promote a better industrial understanding.
>
> The paper seems now to be entering a larger field of activity in taking a stand as a Democratic Labor paper. However, I am not a Democrat, and it has seemed wiser and better all around for me to withdraw from any responsibility for the policy of the paper.[30]

With the IWW still on the minds of many of Manchester's leading residents, Amoskeag managers must have remembered that the radical union *had* briefly made inroads in the city, particularly among workers at the McElwain Shoe Factory. Making matters worse, McElwain had openly opposed Amoskeag over the bridge issue. Unlike the city's other factories, the shoe company announced its Flag Day holiday without waiting for Amoskeag to do so first. Meanwhile, as the strike in the No. 11 Mill and the subsequent unionization meeting had demonstrated, Amoskeag's employees were not entirely content with the company, either.

The problems between Amoskeag and the New England League were an extension of these issues of control and power. The New England League wanted to lease Textile Field, easily the most impressive baseball stadium in New England outside of Boston, so that it might exploit the Manchester fan base that had been built up by the Manufacturers League and the success of the Red Sox, Saint Anselm College, and Manchester High School. Amoskeag continued to see this possibility as infringement on its control of Manchester. A successful New England League club might have drawn fan attention away from the Manufacturers League, which itself had been created to develop loyalty to and unity among the workers of the Amoskeag Manufacturing Company, and might have obscured Amoskeag's role in constructing Textile Field. Amoskeag decided to oppose the New England League's entry into Manchester by representing itself as a paternal figure, protecting its workers and its city from an unstable, possibly corrupt baseball organization.

At the same time, the company did not want to alienate other professional leagues, particularly the majors and high minors—leagues that were not likely to place a team in Manchester, but could send clubs into the city to play exhibition games there. After all, games against the Red Sox, Athletics, and similar teams—particularly if those clubs were persuaded to play their regular line-ups—would be arranged on Amoskeag's terms, and would bring prestige and legitimacy to the Manufacturers League. For such events, fans would have to credit the Amoskeag Manufacturing Company.

The lack of interest generated by Amoskeag's games against independent and college teams forced the Amoskeag Textile Club to change tactics and allow the New England League to use Textile Field. However, the club also used the low attendance for New England League games at Textile Field to suggest that the public would not support minor-league baseball in Manchester. By limiting the team's access to Textile Field, Amoskeag ensured the team's failure.

With the New England League's poor showing in Manchester and disappointing attendance in the exhibition game against the Red Sox, Amoskeag seemed to have proven that the New England League was not wanted in Manchester. However, the Manufacturers League All Stars still had to play an exhibition game against the Philadelphia Athletics. As a political crisis in Europe escalated into war, thereby creating supply and demand problems in the American textile industry, and as Manchester again geared up for state-wide elections, the Athletics game in particular would force the Amoskeag Textile Club to reevaluate its athletic programs and its relationship with the New England League.

14

The End of Big Games

When the Philadelphia Athletics arrived at the Derryfield Club on the morning of September 2, 1914, no one questioned why Connie Mack, baseball's most successful manager since the formation of the American League in 1901, might come to Manchester for an in-season exhibition game. After all, such events were common for major-league teams in the early 20th century. Besides, a year earlier, the Red Sox had demonstrated that a single appearance at Textile Field could earn a major-league team a lot of money. At 75 cents for a grandstand seat and 50 cents for a bleacher or standing-room ticket, and assuming that 3,000 of the 7,000 who attended the 1913 game purchased grandstand tickets, Boston's appearance had grossed the considerable sum of about $4,250 before factoring in concession sales. Newspaper articles do not reveal what percentage of the gate receipts belonged to the Red Sox, but for the club to have started Smoky Joe Wood and played most of its regulars for the entire game, it must have been substantial.

Considering Chicago sportswriter Ring Lardner's estimate that a major-league baseball team's expenditures averaged approximately $169,000 per year, or $463 per day, and that player salaries alone came to $65,000 per year, a chance to play in Manchester probably did appeal to the Athletics' owner-manager. Mack was considered by many to be a "cheapskate" and a "skinflint," a fact that a 1913 magazine feature seemingly confirmed: for all of Mack's success, and even though his four infielders alone were said to be worth $100,000, the article claimed that the Athletics carried the smallest payroll and earned the highest profits in baseball. Whether this was true or not, Connie Mack's finances do not appear to have been in the best of order. He owed Athletics co-owner Ben Shibe $113,000, a debt he had incurred a year earlier in purchasing majority interest in the team. Furthermore, attendance at Shibe Park was down significantly from prior seasons. Even though the club had won the World Series in

14. The End of Big Games

1913 and appeared poised to do so again in 1914, the club drew only 346,641 fans in 1914—off by 225,255 from the previous year, and the second-lowest total in team history to that point.[1]

Financially, the most threatening development of 1914 was the baseball war with the upstart Federal League. The "Feds" consisted of eight teams, four of which played in cities already occupied by the American and/or National Leagues, and the organization had declared itself a third major league not subject to the National Agreement. At first, the outlaw league did not sign players already under contract in the established major leagues, though it did ignore the reserve clause. However, when some well-known players jumped to the Federal League prior to the season, and when the league announced its intention to file an anti-trust suit against organized baseball, any possibility of peace

From left, Connie Mack, coach Ira Thomas, and an unidentified Athletics player or coach at Philadelphia's Shibe Park in 1914. That September, Mack brought his champion Philadelphia Athletics to Manchester to face his former teammate's all-star team at Textile Field. Both the result of that game and fan interest in the contest would be a source of embarrassment to the Amoskeag Textile Club (Bain Collection, Prints and Photographs Division, Library of Congress, LC-B2-3260-7).

among the leagues ended. A bidding war ensued for the services of major-league baseball's best players—including the stars of the Philadelphia Athletics.[2]

Connie Mack's eagerness to bring his team to Manchester may have been financial, and to do so on September 2 obviously was convenient; the club was scheduled to face the Red Sox in Boston the following day. But his visit also may have had a more personal significance, one with roots in another renegade major league. In 1890, the Players' League was established by baseball's first union, the Brotherhood of Professional Baseball Players, to compete with the National League and the American Association. Players who jumped to the new league opposed the reserve clause, the imposition of a set salary structure, and the major leagues' refusal to honor promises to include specific salary figures in player contracts. The rebel organization lasted but one season, and the bitter labor battle resulted in escalating salaries, plummeting profits, and acrimonious court cases for all sides. By 1891 the Players' League had disappeared, and the American Association limped along for only one more year before it, too, folded. This left the National League a monopoly until the American League declared major-league status in 1901.[3]

Though he makes no mention of it in his 1950 autobiography, Connie Mack was a vociferous supporter of the Players' League. He had played for the National League's Washington franchise in 1889, but upon learning of the new league's formation, he invested $500 in the proposed Buffalo club, becoming one of its seven directors. He appeared in 123 games for the team, including 112 at catcher. But he was not the only Players' League veteran at the Derryfield Club on the morning of September 2, 1914. Mack's first baseman in Buffalo—who, like many of their teammates, also had made the jump from Washington—was none other than John Carney, now director of the Amoskeag Textile Club Athletic Association and manager of the Manufacturers League All-Stars.[4]

Nearly a quarter-century had elapsed since Carney and Mack challenged the baseball establishment, and now both were part of that establishment, albeit at different levels. As an owner, Mack had every reason to advocate the reserve clause he once opposed. He also had shown his allegiance to the establishment by supporting professional baseball's boycott of Manchester, even if reluctantly. Carney, meanwhile, as athletic director and baseball manager of what was advertised as the largest cotton textile factory in the world, held many of the same powers as Mack. In that position he *should* have rejected the reserve clause, as it did not apply directly to the Manufacturers League and potentially only hurt his recruiting efforts. When the New England League imposed its so-called "reserve fence" during the boycott, he and the Manufacturers League Board of Directors accepted it, choosing to bow to organized baseball in the hope of maintaining good relations with the established order.

14. The End of Big Games

The reserve clause would not be an issue for Manchester in 1915. However, both the Federal League and the Philadelphia Athletics would be. Few realized that the Athletics game, coupled with November's Holy Cross-Carlisle football contest, would lead to Amoskeag's abandonment of the Manufacturers League and to Carney's departure from the Amoskeag Textile Club. The Federal League, meanwhile, set its sights on Manchester. Encouraged by Amoskeag's William McKay, the rebel league created a bidding war between itself and the financially unstable New England League. The war was not over players and had little to do with the reserve clause. Rather, it was a fight for Textile Field.

On the morning of September 2, the Athletics boarded a train in Philadelphia, arriving in Manchester before noon. Just as with the Red Sox a year earlier, the 1913 World Series champions dined and relaxed at the Derryfield Club and, sometime before 2:00, exited the club wearing their uniforms—loose-fitting grey wool knickers and matching shirts featuring a large, fancy, blue "A" on the left chest. Their caps were unique for that era: grey pillbox-style baseball caps trimmed with three blue horizontal stripes. Outside the building on Mechanic Street, the group met members of the four Manufacturers League clubs and climbed into automobiles, then followed the Textile Club Band to Textile Field.

The city had been preparing for this day for more than two weeks. There were two known mishaps during that time; the first had been on the evening of August 26, when, while readying Textile Field for the big day, a worker fell from the grandstand roof, injuring both wrists and his right leg. The other was an error in planning: the Textile Club arranged for the Red Sox to send a pitcher and a catcher to play for the Manufacturers League against the Athletics, but when the day approached the Boston club found that its schedule would not allow it to comply with its promise. Therefore, the Amoskeag Textile Club arranged a one-day trade with Fred Lake's New England League team: Lake sent the Manufacturers League a battery, and Amoskeag returned the favor to Lake.

Otherwise, everything went as Amoskeag had hoped in the days before the game. All of the city's major newspapers included advertisements for the coming of the Athletics, or "Champions de l'Universe" as *L'Avenir National* called them. American flags and Textile Club banners hung throughout the ballpark. The mammoth scoreboard was ready for the game. The club also arranged for an evening program consisting of the popular Teels Concert Band of Boston, a dancing exhibition by tango specialists Amelia Burnham and Leroy Young, a performance by the Irving Berlin Serenaders, and a fireworks display consisting almost entirely of set pieces which could not be seen from outside Textile Field.

As he had promised, Connie Mack played many of his starters, including Eddie Collins, Jack Barry, Frank "Home Run" Baker, Eddie Murphy, Rube Oldring, and pitcher Jack Coombs. Of course, Coombs was working his way back from injury and was not one of the team's primary pitchers any more, and without Stuffy McInnis the team only featured three-quarters of its $100,000 infield. Still, as Jack Finn noted, "it's customary in exhibition contests for major league managers to trot out a bunch of substitutes … but Connie has long been known as a man of his word."

Unlike the previous year's contest with the Red Sox, the game itself turned out to be an embarrassment for the Manufacturers League. Late in the game, with the visitors leading by a score of 7–0, Athletics players sensed that the crowd had become bored. Therefore, they began a display of "amusing stunts," referred to by some reporters as a "touch of burlesque."[5] As the *Leader* reported:

> In the seventh Murphy, Collins, Oldring, Baker, Walsh and Barry changed positions, and from this start the fun began. First the entire infield would rush nearly to the plate as a Textile man lunged at the ball. The next moment the whole outfit, with the exception of the battery, was hiking pell-mell for right field, chasing a long liner. In the other half of an inning, two Philly base runners were purposely caught between the second and third and first and second bags and the diamond was a hive of running figures for several minutes as the ball was sent first to catch one and then the other of the frolickers. Collins, captured at second, took it into his head to run the bases backwards, and dashing to first, he gave an exaggerated exhibition of sliding.[6]

The Manufacturers League All-Stars finally did score a run in the ninth by hitting the ball beyond the Philadelphia players, all of whom had taken positions in the infield. Fans left the park amused, with a reporter for *The Emerald and Catholic Opinion* suggesting that the Athletics' stunts "would have made good material for a movie director," and Jack Finn writing that it was much better than the "blasé attitude" adopted by the Red Sox in their recent game against Fred Lake's club.[7]

The game revealed a problem even greater than the weakness of the Manufacturers League: fans were not sufficiently interested in professional baseball. According to the *Amoskeag Bulletin*, the contest drew 3,500 people, or about half what it claimed the Dedication Day game had drawn in 1913. Despite *L'Avenir National*'s assertion that the day's crowds totaled 20,000, or the *Union-Leader*'s report that 12,000 had attended the fireworks display, the Amoskeag Textile Club soon admitted that evening attractions brought "nearly 7,000" additional attendees—far fewer than the club had anticipated.[8] What had gone wrong?

The biggest problem may have been one of timing: the Textile Field appearance of the Philadelphia Athletics occurred during the Amoskeag Manufacturing

Company's annual shutdown. Every summer and occasionally at other times, Amoskeag closed its doors for a set period of time, and other city industries followed. If they were lucky, workers would have only a one-week vacation, meaning they would lose just one week of pay. When Amoskeag announced the 1914 shutdown at the beginning of July—nearly a month before the end of the boycott—the company had determined that work would be suspended from Friday, August 28 to Tuesday, September 8.[9] Thus, when Connie Mack confirmed that his team would be available for a game on September 2, his arrival was planned for roughly the midpoint of the break. Many of Manchester's residents typically left the city for the week, and a portion of those who remained were unlikely to spend 50 cents on a baseball ticket while they were not being paid.

Actually, the situation was worse than anyone had anticipated. The start of World War I in July resulted in what the *Amoskeag Bulletin* called "unsatisfactory business conditions." "Up to within three weeks [ago]," announced the *Bulletin* on August 15, "trade conditions throughout the country have been peculiarly unsettled and no one person has been found who could foresee the outcome, consequently the textile industry has been extremely cautious in its every move. Within the past three weeks, however, the European crisis has made the situation still more complicated." Therefore, the annual shutdown actually commenced on August 21, giving workers an extra week of unpaid vacation.[10]

At the same time, Manchester citizens were preoccupied with the war. Many workers retained ties with Europe, so naturally they were concerned with the events occurring overseas. *L'Avenir National* covered Germany's blitzkrieg through Belgium and into France, and seemingly favored America's entry into the war to help the French cause. The *Mirror* concentrated on events in southern Europe, apparently trying to satisfy curiosity among the city's Greek community, though it also carried reports about other major events throughout the continent. Likewise the *Union-Leader*, while expressly promoting American neutrality and differentiating between the Kaiser and the German people, reported on major events on its front page.[11]

Given the city's diverse population, German immigrants in the Eighth Ward grew concerned about a possible anti–German backlash. Therefore, on August 16, many of the city's German residents met in the city's *Turnhalle*, or Turner Hall, to discuss the situation. Ultimately the group approved a series of resolutions, to be delivered to every newspaper in Manchester, reaffirming the considerable German heritage of the United States while reiterating the patriotism of the city's German enclave. The group, which identified itself as being composed of "American citizens," insisted:

The American press shall present its information [about the war in Europe] in an unbiased and impartial manner, and that the editorials shall as far as possible be without prejudice or hatred toward any class of American citizens, for this, though an English speaking country, is not an English nation and it is but fair in these trying times that the American spirit of fair play shall be exercised to further good feelings among American citizens of every extraction and creed.[12]

Perhaps as a result of the war and heightened ethnic tensions in Manchester, Philadelphia's arrival in the city received limited coverage in local newspapers. In fact, baseball in general seemed to have lost popularity in the city in August. The Amoskeag Manufacturing Company won the Manufacturers League championship, finishing the season four games in front of the Beacons and nine ahead of McElwain. After expenditures totaling $1,145.47, the Manufacturers League netted $4,137.38. But according to the *Bulletin,* the last month of the season (which corresponded with the arrival of the New England League and the scheduling of single-admission double-headers for the Manufacturers League) saw a "falling off in the gate receipts." So even though it had been $800 ahead of the previous year's pace at the start of August, the league ended the season with $500 less than it had in 1913. Because profits could be correlated with interest in the Manufacturers League, the season clearly had been a disappointment. As a result, the *Bulletin* suggested that the league might not operate in 1915: "A great deal will depend upon the disposition of Textile Field by the Amoskeag Textile Club."[13]

Fred Lake's New England League team saw even less success. The club was awful, finishing the season with a .293 winning percentage, 48 games behind the champion Lawrence club. Jack Finn called it a "joke outfit" and claimed that "Lake has not made money this year." After his team dropped its final two games to Lowell, the owner of Manchester's minor-league baseball team abruptly left town, leaving fans to wonder if the New England League would return to the city in 1915.[14]

Following the end of the local baseball season, Amoskeag's economic situation worsened again. On September 22, the company announced that its 6,500 cotton weavers would be placed on a four-and-a-half-day schedule, meaning the cotton division would shut down on Friday afternoons and Saturday mornings and that operatives would be paid accordingly. Company managers blamed the cutbacks on World War I: specifically on uncertain business conditions, problems in the supply of dyestuffs, and yarn shortages resulting from the conflict. Amoskeag would not restore the 55-hour workweek for its cotton division until December.[15]

Meanwhile, New Hampshire entered the 1914 election season. Unlike in 1912, however, this year's elections were relatively quiet and uneventful. Robert Bass's pronouncement that "the Progressive party has a really vital purpose to perform in this state" notwithstanding, the Progressives were much less of a force than they had been in 1912.[16] The *Union-Leader* limited its coverage of the party's convention, Frank Knox already having decided to seek reconciliation with the Republicans, and Progressives themselves came out in support the 48-hour workweek at a time when many Amoskeag workers wanted *more* work. The state Republican Party did not attempt to scare voters with visions of Amoskeag's closing, as it had done two years earlier. This time, its ads merely pointed to the shortened week for cotton workers and blamed the situation on the Democrats.

Ultimately, the Democrats were swept from power at all levels. Even locally, Republican lawyer Harry Spaulding defeated the incumbent, Democrat Charles Hayes, in a close election for mayor—despite the fact that, according to the *Advocate*, Spaulding knowingly utilized non-union shops to produce printed materials.[17] The Progressives, meanwhile, could not find enough candidates to run for all of the offices on the ballot. Open positions in the United State Senate and the House of Representatives went to Republicans, and the GOP picked up the Governor's office and majorities in both of the state's legislative houses. The win was convincing enough that Knox claimed Republicans and Progressives to have been united as one party.[18]

With the events in Europe weighing heavily on the minds of Manchester's residents, Frank Knox took it upon himself to promote a diversion for his readers: the World Series. As had been widely expected, the Philadelphia Athletics won the American League with ease. Their opponent would be the surprising Boston Braves, a team that featured George "Lefty" Tyler of nearby Derry. Boston earned the National League pennant despite having occupied last place as late as July 18.[19] In an October 5 editorial entitled "Let's Follow the World's Series," the *Union-Leader*'s editor wrote:

> The American public always has a-plenty to occupy its attention, and this year, what with its interest in the war in Europe, it is extraordinarily preoccupied; but the American public is never too busy with other things, however important or sensational, to take a lively interest in baseball, and particularly in that of the major leagues. The opening of the World's Championship series, on October 9, between the Boston Braves and Connie Mack's team, will prove this to a nicety. Not even the battlefields of Europe will eclipse in popular interest over here the cities of Boston and Philadelphia. When once this annual tournament of the victorious experts of the national game begins, it will surely and properly command first place in the American mind, collectively.... The people of this neutral country would be foolish indeed if they permitted the sad reflections inspired by the European conflict to monopolize their minds to the exclusion of all other intellectual, sentimental or recreative considerations. The American liking for baseball is a sane and beneficial indulgence, and there is no reason under heaven why an attachment so conducive to mental and physical health should be suspended simply because events of the first magnitude are progressing in another quarter of the globe. He is an unfortunate man who cannot give some time and attention to the lighter, as well as to the graver, things of life.[20]

The World Series opened at Shibe Park before a capacity crowd of 20,562. Experts predicted that the Athletics would win the series easily, but that did not stop Boston's Royal Rooters from traveling to Philadelphia to shower the home team with taunts and renditions of "Tessie." The Braves shocked the home crowd by winning the first game handily, 7–1. The second game was much closer, but Boston won again, 1–0, and headed home with a 2–0 lead in the best-of-seven series.[21]

On October 12, the teams reconvened at Boston's Fenway Park. The Braves had started the season at the South End Grounds, a 20-year-old wooden ballpark on Walpole Street, but because of growing crowds the club moved to the more spacious home of the Red Sox in mid–August. The change of venue did not hurt the Braves much. After tying the third World Series game with two runs in the ninth inning, the team defeated Mack's team in twelve innings, 5–4. One day later, the club defeated Philadelphia 3–1 to complete the first-ever four-game sweep in World Series history.[22]

Both the *Mirror* and the *Union-Leader* covered the series extensively on their front pages. However, the *Union-Leader*, which noted the second anniversary of the *Leader*'s founding on the first day of the World Series by thanking its readers for its success, again outdid its rivals. In addition to keeping an up-to-date scoreboard in the window of its headquarters, the *Evening Union* carried seven-column headlines just below the banner and an up-to-the-moment-of-publication score, just as the *Leader* had done two years earlier. "BRAVES TACKLE ATHLETICS," read the first day's headline, just above an inning-by-inning line score (the Braves led 3–1 after five innings) and, occupying two columns to the right of the newspaper's war coverage, photographs of Mack and Braves manager George Stallings. On October 10, the newspaper actually put the headline—"JAMES AND PLANK BATTLE"—*above* the banner, with the scoring summary below. Two days later the headline, "BOTH TEAMS SCORE QUICKLY," was restored to its normal location, and on October 13, in an "extra" edition, the newspaper proclaimed "BRAVES WORLD CHAMPIONS."[23]

With that, baseball was virtually over for the year. The Manufacturers League All-Stars did play an exhibition game in Derry in late October to benefit Joe Ricord, a player who broke his right leg in a game two weeks earlier; the Derry team enlisted Lefty Tyler to pitch and draw more fans.[24] Yet this game received little media attention as the city's sports writers attempted to coax their readers into the next season's sport: football.

The big game for Manchester, of course, was the contest arranged by John Carney between the College of the Holy Cross of Worcester and the Carlisle Indian Training School of Pennsylvania. Before the National Football League

14. The End of Big Games

or the National Collegiate Athletic Association came into existence, football fans followed regional college teams. New Hampshire residents were particularly interested in the Dartmouth College football club, though in Manchester fans also followed the exploits of Harvard and Saint Anselm College. The Holy Cross team also was well known throughout New England, and reporters saw Carlisle as one of the country's elite football clubs.

In the weeks before the game, and in the wake of the disappointing Philadelphia Athletics contest, the Textile Club made the Holy Cross-Carlisle game a referendum on its policies regarding Textile Field. "The support which the public gives this Carlisle-Holy Cross game will determine whether or not other big games will be played here in the future," claimed the *Union-Leader*. But with end-zone seats selling for a dollar and tickets for seats along the sidelines at $1.50, interest in attending the game was limited.[25] And even though the *Union* claimed while the game was in progress that a "record crowd" filled Textile Field, both Jack Finn and the *Amoskeag Bulletin* admitted after the fact that attendance had been sparse.[26]

With the poor attendance, the Amoskeag Textile Club believed the people had spoken, though in a front-page article appearing in the *Amoskeag Bulletin* it seemed bitter about the message it had received:

> The public of Manchester has been given "big football" as it demanded. It has also shown that it did not really want what it was demanding.
> However, be that as it may, the Amoskeag Textile Club has nothing to regret in its action in bringing to Manchester an attraction which the city failed to support. Textile Field was built in the interests of athletic sports and the Textile Club has made a constant endeavor to promote clean sports. And when it was evident several weeks ago, that the Holy Cross-Indian game would not be a money-making proposition, there was no thought of canceling the game or of transferring it....
> The Amoskeag Textile Club has ever tried to give the people of Manchester what it [sic] wanted. They heard the call for a "big game." They could not know that the public did not really want the game and would not pay the price to see the game, (for big games cannot be obtained for a song)....
> The Textile Club has done nothing which it would not do again under similar conditions. It has put forth its best endeavors to serve the public by answering to a so-called demand and the fact that the public was not sincere in its demand is by no means a reflection upon the business judgment of the club.
> The Textile Club has nothing to regret.
> The Textile Club has nothing to regret.[27]

By declaring its lack of regret in no uncertain terms, the club was, in part, responding to criticisms that had appeared in the *Manchester Mirror*. The *Mirror* claimed that with the failure of the recent football game and the curious silence of Fred Lake since September, a "death knell" had been "sounded for big games in Manchester." It told its readers that Fred Lake was "anxious to get the

Manchester franchise off his hands" and join the Federal League as a scout. "This disposes of that franchise," the reporter posited, "...for when it is sold it is more than likely to go out of town." About the Manufacturers League, the *Mirror* claimed that it had made less money than it had the year before, indicating a "lessening of interest, and the league was formed for the purpose of supplying good baseball to workers in the mills and shops." Unfortunately, players had squabbled publicly too often, and those arguments sometimes "carried even into the meetings of the clubs, ... [sounding] the death knell of the league."

Finally, the newspaper commented on the Textile Club's policy of scheduling sporting events featuring regionally and nationally known teams, claiming that most of the contests were not well attended. "There are, of course, two sides to this question and the people who like sports are not wholly to blame. They feel that they cannot afford to pay the prices asked for these games, and on the other hand the club is compelled to charge high prices to realize even bare expenses."

Based on these problems, the *Mirror* suggested, the Amoskeag Textile Club was unlikely to schedule any "big games" at Textile Field in 1915. With no college football, no major- or minor-league baseball, and likely no Manufacturers League, Textile Field, which represented "too much of an investment to allow it to lie idle," would remain underutilized.[28]

The annual off-season baseball rumor mill exacerbated the situation. In fact, those reports suggested that the Textile Club would purchase Fred Lake's franchise and install John Carney as its manager. Through the *Bulletin* the club did confirm that Lake had not contacted it about use of Textile Field for the 1915 season. But it also issued a terse response to the rumors surrounding it and the New England League: "The Amoskeag Textile Club is not considering, in any form or manner, taking over a New England league franchise."[29]

Amoskeag also had an answer to the rumor that Carney would manage the team. "[Carney's] contract expires on December 1, and he has already been notified by the board of governors that it was not deemed advisable to renew it."[30] The future of baseball in Manchester in any form now seemed in doubt.

John Carney's apparently forced departure resulted from a disastrous year in Manchester. The Athletics game was a disappointment, but less so than the other games involving big-name teams had been. The New England League's reserve fence and the professional baseball boycott of the city had embarrassed the Amoskeag Manufacturing Company, as did the poor showing at the Carlisle-Holy Cross football game. The Textile Club's relationship with local high schools and colleges had suffered over the use of Textile Field. At the same time, the Manufacturers League virtually fell apart; on- and off-field squabbles, rumors of players refusing to report to work, and other incidents clouded the league's future. Whether responsible for these problems or not, Carney was a convenient scapegoat.

Barely a month after Carney officially left Amoskeag to return to coaching in Exeter, the Amoskeag Textile Club held its annual meeting. Members arrived at St. Cecilia Hall to find a "bountiful spread" of "Dutch things," prepared by chef Oscar Schonniger, waiting for them in the basement. After the feast, club members climbed the stairs to the main hall where, as the Textile Club orchestra performed a program of popular music, each was presented with a clay pipe and package of tobacco.

After a short time, the curtain rose and William Parker Straw appeared on the stage. Straw, known to his friends as "Parker," was the son of Herman F. Straw, the Amoskeag Manufacturing Company's top official in Manchester, and the grandson Ezekiel Straw, who planned out the city of Manchester before serving two terms as governor of New Hampshire in the 1870s. Born in 1878, Parker Straw had been the Amoskeag Textile Club's president since its founding, and currently served as its superintendent, the second-highest-ranking Amoskeag official in Manchester. As such, he was expected to take over as agent when his father retired (Herman Straw turned 65 in 1914 and had been Amoskeag's agent since 1885). But the younger Straw was more introverted and businesslike than his charismatic father. "He was nice enough personally, but he was a long way from H.F.," remembered one former employee in the 1970s. Although he would prove successful in business in his own right, comparisons to his father would plague Parker Straw for the rest of his time at Amoskeag.[31]

As the applause died down, Straw announced that the meeting was about to begin. Then he delivered his address on the state of the club:

> Now this is the time when we should look back on the work that has been done, analyze it, consider the mistakes that have been made, and lay out the plan of our work for the coming year, based upon our experiences. It is my intention tonight to speak of the mistakes we have made that seem particularly obvious and serious, and to give briefly some of the plans your Board of Governors has laid out for the future.

The club had made its "gravest mistakes," Straw believed, in the area of athletics. "[T]he mistake at the bottom of all the others was in making too much of a few athletes," he told the crowd, "for I believe it is better to have a thousand men actively contesting and twenty watching, than to have twenty men actively contesting and a thousand watching." Straw suggested that the club should sponsor informal teams and leagues in a variety of sports for its employees, and to demonstrate both "the glory of physical exercise" and the "shallowness and the folly of idleness that begets selfishness and aimlessness that means sickness and irresponsibility." With these words—and at a time when the world was falling into war even as Amoskeag fought both nationalism and economic challenges—Straw emphasized the purported goal of Amoskeag's athletic programs: to encourage activities that produced good American citizens.

Regarding the baseball team, Straw hoped the club would continue to support one, but he suggested that the ATC "will, I think, professionalize it less." No longer would the club hire outsiders; instead, it would recruit from among its employees. Then, making an indirect reference to the company's former athletic director, he told the club, "I believe there are men right here tonight who can run a team as well as anyone we can hire, and bring home any pennants we go after." He was not specific about winning a Manufacturers League pennant.[32]

15

Amoskeag and the Federal League

About a month before Parker Straw's pronouncement that the Amoskeag Textile Club would no longer recruit professional baseball players, a rumor circulated that Fred Lake was looking to sell his New England League team. "Lake sometimes declares he's ready to dispose of his holdings here, and again he intimates that he will have Manchester in the league next season," reported the *Leader*. When Lake did not contact the Amoskeag Textile Club to negotiate for use of Textile Field in 1915, Jack Finn speculated "that he is waiting for a purchaser to turn up." The *Mirror* concurred, adding that Lake "certainly can have [Textile Field] if he will pay the price."[1]

Even Amoskeag Textile Club officials seemed surprised when no one in the New England League approached them about leasing Textile Field. This time they were willing to negotiate, even cancelling the Manufacturers League organizational meeting set for January 6 as they awaited the results of the New England League's annual meeting in Boston the following night. At the Boston meeting, Lake indicated that if he could not sell his club he would be back in Manchester, and he promised to negotiate for use of Textile Field. Tim Murnane told reporters he would run the team himself, if necessary, to keep it in Manchester. Nevertheless, the ATC heard nothing from Lake or anyone else. On January 13, the Manufacturers League canceled another organizational meeting.[2]

The New England League's reluctance to commit to Manchester may have stemmed from the declining fortunes of professional baseball region-wide. The World War I–related recession that had hurt New England's textile industry over the summer had damaged the New England League as well. It also found itself in competition with the outlaw Federal League, which threatened to sign major- and minor-league players already under contract, creating instability throughout organized baseball. Meanwhile, behind the scenes, unnamed league officials looked to merge their organization with another regional minor-league organization, the Eastern Association. The idea was to take the strongest teams in the region—Worcester, Lowell, Portland, Fall River, New Bedford, Hartford, Springfield, and New Haven—and create a new league from them. Manchester was to be abandoned by the new league. One rumor even had the merged organization withdrawing from the National Agreement to become a "feeder league" affiliated with the outlaw Federal League. The plan was dropped almost immediately, but the ideas of a merger between the two existing minor leagues based in New England and of a Federal League interest in the region persisted.[3]

The New England League did remain in Manchester for the 1915 season, and prior to the season team owners worked closely with both the *Manchester Leader and Evening Union* and officials from the Amoskeag Textile Club to ensure the team's success. The process of bringing the sides together was arduous, however, particularly when the Federal League itself presented Amoskeag with an opportunity to spurn the New England League.

Federal League executives in 1912. In 1915, the outlaw baseball league's officials hoped to establish a minor league in New England, with one team playing in Manchester's Textile Field. Hugh McKinnon (second from right) expressed surprise at the Amoskeag Textile Club's openness to leasing the grounds to the Federal League (Bain Collection, Prints and Photographs Division, Library of Congress, LC-B2-2380-13).

15. Amoskeag and the Federal League 169

The 1914 season had not been easy for the Federal League. Owners successfully induced several American and National League players to jump to the Federal League, but they could not convince the game's most established stars—including Walter Johnson, Christy Mathewson, and Tris Speaker—to follow. Some of the players the league *did* entice away from organized baseball defected back, forcing the Federal League to go to court to enforce its contracts. As legal fees mounted, Federal League owners determined that their best course of action would be to sue the American and National Leagues, as well as the National Association which oversaw the minor leagues, for antitrust violations.[4]

The Federal League filed its lawsuit on January 5, two days before the New England League met to discuss the future of Fred Lake's Manchester franchise. The judge in the case, Kenesaw Mountain Landis, appeared to be a progressive "trust-buster" who often sided with the underdog, and Federal League owners believed he would rule against organized baseball. They were wrong, however. The trial began on January 20 and was over quickly, so most observers believed the judge would rule on the case prior to the start of the 1915 baseball season.[5] But Landis was an ardent baseball fan and apparently reluctant to rule against the established major leagues. Instead, he delayed issuing any ruling whatsoever.

Nine days before the trial's start, *L'Avenir National* reported that Federal League representative Hugh McKinnon had been in Manchester to investigate the possibility of placing a team at Textile Field. The proposed club would not play in the Federal League, but rather in a new minor league affiliated with the Feds. McKinnon spoke with William McKay and other Amoskeag Textile Club officers, as well as local business leaders who might be interested in investing in the club. Before leaving the city, he assured the reporter that the new league would be "absolutely of the same quality as the International League," which occupied the highest minor-league classification level under the National Agreement.[6]

No one in Manchester's English-language media took McKinnon's visit seriously. Nearly a week after his visit with McKay, the *Mirror* reported that "Manchester does not appear to be involved in the plan of the Federal League officials to buck the New England league...." Jack Finn did not believe the outlaw minor league could succeed without inducing some of the New England League and Eastern Association teams to jump leagues—and Manchester was not one of the cities Finn believed would be represented in such an endeavor.[7]

On January 21, however, Finn abruptly reversed course. "We wouldn't be a bit surprised if the Federal league puts a team in this city," he wrote, "and neither would it be astonishing should the Textile club prefer turning over its fine plant to the outlaws rather than to the New England league." Earlier that day, Hugh McKinnon returned to Manchester with news that a league was being formed, and that it would consist of Manchester, Worcester, Portland, either Lowell or Lawrence, Hartford, Springfield, New Haven, and Bridgeport. He also commenced negotiations with the Amoskeag Textile Club for use of Textile Field. Because of this new development, the Manufacturers League again postponed its annual meeting until "negotiations which are under way for the lease of Textile Field are completed."[8]

McKinnon's reappearance, coupled with a letter from Federal League president James Gilmore confirming the league's intentions, finally brought New England League secretary John Moore to Manchester. His trip was arranged in haste, for when he arrived in Manchester he found that William McKay was out of town. Instead, Moore spoke with a *Union-Leader* reporter about his and Lake's plans to develop a "high class" team for Manchester in the coming year.[9] Still, Jack Finn believed the New England League would be shut out of Textile Field. "The New England men have been lax in their methods, very lax, and the Feds have at least beaten them to it, to the extent of getting their agent here with a view to making a deal for the grounds."[10]

On January 30 in New Haven, Connecticut, Gilmore met with potential owners "and other interested parties" in the new organization, dubbed the "New England States League" by some publications. At the meeting, the Federal League president told participants—who included representatives from Providence, Springfield, Danbury, and New Haven, as well as William McKay of Manchester—that the Feds would furnish each club with six players. The teams promised to pay their major-league sponsor $200 per player per month, "with the parent league paying the difference when the player's salary is in excess of that amount."[11]

McKay left the meeting with no doubt that the Federal League was serious in its intention to help start a new minor league in New England. Even so, he told the *Mirror* that he was not ready to back its overtures for Textile Field over those of the New England League. "[W]ho gets it will depend upon which of these two leagues will bring the better baseball to Manchester.... I attended the meeting in behalf of the Textile club to see what the Federals proposed to do." Perhaps as a result, a reporter for the *Manchester Advocate* believed the meeting set up a conflict between the Federal League and the New England League that, while small compared to the Federal League's antitrust lawsuit being considered in Chicago, "will prove to be ... one of the biggest factors in the game in this vicinity from this time on."[12]

Tim Murnane's *Boston Globe* claimed little money could be made in New England baseball as it was, and that the Federal League's proposal was neither financially responsible nor realistic. As the *Sporting News* urged a merger of the New England League with the Eastern Association, league officials considered dropping two clubs—Manchester and Lowell—and, to boost attendance, discussed creating a split-season format, with the winner of the first half meeting the winner of the second half in an end-of-the-season playoff. Owners rejected the changes in a February 4 meeting in Boston, causing the *New York Times* to remark that the "New England League of Baseball Clubs today decided to present an unbroken front against the threatened invasion of its territory by Federal League interests."[13]

The meeting did produce a notable development: Lake was prepared to sell his Manchester franchise to Tom Keady, a former Dartmouth and New England League pitcher who currently coached baseball and football at Lehigh University. The sale was not yet complete; as Tim Murnane explained, Keady had an option to purchase the club, and the sale would be closed as soon as he had arranged to lease Textile Field. Immediately, Keady and Lake conferred with McKay, who attended the meeting on behalf of the Amoskeag Textile Club. In the end Keady agreed to travel to Manchester to look over the ballpark and make arrangements. "There is nothing definite to be said either way," claimed McKay. "The use of the park has not been promised to either the Federal or the New England league."[14]

Despite the McKay's claim, not everyone believed that the New England League would succeed in its negotiations for Textile Field. Jack Finn repeatedly wrote that the Federal League was more likely to get the park because of the New England League's recent history with Amoskeag. A rumored co-owner of the Federal League team in Worcester, Narcisse Lavigne, also claimed that the league had finalized plans to place a team in Manchester. The Textile Club responded with another denial, stating that no party had been granted use of the ball grounds. Still, the *Leader* certainly believed the official, suggesting that "he should know something about the conditions in other cities, and it looks very much as if he spread the news before some of the men higher up wished it to get out. Hence you get the repeated denials."[15] When asked about Lavigne's comments the next day, Hugh McKinnon responded that "a few things were revealed which President Gilmore wished to keep secret for some time."[16]

Tom Keady clearly worried about his chances for Textile Field, so he reopened negotiations with Fitchburg. However, he also continued speaking with the Amoskeag Textile Club about Manchester. Then, Louis Pieper complicated the situation for Keady with an outburst, apparently in response to the Federal League's claims of success and Keady's continued problems in the city:

> On two occasions, says Pieper, he [William McKay] told me that there was absolutely no reason why the New England league could not get into Manchester. He also told me

that as between the New England league and the Feds, the sentiment of the Textile club as well as the people of Manchester was for the New England league.

Later he informed us that nine out of 10 fans in that city wanted the Federal league to come in. Of course the Textile club had a perfect right to let Textile park to the Feds, if it chose, but this seems like double dealing.

The city of Fitchburg has shown that it has real possibilities as a Class B baseball town. Last year, with a tail-end team and the people dissatisfied, Fitchburg turned out more than the average mid-week attendance. I am out to lick Manchester and I don't care who knows it.

Jack Finn joked that "we're about to have another of those New England league boycotts wished off on us." He did not take Pieper's words too seriously, believing that the Lynn owner "has a rather well founded idea that the Federals are going to get the park here, and rather than await the verdict, he thought it proper to cut loose in advance." Tom Keady, though, responded with a letter to the *Union-Leader* distancing himself from Pieper and stating his opinion that "an injustice has been done to Mr. McKay in this matter." He also wrote that whatever happened with his application to put his team in Textile Field, he would be "glad to help" the city and its clubs "to secure big football games, track meets or any other branch of sporting events."[17]

When the Amoskeag Textile Club's new board of governors met on February 16 to decide the Textile Field situation, Keady attended without Pieper. Hugh McKinnon planned to arrive in the afternoon. Reporters for all of the city's daily newspapers expected that the Federal League would receive permission to place a team at Textile Field because it promised more highly skilled players, besides which "the high-handed methods employed by the New England League in the past and the recent fiery statements of Louis Pieper" worked against the established minor league.[18]

To everyone's surprise, the club made no decision on Textile Field's immediate future. New rumors circulated that Keady would be coaching at Dartmouth that year, and he had allowed his option to purchase Fred Lake's team to lapse. More startling, the Federal League revealed that, after the International League threatened to place its own teams in Springfield, Hartford, and Worcester, it would cancel plans for a minor league in New England. Instead, the Feds opted to finance the Colonial League, which was based in southern New England. In the words of the *Mirror*, "the baseball situation for Manchester … is clouded by a haze just now."[19]

The sudden and, for Manchester fans at least, unexpected demise of the Feds' proposed "feeder league" brought Jack Finn to write, "We're all glad the thing has taken some kind of form, as that uncertainty is killing on the nerves." However, the city still was not assured a New England League team. The fact that the Manufacturers League had not rescheduled its organizational meeting was promising, as it suggested that the Textile Club expected to resolve the situation with the minor league.[20] But the New England League also had to assure the club of its willingness to field a competitive team.

Rumors about Keady's future quieted when the former Lehigh coach announced he would meet with the Amoskeag Textile Club on Thursday, February 25, to secure a lease for Textile Field. At the same time, the New England League proclaimed that the Haverhill franchise would move to Fitchburg, giving the Manchester team no other viable city to which it could to relocate and bolstering the likelihood that its team would stay.[21] Keady's meeting confirmed these hopes, when the Amoskeag Textile Club agreed in principle to lease its grounds to the New England League club.

In the previous two years, nothing between the New England League and Amoskeag Textile Club had been simple, and this apparent agreement was no exception. Before he could accept the offer, Keady had to clear up "a misunderstanding over the transfer of the franchise." Apparently, Lake was holding up the transfer over money.[22] Otherwise, he claimed to be happy. That afternoon, however, the New England League convened an owners' meeting that lasted ten hours, with most of the discussion pertaining to Manchester. When it was over, Keady announced that he was unhappy with the deal, had given up his option to buy the Manchester team, and would return to Lehigh to coach.

Rumors swirled as to the reasons for Keady's change of heart. Most centered on the Textile Club's proposed rent for Textile Field: $2,500, a high sum that Jack Finn blamed on Louis Pieper's recent outburst. Keady himself believed Pieper's tirade to have added $1,000 to Amoskeag's proposed rental fee. According to league president Tim Murnane, "The rent was exorbitant ... and the owners [of Textile Field] wanted the privilege as well as the right to say whether the baseball provided was satisfactory to their different tastes."[23] William McKay, on the other hand, claimed that "the fine Italian hand of Fred Lake" was responsible for Keady's change of heart:

> When Mr. Keady was here this week, and our conference was over, said Mr McKay, Mr. Keady was perfectly satisfied with the price of the Textile Park. He phoned me last night that there was no question that the price was all right, and when he left here day before yesterday he said to me, in the presence of witnesses, that the only trouble he would have would be on the other end of the line—in the matter of the franchise on which he had an option....
>
> [At the Boston meeting,] in endeavoring to keep the price down on the franchise—with which nobody in Manchester had the slightest concern—Keady pleaded that he had the additional expense of the Textile park rental to meet.... At once the element in the New England League, which had it 'in for Manchester,' raised the cry that we were squeezing Keady up here on the park rental, which was not so at all....

Thus, in McKay's view, Lake and the New England League wanted to keep Keady from claiming that the ballpark rental reduced the value of the franchise. He added that Lake's asking price for the franchise had been $1,200 when the organization was competing with the Federal League for Textile Field, but that the price had more than doubled when the threat of an outlaw minor league vanished.[24]

In response to this latest crisis, the New England League formulated a schedule in which Haverhill, not Manchester, would be represented in the eight-team circuit. Disappointed, Jack Finn prepared for a year without professional baseball. The *Mirror*, however, was willing to wait a year, believing a successful venture could not take hold in the city until the local economy improved. "[F]or this year at least Manchester wage-earners will have none too much in surplus earnings to enable them to live and enjoy some of the comforts of life. We believe it is better to wait another season, when the tide of coming prosperity will have gained volume, before making a venture in professional baseball in this city."[25]

The saga was not over, of course, for Keady continued to speak with New England League officials, and apparently was able to strike an acceptable deal to purchase the team from Lake. Then, on March 2, he went back to Manchester one final time, stating, "I will head a team in Manchester if I can get Textile park for a figure less than the one now named." He also set a deadline of March 3 to finalize a settlement.

To everyone's relief, Keady and the Amoskeag Textile Club finally did come to a reasonable compromise, apparently at a much lower figure than the one quoted by the club a week earlier. "Yep, it's a fact!" declared the *Mirror*. "After the boycotting and the criticism in which the directors of the Amoskeag Textile club were rated as 'pirates and buccaneers,'" the New England League had returned to Manchester.[26]

The New England League and the Amoskeag Textile Club appeared to have called a truce in their ongoing war for Textile Field. As newspapers bickered over who broke the story first and who had been more accurate than whom—at the height of the squabble, a *Mirror* reporter resorted to calling the *Union-Leader*'s staff "ivory-headed sporting writers"[27]—Tom Keady still had to put together a team. Fred Lake sold Manchester's two best players to Portland during the off-season, besides which the team had been horrible in 1914, leaving few viable candidates for positions in 1915. As a result of the confusion over ownership and where the team would play, Keady had not begun to rebuild the club. Nevertheless, the new owner and his manager, Jack Kiernan, promised local fans a pennant contender. They fanned out across the Northeast, with Kiernan traveling to New York to sign two highly regarded players and Keady—who was contractually obligated to coach at Lehigh after all—scouting talent around Bethlehem, Pennsylvania.[28]

15. Amoskeag and the Federal League

Despite the truce, hard feelings remained between officials of the New England League and the Amoskeag Textile Club. If the minor league wanted Manchester's team to survive financially, schedule makers did the city no favors. Of nineteen possible Saturdays during the season, Manchester played nine home games on seven dates, and only one Saturday home game after July 24. Including contests scheduled on three holidays—Manchester received the morning half of each holiday home-and-home series, though the afternoon game allegedly was a better draw—some local fans had just ten opportunities to see the team. Schedule makers also seem to have had a sense of irony; Keady's club began its 126-game season on April 30 in Fitchburg, and opened its home season at Textile Field against that same Fitchburg team.[29]

League officials also shut Manchester out of decision-making positions. In mid–March, the organization announced the creation of a five-man executive committee to oversee the league's business affairs. The committee consisted of Lynn's Louis Pieper, his brother-in-law Dan Noonan of Fitchburg, Portland owner Hugh Duffy, John O'Donnell of Worcester, and Andy Roach of Lowell. "The affairs of the Lynn, Fitchburg, Worcester, Portland and Lowell club[s] will receive particular attention," predicted the *Leader*, "but Manchester, Lawrence and Lewiston is [sic] without representation, so there's no telling what the teams in these cities will receive." The newspaper pointed to the recent schedule as proof; the committee had drawn up the calendar, and "did not give the three cities who are without a representative on the committee, any the best of the dates."[30]

Despite these problems with the league, Keady and Kiernan did bring players to Manchester. Including six holdovers from 1914, 26 players reported to training camp at Textile Field in April. Players came from throughout the northeastern United States, but the team carried a heavy Massachusetts contingent. Fifteen players came from the Bay State, compared with four from Pennsylvania and one each from New York, New Hampshire, Connecticut, New Jersey, Ohio, Maryland, and Maine. Kiernan still wanted to add two or three well-known local players to the roster, and hoped to invite Joe Holcomb of McElwain and former Amoskeag standout Emil Pernod to try out for the team. Yet money would be tight, and the team refused a raise to one of the previous year's best players, Joe Kane. "This season is a poor one for players to seek increases," wrote Jack Finn, "for with half a dozen leagues out of commission and the majors cutting down to the 21-man [roster] limit, ball players will be plentiful and at moderate salaries."[31]

Holcomb did eventually join the local team. Pernod, however, was unavailable. The former Amoskeag catcher from Ohio had left the corporation to work for the Stark Mills in the Mill No. 4 rolling room. In February, while working on a rolling machine used for winding cloth, Pernod slipped and a roll fell on him, causing injuries to his back and pelvis. "[T]he muscles, tendons and ligaments thereof were bruised, torn, stretched and mangled, the bones and joints thereof bruised, broken and dislocated and the spine and nervous system were seriously injured." Because he had earned between $100 and $125 per season as a baseball player, was only 26 years old, and appeared to have been capable of playing several more years prior to the injury, Pernod sued the Stark Mills for $15,000. His former employer, the Amoskeag Manufacturing Company, placed a copy of the *Mirror*'s article about the lawsuit in his personnel file, effectively blacklisting him.[32]

Even without Pernod, players and reporters alike excitedly talked of how the still-unnamed local team would compete for the 1915 pennant. Meanwhile, many other veterans of the defunct Manufacturers League searched for professional and independent teams with which to play. Besides Pernod and Holcomb, some of the better players received offers to try out with minor-league clubs. George McCarthy, who replaced Pernod as Amoskeag's catcher in 1914, traveled to Milwaukee to join the minor-league Brewers. McElwain, meanwhile, put together an independent team, and advertised that "managers desiring dates will be accommodated by addressing F. G. Flood, care Central Plant, McElwain Company, Manchester." An independent club based in West Manchester also formed under the direction of manager Tom Werner, who claimed to have "secured the pick of the players of the Manufacturers league teams."[33]

But the question remained: could the Amoskeag Manufacturing Company and the New England League coexist in Manchester, especially considering Amoskeag's history of control over the city and desire to use baseball to Americanize its own workers? The days leading up to the season seemed to indicate that they could. On April 13, the *Manchester Leader and Evening Union* announced a contest to name the minor-league team, with the winner receiving two season tickets. Two days later, the *Union-Leader* revealed the names of the men who composed the committee to choose the winning entry: Jack Kiernan, Jack Finn, and William B. McKay.[34]

The newspaper received hundreds of entries. Some of the suggested names include "Rabbits," "Hustlers," "Midgets," "Hopefuls," "Fly Catchers," "Mugwamps," "Millers," and—perhaps attempting to appeal to the newspaper that sponsored the contest—"Leaders." On May 1, the *Union-Leader* announced the name it would use: Textiles. "[I]n the opinion of the three judges, ... the 'Textiles' is the most appropriate title. The Textile industry is the chief business in this city, the greater part of the population are Textile workers, and the ball park where the Manchester players will hold forth is known as Textile Field."[35]

Thus, the city's team finally had a name, one that inevitably linked the team to Amoskeag in most people's minds. While *L'Avenir National* referred to the team using a French translation—"Les Textiles"—the *Mirror* refused to utilize a name devised with the help of its chief rival. Instead, the newspaper would continue to refer to the club as "Manchester."

The Amoskeag Textile Club's reconciliation with the New England League was superficial at best. The club claimed to have listened to the fans in Manchester, and now was working with the local baseball club to ensure its success—or, at the very least, doing enough to avoid any suggestion that the company had sabotaged professional baseball in Manchester. Perhaps it was intended as an experiment, another attempt to retain control over baseball audiences in Manchester. Still, the placement of a New England League club at Textile Field did little to help Amoskeag in its efforts to Americanize workers and promote company unity and allegiance, something that was becoming more important as war made the world textile market less predictable. The Amoskeag Textile Club, after all, had little control over Keady's team, despite the fact that the team's uniforms read "Textiles." Besides, William Parker Straw had expressed his hope that the company would support a baseball team outside of professional baseball.

Ultimately the company would field a team, though not in a city league. At the same time, as baseball competed with other games for the public's attention, evidence began to mount suggesting that the baseball creed was not as effective as many observers claimed it to be. Thus, even as local leaders extolled the virtues of a progressive Manchester and worked to diversify the city's economy, problems of race, ethnicity, and poverty still afflicted the community as Amoskeag's powerful influence over its workers and the city continued to erode.

16

Frank Knox's Manchester

As May approached, Manchester prepared for the new baseball season. Although manager Jack Kiernan's preseason prediction for his team began with the line, "I'm not claiming any pennant," expectations ran high.[1] The New England League team impressed observers in its exhibition wins against Portland and Dartmouth College, and it apparently played well against an International League club from Buffalo. After the Buffalo game the *Mirror* reported, "There were many at Textile park who were heard to say that in some ways the team reminded them of the one which represented Manchester the year that the New England championship was brought here" in 1902 under Phenomenal Smith.[2] To educate local residents about their new team, the newspaper included a copy of the New England League schedule in its annual baseball booklet, "Facts for the Fan."

The *Amoskeag Bulletin* also actively promoted the team. On its front page the newspaper advertised that the home schedule would begin with a parade featuring players from the Textiles and the Fitchburg club, joined by the various Manchester dignitaries and business leaders who supported the local New England League team. William McKay himself promised to back the Textiles with a monthly column, "Bill's Baseball." Throughout the coming season readers would be treated to insights such as, "It certainly is satisfying to see a real bunch of ball players in Manchester uniforms. The present outfit is some different from the dilapidated club wearing the local colors last season."[3]

In promoting the team through the company newspaper, perhaps the Amoskeag Textile Club hoped to at least appear to be in control of the minor-league team to which it was committed. The New England League club did, after all, carry the name "Textiles," and called Textile Field home. The arrangement was not ideal, at least from Amoskeag's perspective, because an outside force ultimately controlled the on-field product. But in its support, at least

Amoskeag seemed to be carrying out the will of the city's baseball-loving public, an image seemingly designed to foster "American-style" loyalty in Amoskeag's workers—and perhaps in the city's business leaders as well.

As the season approached, Manchester remained a city with significant problems. Amoskeag's economic dominance was foremost among them; the national downturn in the textile industry threatened Amoskeag's—and therefore the city's—prosperity. As Lawrence had shown three years before, poverty could lead to unionization, radicalism, and ethnic conflict. Furthermore, baseball itself competed for popularity with other sports, such as boxing; this development meant that the baseball creed might not be helpful in alleviating the city's labor situation should conditions worsen. Thus, as the international worker's holiday of May Day and the coincidental start of the minor-league baseball season approached, Frank Knox and other city leaders searched for ways by which to promote both baseball and the diversification of the city's economic base. The *Union-Leader* and the merchants and professionals of the Manchester Publicity Association became central players in their campaign.

In the late nineteenth and early twentieth centuries, business leaders throughout the United States learned to be wary of early May, and May Day in particular, at least in the area of labor relations. The reason for this can be traced most immediately to 1884, when the Federation of Organized Trades and Labor Unions—precursor to the American Federation of Labor—unilaterally declared that as of May 1, 1886, workers should no longer be required to work more than eight-hour days. When the appointed day arrived, hundreds of thousands of workers throughout the United States met it with strikes and pro-labor demonstrations, particularly in Chicago where about 40,000 laborers walked off their jobs. But on May 3, 1886, the Chicago protests turned violent as police fired on strikers at the McCormick Harvesting Machine Company plant, killing two. Outraged, local anarchists organized a demonstration.

The following night in the rain, protestors headed for Haymarket Square. As police watched from the edges and undercover agents from within, August Spies, Albert Parsons, and Samuel Fielden took turns addressing the crowd of about 3,000 people. Initially the gathering was peaceful, and by 10:20, as Fielden wound down the night's final speech, only around 500 people remained. But then additional police arrived on the scene and ordered the crowd to disperse. Without warning, someone in the crowd tossed a homemade bomb into the formation of police. The bomb exploded, killing one officer instantly and wounding several others, after which police and demonstrators drew guns and fired on each other. Within five minutes the square had been cleared. In the end, seven police officers and four workers lay dead, and about sixty officers and an unknown number of protestors were wounded. In the aftermath, mostly on the basis of dubious evidence, seven defendants were tried and found guilty of conspiracy to commit murder. Spies and Parsons were hanged in 1887, as were George Engel and Adolph Fisher; a fifth man, Louis Lingg, committed suicide while awaiting execution. Fielden and Michael Schwab saw their death sentences commuted to life in prison.[4]

May Day and the Haymarket Affair became important symbols in labor circles worldwide. In 1890, at the suggestion of the American Federation of Labor, the founding congress of the Second Labor and Socialist International in Paris adopted May 1 as a day on which to demonstrate for the eight-hour workday. Essentially, this guaranteed that Haymarket would reverberate in the international labor movement and that Parsons, Spies, Engel, and Fisher would be its martyrs.[5] In the United States Bill Haywood called the Haymarket Affair "a turning point in my life," and Lucy Parsons—Albert's widow—dedicated the remainder of her life to the anarchist labor movement. In fact, many of the socialists and anarchists who joined Haywood, Lucy Parsons, Eugene Debs, and William Trautmann in organizing the Industrial Workers of the World in 1905 assumed continuity between their work and that of the Haymarket demonstrators.[6]

Frank Knox was well aware of May Day's importance to the pro-union movement, particularly to socialists, anarchists, and other radicals. But as a pro-business Republican who was becoming increasingly familiar with Manchester, he seemed to support a union-free Amoskeag. Therefore he chose May 4, 1915—the 29th anniversary of the Haymarket Affair—to reflect on labor conditions in his adopted city. "It is one of Manchester's boasts and her mighty good fortune that labor troubles have been infrequent and of inconsequential proportions," he wrote. "No costly and long-drawn out strikes have marred her industrial record. Instead there is a long and creditable history of harmonious co-operation and good will."

Knox believed two factors were responsible for Manchester's history of labor peace. The "quality of labor" was obvious to the editor; he pointed to the number of savings accounts in local banks as evidence of that fact. But he also credited the benevolence programs of companies such as Amoskeag and McElwain for keeping the peace:

> Next in importance has been a spirit on the part of the larger employers, and they have set the pace for the rest, that one of the best investments they could make was in insurance against dissatisfaction on the part of the people in their employ. As a result Manchester has seen more intelligent and constructive welfare work undertaken than in any other industrial center in New England.

In particular, the *Union-Leader*'s editor mentioned the city's housing conditions and the work of the Amoskeag Textile Club and McElwain Athletic Association in maintaining that positive relationship. "The most serious injury which could be done to Manchester would be to disturb, or disrupt, the progress toward a still better understanding between workers and the men who employ them," wrote Knox.⁷

Despite Knox's assertion that all was well in Manchester, problems were visible to anyone who cared to look for them. By most indications, poverty had improved only slightly, if at all, since 1912. In fact, from 1913 to 1916, food prices rose by about 12.9 percent, while Amoskeag workers saw an increase in wage rates of about 14.9 percent over the same period, resulting in just a slight gain for the city's workers.⁸ The city's economic base still was tied to the Amoskeag Manufacturing Company, which continued to suffer as a result of the economic downturn that arrived with the war in Europe. In 1914 the company had made clear that its problems were related to the ongoing problems overseas, despite the fact that publications such as the *Mirror* continued to blame the "un–American policy of the Democratic party" regarding the protective tariff. Admittedly, the two most dramatic expressions of this poverty were still to come: first, in July 1915 when Amoskeag announced that its annual late-summer shutdown would stretch for three weeks; and second, in August when 3,152 Manchester boys and girls attended the Joseph A. Brown picnic for poor children at Pine Island Park, a local amusement park.⁹

If Knox saw the larger problem of poverty, he did not directly acknowledge it on the *Union-Leader's* editorial pages. Yet family-based economic problems appear to have been at the root of one of his progressive campaigns in 1915: the hiring of women to serve as police matrons. Knox believed Manchester "has its share" of problems relating to Manchester's young women. Some women, he felt, were "recklessly or thoughtlessly following paths which ...

Frank Knox, circa 1910. Knox arrived in Manchester in 1912 to promote the programs of the state's Progressive Party through the *Manchester Leader*. By 1915, he had returned to the Republican Party and was one of Manchester's important and respected community leaders (Bain Collection, Prints and Photographs Division, Library of Congress, LC-B2-3460-11).

inevitably lead to disaster," while others were led astray by "the contemptible specimens of manhood who prey upon young girls, found in the streets, unprotected at night." Knox believed that by hiring women as police matrons, the department could handle homelessness, prostitution, and general immorality among girls and young women better than could an exclusively male police force.[10]

Though not opposed to the idea, Chief Michael Healy was decidedly less enthusiastic, saying only, "a good woman would do a vast amount of good, and a woman who was not good, a vast amount of harm."[11] But he had other problems on his mind; specifically, he found that sensitive information about crimes and police investigations in Manchester routinely found its way to the city's media outlets. He investigated the problem for several weeks without resolution. Then, in early May, Healy initiated a ploy to trap those who were releasing the information. He reported to his officers that his house had been robbed of a gold watch, a diamond ring, a pendant, an emerald ring, and $110 in cash. "Within an hour the story was out," reported the *Union-Leader*. "Inside of another hour the whole town was fairly buzzing with the story.... Everybody knew just what the robber had secured, too, and where he got it and when and all about it. It was very interesting."

Through his false report, Healy was able to implicate five of his officers, all of whom confessed their indiscretion. Healy was most impressed with Patrolman James Dunn who, when asked to whom he had given the information about the supposed robbery, answered, "everybody." "To him," said Healy, "I take off my hat. His judgment was poor but he is honest." Even so, Healy suspended Dunn and the other officers. "I do not propose to be made the laughing stock of this city or any other," Healy told the *Union-Leader*, "and I do not propose to have the department so made, nor its efforts in the line of law and order set at naught by any man who hasn't learned the important lesson of keeping his mouth shut."[12]

Order in the Manchester Police Department remained a high priority in no small part because the ethnic problems which had plagued the city throughout Healy's tenure as chief had not improved by 1915—nor had Healy's treatment of them changed. The Manchester Police Department still noted when a complainant or an alleged criminal was "a Greek" in its records. According to local historian John Patrick Jordan, by 1916 Healy would go so far as to order Greek coffee shop owners to keep their windows clean so that police could more easily look into the shops. He also prohibited them from hiring female employees, because the motivations of women and girls who sought such work could not possibly have been moral.[13]

By 1915, in fact, anti–Greek bias occasionally seeped onto the *Union-Leader*'s pages. For instance, the most celebrated murder of the previous year had involved a West Side resident named John St. Denis who, while drunk, killed his wife Lenna. In reporting that homicide, the *Union-Leader* listed other murderers in Manchester's history: James Myers in 1867, Dennis Shay in 1872, Fred Stockwell and "Slasher" Welch in 1895, Willard Green in 1899, Orlando Underhill in 1901, and Martin Conroy in 1911—none of them Greek. On its list, the newspaper did include one murder committed by a "Manchester Greek" named Spiropolis—and that had been perpetrated in Arlington, Massachusetts. It was the only Manchester murder on the list that did not occur in the city, and the only one committed by someone identified by ethnicity.[14]

The police investigated other homicides and murder attempts in the year following the death of Lenna St. Denis. For example, in September 1914, police arrested Ekem Myor for attacking Stephen Perok with a knife; the two Russian immigrants had been vying for the affections of the same woman.[15] Six months later, the *Amoskeag Bulletin* reported that an Amoskeag yard hand named John Dudziak killed his estranged wife, Angela, also an Amoskeag employee, in front of her house on Stark Street. None of the perpetrators or victims was Greek.[16]

This was a difficult period during which to belong to an ethnic or racial minority group anywhere in the United States, and Manchester was no exception. African Americans had been ridiculed in local media for decades, and even Manchester's newspapers were not above referring to the Brooklyn Royal Giants as "darkies" in 1914. With the country's ongoing troubles with Pancho Villa and Mexico, reporters used derogatory terms such as "greasers" to describe all Mexicans. The start of the war in Europe, meanwhile, combined with union opposition to immigrant workers, caused some Americans to demand that all people who lived in the United States, including ethnic minorities, be "one-hundred-percent American"—a slogan that would become a movement by war's end.

Helping to promote ethnic identity in Manchester was arguably the city's *other* most popular sport, boxing. As Manchester's baseball fans wearied of the battle for Textile Field, of clashes between the Federal League and organized baseball, and of reports of escalating salaries among major-league baseball players, newspapers—particularly the *Union-Leader* and *L'Avenir National*—heavily covered pugilistic contests from across the country. Locally, Manchester fans were treated to weekly bouts involving prominent white boxers from throughout the eastern United States, including Taunton's Freddie Yelle, Boston's Joe McDonald, Danny Ridge of Brooklyn, and others whose names were better known then than they are today. Occasionally, boxing fans also witnessed bouts involving African American pugilists, but interracial fights were rare in the city. The news that Sam Langford, known in the press as the "Boston Tar Baby," might come to Manchester for a bout with Joe Jeanette of New York was of particular interest, as both fighters were well known and black.[17]

Perhaps this interest in seeing African Americans pound each other with their bare fists related somewhat to the situation of Jack Johnson, the first African American heavyweight champion. Johnson's success against white opponents made many white Americans uncomfortable, and his relationships with white women enraged many whites in a time when lesser conduct incited lynchings and other violence against African Americans in much of the United States. In fact, one of Johnson's relationships brought the boxer afoul of the Mann Act. As a result, Johnson fled the United States.

By early 1915, as Johnson negotiated his return home, the *Union-Leader* weighed in on the boxer's plight. Much of Frank Knox's April 12 editorial disparaged Johnson for "the blatant and unashamed immorality which characterized this negro." While he believed "the offender ought to meet with the most vigorous treatment the law permits," Knox also claimed that race had nothing to do with his opinion, for "a Jack Johnson, with a white skin and similar lack of decency and morals, would be as objectionable and as worthy of punishment as is the negro who was the actual offender." Even so, in Knox's mind Johnson and other African Americans occupied the lowest levels of an ethnic and racial hierarchy. But southern Europeans were only moderately better:

> The capability of taking care of one's self with one's fists, backed up by muscle and courage, is distinctively an Anglo-Saxon characteristic. Contrasted with the employment of the knife, sword, or stiletto, so common among southern Europeans, self defense with the weapons nature provided, is both more harmless and requires greater courage. But this Anglo-Saxon trait is damned rather than exemplified by such a degenerate as Johnson. The sooner he is treated for what he is, the better for society and for the wholesome sport of boxing.[18]

If boxing were an "Anglo-Saxon trait," as the *Union-Leader*'s editor claimed, one would think that the Amoskeag Textile Club might take advantage of the sport's popularity and promote it to Americanize its employees. However, if the Textile Club wished to create an Amoskeag-based *community*—an association of people who share a common identity—among its disparate employees, then boxing would have been a poor choice by which to do so.[19] Boxing is an individualistic sport, one that highlights the character and characteristics of individual boxers. Boxers often did earn the respect of fans in their home communities, but Manchester had no notable pugilists to represent it. All too often, the combination of individualism and lack of geographical attachment encouraged reporters to highlight racial and ethnic characteristics of particular boxers. As a result, boxing promoted racial and ethnic pride—in fact, by viewing bare-knuckled boxing as an Anglo-Saxon trait, Knox, too, was simply projecting his own ethnic values on the sport. Little about boxing promoted unity or devotion to one's workplace or home community.[20]

Although Amoskeag's goal of Americanizing workers and reducing ethnic problems through baseball does not appear to have been working, the company clearly could not turn to boxing. Instead, it stepped up efforts in other sports; for example, the Amoskeag Textile Club sponsored bowling leagues and basketball teams in the winter. But it also continued to pin its hopes on the so-called National Pastime. This time, however, the ATC team would join clubs from Franklin, Nashua, and Concord to form the Merrimack Valley League. At the league's organizational meeting on April 24, representatives from Amoskeag and the three communities chose William McKay to be president of the league. All league games were scheduled for Saturdays. Teams would also be decidedly less professional than those of the Manufacturers League; for instance, Amoskeag asked a current Amoskeag employee, Jack Fraser—a holdover from the previous season—to manage the club. The ATC would not hire ringers to play for the team.[21]

William McKay behind the wheel with six unidentified women, 1915. McKay, the former Manufacturers League president and editor of the *Amoskeag Bulletin*, attempted to work with the owners of the Manchester Textiles to ensure the success of the New England League in the city (courtesy Manchester [New Hampshire] Historic Association).

Local media reaction to the new league was positive. Jack Finn wrote, "such a league is a far better venture than to have a circuit existing in one city only."[22] By creating a four-team league in which Amoskeag's opponents would be clubs representing towns and cities—in other words, political and, to a lesser extent, social communities—the Amoskeag Textile Club created an environment in which the corporation would be a community as well. Thus, its baseball team would exist on par with those from Franklin, Nashua, and Concord. Unlike the Manchester Textiles, which came to represent the city's business and professional community, the ATC team would encourage its fans to form an allegiance with the Amoskeag Manufacturing Company. This had been Amoskeag's goal in creating the Manufacturers League, of course. But now, with only one team from Manchester represented in the Merrimack Valley League, the company seemingly could control local interest in Amoskeag's non-professional baseball ventures.

By 1915, the *Manchester Leader and Evening Union* was unquestionably the most dominant newspaper in the city. And though Frank Knox had been interested in the welfare of Manchester and its residents since he first arrived in the city, by 1915 the tone he took in his editorials was one of outright boosterism. "Watch Manchester Grow," read the title of one editorial which began, "If you have ever been so feeble-hearted as to entertain for one little minute a doubt of the splendid future of Manchester; ... if you have ever hesitated to compare Manchester favorably with the most enterprising, most hustling and most thrifty cities in the entire country, confess now that you were in error, or forever hold your peace."[23]

Perhaps Knox's display of enthusiasm came from his participation in the activities of the Manchester Publicity Association and Chamber of Commerce, or MPA. Founded in 1914 by local merchants, government leaders, and professionals, the organization of Manchester businesses had offices in the new Amoskeag National Bank building on Elm Street. Although the city already had a Chamber of Commerce, this one promised to take a more active and visible role in promoting the city to outside business interests. To ensure it promotional success, the organization appointed Frank Knox as its vice-president.

Knox's membership in the MPA may have stemmed from their shared belief in economic diversification. Politically, as the Queen City Bridge issue had proven in 1914, Amoskeag and its "outsider" managers held tremendous power over Manchester's affairs. As the recession that accompanied World War I also demonstrated, a local economy composed of many different industries is better able to withstand economic problems than one dominated by a single company. "This is why, in large measure, diversified industries are so stoutly urged by those who have the genuine interests of their respective communities sincerely at heart," Knox asserted. "It is one great reason why Manchester ... not only welcomes, but clamors for, new industries."²⁴

Both Knox and the MPA agreed that professional baseball could play an important role in promoting the city to outside businesses. According to the *Union-Leader*'s editor:

> The advantage to a city of having a winning baseball team are hardly to be over-estimated. The popularity of the game itself admits of no question, and the team which best exemplifies the game is proportionately admired and correspondingly valuable as an advertisement of the city which it represents. But no team can play winning ball consistently, any more than a civic organization like the Manchester Publicity association, for example, can succeed in its beneficent efforts, without the help and encouragement of the public.²⁵

Knox's statement of support echoed that of MPA President and F.M. Hoyt Shoe Company managing salesman Arthur B. Jenks, who endorsed the Manchester Textiles in a statement that appeared prominently on the sports page of the *Leader* two days earlier. (A French translation appeared in *L'Avenir National* that same day). "[I]t is the duty of every citizen, who believes in wholesome sports, to lend his assistance to make the undertaking profitable to the owners of the club, to the end that the franchise will be retained," wrote Jenks. "We believe a club representing Manchester would do more to advertise this city than anything this association could do," he claimed, for "wherever there is a live baseball team, there you will usually find a progressive city."²⁶

Unfortunately for Manchester, the business community's support for baseball backfired badly in 1915. Economic conditions, perhaps combined with fatigue over the city's baseball situation, took a financial toll on both the New England League and the Amoskeag Textile Club. As a result, by the end of the 1915 baseball season, the fight for control of Textile Field—and, simultaneously, for the attentions of Manchester's baseball fans—would lead them to question the wisdom of fielding teams in Manchester.

17

The Demise of the Textiles

On May 1, 1915, with Jack Kiernan as manager, the Manchester Textiles won their first game in Fitchburg, 4–2. Two days later, the same two clubs were in Manchester to open the Textiles' home schedule. Before the game, automobiles carrying Textiles players and their Fitchburg opponents paraded from City Hall to Textile Field and around the park's track. Heavy rains had fallen over the previous few days, making the grounds wet and muddy. Both sides warmed up until shortly before 3:15, when they formed a line and marched across the field to a flagpole near the scoreboard. There, as the band led the crowd in the National Anthem, representatives of the two teams assisted each other in hoisting the American flag on the pole before new Republican Mayor Harry Spaulding, a 40-year-old lawyer who had defeated incumbent Charles Hayes in December by just 386 votes, threw out the first pitch.[1]

Behind the Manchester Publicity Association, Manchester's business community looked to the Textiles to represent and promote their city and its business interests. "Manchester owes it to herself to present a large and enthusiastic crowd at the park for this first home game," wrote Frank Knox. Not only did he want fans to support the team; he also hoped to "demonstrate to other New England cities and towns that Manchester has the sporting blood to support a baseball team after the most approved fashion. It is a mighty good reputation for a city to have."[2]

But the business community allied itself with a poor partner. The team's 1915 season, which started with such high expectations, quickly devolved. The business leaders and newspapers that supported the baseball team and counted on using it to promote Manchester were disappointed as the Textiles struggled to win games against better-organized clubs in the New England League. By mid-season the club even used the MPA's efforts to promote the city against it, effectively extorting money from local interests to keep the team afloat. What had begun so promisingly at the beginning of May ultimately resulted in the end of minor-league baseball in Manchester for more than a decade, and a loss of money and prestige among Manchester's business and political leaders.

Although the Manchester Textiles had won their first game in Fitchburg, and while they were much better than they had been under Fred Lake in 1914, the team still only hovered around .500 in the opening weeks of the season. In fact, despite the media's preseason excitement and business community's backing, few fans seemed interested in minor-league baseball. In one three-game span in May, the team attracted a total of 1,500 fans, at least 100 per game fewer than necessary for the team to break even. "It doesn't look as though the fans who were yelling for baseball were justified in their statements that the city would heartily support a winning team," complained the *Mirror*. In his *Bulletin* column, McKay noted that "attendance at the games ... has been nothing to be proud of," and he felt that "as the season gets a little further advanced there is no question but what it will pick up in good style." But since this was an era when women were pushing for suffrage and equal rights, he also recommended that, for practical reasons, the team do more to promote the game to women. "There is considerable talk going the rounds about the scarcity of females at the league games," he wrote. "Perhaps it would be a good idea for the management to cater to them a little more, during the mid-week games, and then they will more than likely be there strong on Saturdays—and with the 'steady.'"[3]

Although the Textiles ignored McKay's advice, the club did attempt to improve its attendance figures by shifting start times from 3:15 to 3:30, a move management hoped would "give the banking and insurance men a chance to get to the grounds." Its record remaining around .500 throughout May, though, the team's play did not inspire any more fans—already hurting from economic conditions in Manchester—to purchase tickets to see the Textiles. Soon, rumors began to surface that the Textiles would move, perhaps to Biddeford, Maine or North Attleboro, Massachusetts. Complaints also circulated about the poor condition of the Textile Field playing surface, which unnamed Lawrence players dubbed "the worst infield on the circuit."[4]

Aside from its winning percentage and, of course, the local economy—economic troubles would continue for the textile industry for at least another year—perhaps the biggest factor working against the Textiles was the ongoing war in Europe.[5] Despite the fact that the United States had not gotten involved, the start of the 1915 baseball season virtually coincided with Germany's sinking of the *RMS Lusitania*, a British-based cruise ship which was well known for carrying passengers (including a team of major-league all-stars in 1913–1914) across the Atlantic. More than 1,100 people died in the attack, many of them Americans. *L'Avenir National* was particularly good about covering this and other events on its front and editorial pages, bringing the French-speaking population news of gas attacks, torpedo attacks, and other brutal images of war, both in print and in photographs. And while the *Leader* and *Mirror* continued to cover the war, they also tended to emphasize baseball as an escape from real-world horrors, something that must have seemed inappropriate to some readers.[6]

Both the Manchester Publicity Association and the *Mirror* registered their concern about attendance at Textiles games. Arthur Jenks asked members of the MPA to give "moral and financial support" to the team to help it succeed both on and off the field, thereby assuring that the city would retain the Textiles in 1916. "That a ball club is a great factor in advertising any city, I think you would not question," he wrote. "I feel we should do all we can consistently to support the club." The *Mirror*, meanwhile, appealed directly to the fans, though its editorial writer apparently did not realize that Tom Keady was not yet in Manchester: "Manager Keady and his players are entitled to the solid support of those who are interested in the national game in this vicinity."[7] At the time, the Manchester textiles had won five of its ten games and sat in fourth place, three games behind first-place Lawrence.

The return of Tom Keady to Manchester during the week of June 7 created another problem for the team. Responding to rumors that may have originated with Louis Pieper, who seems not to have gotten along with the Manchester owners, Keady told the *Leader* that "Kiernan is going to manage the team in Manchester throughout the season ... and no one is going to butt into his affairs in any way." However, Keady did promise to "look after the financial end of the club." The *Bulletin*, meanwhile, welcomed Keady's reunion with Kiernan: "With two such aggressive fellows on the job we can expect some surprising developments."[8]

The Amoskeag newspaper was right. Within three weeks, his team having lost a reported $3,000, Keady went back on his word and announced that the Textiles were moving to Greenfield, Massachusetts.[9]

Despite the team's season-long attendance problems, Tom Keady's announcement came as a shock to anyone who followed the Textiles. Manchester newspaper reporters were stunned; Jack Finn had not seen it coming, and the reporters for the *Mirror* learned of the proposed move from Boston newspapers. When he arrived in Manchester, Keady himself had promised to "give this city a good chance to show its worth as a league ball town and will stick to the end of the season."[10] Now, less than a month later, Keady and Kiernan both complained that the "transfer was imminent on account of the failure of the people of Manchester to support the team," and they believed that the situation in Greenfield would prove better. In fact, Greenfield already had raised

$500 in the effort to bring the team to that community, and according to Manchester's newspapers, promised to raise at least $1,500 more.[11]

The choice of Greenfield as the team's proposed destination probably was a bluff, one designed to embarrass Manchester into supporting the team. Greenfield's population was only 10,427 in 1910, which amounted to less than 15 percent of Manchester's population according to that same census—and less than two-thirds the number of employees working at Amoskeag (though again, Amoskeag workers could not attend weekday games). Besides, the Manchester Publicity Association and Manchester's newspapers already had claimed the team was of value in promoting the city. By their own statements, for the team to move to a small town such as Greenfield would have been a tremendous blow to city leaders.[12]

If Keady and Kiernan sought to mobilize Manchester's business community, they succeeded. The *Mirror* took the lead in promoting the New England League club, imploring, "By all means let us keep the team in Manchester by rallying to its support." Meanwhile on June 25, a day after the owners announced their plan to move the Textiles, a small group of business leaders held what *L'Avenir National* termed a "secret meeting" to determine how to raise funds in an effort to keep the team. Subsequently an attorney and a local coal dealer, apparently with the help of an unnamed club official, responded with an effort to raise the $3,000 that Kiernan, Keady, and co-owner James Smith claimed to have lost on the team thus far, with the aim of buying a controlling interest in the club. Within three days, behind the motto "Boost Manchester," the trio raised $505 from 21 people. One day later, on June 29, the group had raised nearly $1,400 toward purchasing control of the club, and Mayor Spaulding, A. B. Jenks, and team official William C. Carroll met to discuss how to raise the remaining $1,100. They decided to hold a mass meeting the following night.[13]

Prior to the meeting, New England League officials met in Boston and voted to allow the owners of the Textiles to move the team to Greenfield if they chose. Spaulding and Jack Finn together sent a letter to the league supporting the efforts of local business leaders to raise the funds necessary to keep the team. Then that evening, Spaulding hosted his mass meeting at City Hall. The gathering attracted an overflow crowd, and when it was over, the funds had been raised. The *Leader* extolled the efforts of the business community, particularly men like Mayor Spaulding and Arthur Jenks. Frank Knox wrote,

> The result is just cause for gratification and pride: gratification that Manchester has maintained her reputation as a live town and is not to sacrifice the benefit of the publicity which accrues from representation by a good team in league baseball; and pride that her business and professional men not only appreciate those benefits, but are willing to match their money against that of the highest bidder elsewhere.[14]

The *Mirror* was more to the point: "It was a remarkable and impressive manifestation of Manchester spirit and aggressiveness. The control of the team will be in the hand of Manchester people with Mayor Spaulding on the board of directors."[15]

The final agreement between Manchester's business leaders and the owners of the Textiles was that the team's ownership would be broken into six stakes worth $1,000 each. Keady, Kiernan, and Smith would each own one stake by virtue of the $3,000 they already had lost. The remaining three stakes would be broken into 120 shares, each worth $25.00, to be purchased by Manchester residents. Spaulding was said to be the largest local shareholder, while Jenks arranged for members of the MPA to buy another twelve shares and the remainder was held by other businessmen in the city. The club would be run by a six-member Board of Directors that included Keady, Kiernan, and Smith. Spaulding served as the seventh member who would vote only in case of a tie. To allow for the sale, the shareholders created the Manchester Baseball Association and planned to incorporate under New Hampshire law.[16]

The situation would be even more complicated than the new owners had realized. Thanks to well-attended exhibition games at Textile Field, the team had been profitable in April to the point of allowing Keady, Kiernan, and Smith to pay player expenses and $150 toward rental of the grounds. When the new baseball association bought into the team, however, the new owners found that players were owed ten days' back pay, uniforms had not been paid for, and the team had not made any subsequent payments for use of Textile Field. Additionally a number of other expenses, including Kiernan's telegraph bills, had not been paid, nor had the team's scorekeeper received any compensation for his work. Therefore, the team's new subscribers gave Kiernan a check for $1,000 to pay his players, and after July 1 paid all expenses (above gate receipts) relating to the team. They also opened negotiations with the Amoskeag Textile Club to try to get more favorable terms on the team's lease of Textile Field.[17]

Throughout the drama surrounding the Textiles' future, the Amoskeag Textile Club remained silent. The club could have pointed out that its directors had warned Manchester residents of the perils of dealing with the New England League as far back as December 1912, but it did not do so. Tellingly, though, the June 15 edition of the *Amoskeag Bulletin* was the last to feature William McKay's "Bill's Baseball" column. Thereafter, in the wake of Keady's threat to move the team to Greenfield, the *Bulletin* never again promoted the Manchester Textiles.

Around the time the New England League season began, the Amoskeag Textile Club's officers realized that with two different tenants, the two primary baseball grounds, Textile Field and the Rock Rimmon Grounds, would require two different oversight committees. Therefore, in early May the ATC appointed two such committees, with William McKay and two other club members responsible for Textile Field. Their charge was to "see that everything is conducted in a proper manner at the park" such that the grounds remained clean and all bills were paid, but they also promised to "furnish a series of entertainments during the summer that will be enjoyed by the public."[18] The Rock Rimmon Grounds, meanwhile, were to be prepared for the Amoskeag Manufacturing Company's annual Field Day and the opening of the Merrimack Valley League season.

Field Day and the Merrimack Valley League season both arrived on May 22. Amoskeag's mills closed at noon and about 1,500 employees marched up to Rock Rimmon for the annual company picnic. This was followed by track and field events, trap shooting, a tennis exhibition, and finally, the league game between Amoskeag and Nashua. Before the game McKay led a procession of players across the baseball field to raise the Amoskeag Textile Club banner "next to a huge American flag while patriotic airs were played." William Parker Straw tossed the first pitch, and Amoskeag won the game, 12–1.[19]

The Merrimack Valley League never captured Amoskeag employees' interest. As planned, teams played weekly on Saturdays, with Amoskeag generally playing at the Rock Rimmon Grounds except when the Textiles were out of town, when Amoskeag used Textile Field. On some weekdays, Amoskeag arranged for exhibition games against non-league teams, including York Beach, Maine, and Portsmouth and Milford, New Hampshire. Yet fan interest in the league seems to have been lacking, and most newspapers, including the *Amoskeag Bulletin*, covered the league only sporadically.[20]

On the field, Amoskeag's season was successful; by early August, the team was tied with Franklin for the league lead. But the league itself had its share of problems, most notably when Nashua was dropped after it failed to show up for a game in Concord on July 24. The *Bulletin* stopped covering the league altogether after August 2, and while it did announce that Amoskeag would be at York Beach for several games during the annual shutdown, fans had to read the city's other newspapers—such as *L'Avenir National*—to find the box scores. According to *L'Avenir National*, Franklin won the Merrimack Valley League championship.[21]

Although Amoskeag ended the season in second place, the Textile Club labeled the season a disappointment for other: simply, local support "was not sufficient to make the season a financial success." The Amoskeag team took in $643.75 in gate receipts, which more than covered its traveling expenses ($580.66). However, after factoring the time lost for work, equipment, federal taxes, printing and advertising costs, umpires' pay, and other expenses, the baseball program lost $362.49 in the Merrimack Valley League.[22] This emphasis on finances was unusual for the ATC, given that the club was not out to make a profit. But to emphasize its fiscal independence from the Amoskeag Manufacturing Company and to justify its continued operation, the club did have to at least break even. The league disbanded that winter, making it the Amoskeag Textile Club's second failure in bringing club-controlled baseball to Manchester.

As Amoskeag's baseball team suffered at the gate, a new enthusiasm briefly took hold among fans of the Manchester Textiles. The *Leader* claimed that reporters in other cities who had been "knocking" Manchester "can't say too much about the get-up-and-go-at-it spirit manifest at the mass meeting ... when $3000 was raised to keep the New England league in New Hampshire." Even better, the team won four straight games after local business leaders purchased their shares of the team, leading Jack Finn to claim that interest in the team was becoming more evident. But Finn also believed that conditions in Manchester were not supportive of the team, to the point at which he suggested that local business owners, like those in other league cities, should give their employees a half-day off on Wednesdays. That idea never took hold because, as Finn later admitted, fans did not want to pay to watch baseball even as they lost wages for their half-day off each week. But another idea—to hold a "boosters day" and ask fans to show up at the ballpark to support the local owners—attracted about 3,000 fans.[23]

The mid–July "boosters day" game may have been the season's high point. As the team limped through the season's final month and a half, fans became disenchanted with the team and the league in general. As was apparently common in the New England League, in August Manchester loaned some of its better players to other teams, including first-place Lawrence. Louis Pieper, meanwhile, was accused of syndicalism. Pieper appeared to have tremendous influence over the Fitchburg team after his brother-in-law, Fitchburg's owner, passed away during the season; the number of trades benefitting Pieper's Lynn team seemed to prove his control over Fitchburg. And unlike in 1913 and 1914, when the Red Sox and Athletics came to town, the hoped-for game between the Textiles and the Boston Braves, defending World Series champions, never materialized. As fans stayed away and the Textiles sank in the standings, rumors circulated that Manchester would be dropped from the league in 1916.[24]

The Textiles finished the year in seventh place at 48–67. Few seemed to notice when the season ended; in fact, a week after the season's end, the *Leader* allegedly received a letter from a fan who complained about the lack of New England League box scores over the previous five or six days. At the same time, Jack Finn began analyzing the reasons for the team's failure, specifically blaming the unfavorable weather, bad scheduling, and the team's poor play for attendance problems and noting that only Portland had made a profit in 1915. "We're hammering all this out because we do not believe the present season has proved a real test of Manchester's worth as a baseball city," he wrote, "and that much of the criticism heaped upon this town, was unmerited in view of the existing conditions and the handicaps ... which had to be met. Things will be different in another year."[25] Finn was worried—and for good reason.

By September 11, new rumors began to circulate that the New England League sought to merge with the Eastern Association. The idea was for the New England League to drop Manchester, Fitchburg, and at least one other club and to replace them with three to five Eastern Association cities chosen from among Bridgeport, New London, New Haven, Springfield, and Hartford. The rumors seemed to be coming from Lynn, home to Louis Pieper's team, and Worcester, whose owners dubiously claimed that their team's poor attendance in 1915 was a result of fans desiring better opponents. Tim Murnane denied that the two leagues could consolidate, but when league owners met in late September, several of them promised to pursue a merger.[26]

Jack Finn attended the September meeting in Boston in place of Mayor Spaulding and told the owners that "Manchester wished to retain its league team and any attempt to drop the city in the event of a merger would be vigorously fought." A surprising figure also defended the team: the New England League's supervisor of umpires, Fred Lake. "I failed in Manchester and other outsiders will also," he said, "but with Manchester men behind the club, the city will be a paying proposition.... No one can tell me Manchester isn't a good ball town, for my experience in the old days when Manchester men held the reins were sufficient to convince me the city can be made a success." Murnane promised to give Manchester's owners "full consideration" as league owners pursued the merger.[27]

In October 1915, as the professional baseball situation in Manchester was being sorted out, the Boston Red Sox returned to the World Series to play the Philadelphia Phillies. Taking the *Leader*'s example from 1912 and 1914, the *Manchester Daily Mirror and American* published front-page headlines and updates relating to each game. It also offered fans a wire service, with an inning-by-inning score posted in the window of the newspaper office and plays announced by megaphone from a balcony. In an editorial, the *Mirror* claimed that between 6,000 and 7,500 people gathered on Hanover Street, and described their activities in terms not unlike those used in Albert Spalding's 1911 description of the baseball creed:

> Unquestionably, it was the largest gathering of people ever assembled in "Newspaper Row" on Hanover Street. It represented people in all walks of life, from the prosperous banker, merchant, lawyer, doctor, down to the most humble workman. All stood shoulder to shoulder,

intensely interested in the outcome of this mighty contest on the diamond, with the championship of the world at stake. It places baseball at the pinnacle of outdoor games as a clean, healthy, wholesome and alluring sport to which the people can flock and where for two hours they can forget their troubles and the vexatious problems of the time and hour.[28]

Despite the popularity of the Red Sox, who won their second World Series since 1912 (and third since 1903), fans seemed tired of the game locally. After the series, Ed Maynard of the Plymouth-based Draper-Maynard sporting goods company traveled to Squam Lake, New Hampshire, along with Red Sox outfielder Tris Speaker, pitcher Ernie Shore, and several Royal Rooters including Tim Murnane. On their way northward, they stopped in Manchester where Mayor Spaulding entertained them at the Derryfield Club. The luncheon was not covered in local newspapers; in fact, no one seemed to notice the arrival of some of New England's most prominent baseball personalities.[29]

The visit came in middle or late October, shortly before the end-of-the-month meeting of the New England League in Boston. By this time a rift had developed among the Manchester Textiles' owners—Kiernan, Keady, and James Smith on one side and local owners on the others. To represent the latter, Finn and Phenomenal Smith attended the meeting. "The local citizens who have money invested and far more local capital was put in by them than the outsiders invested in spite of their claims, are going to have a little to say about the Manchester franchise and when the time comes for saying it they'll be on deck and won't mince words about the situation," Finn wrote prior to the meeting.[30] When the league named a committee to investigate the Eastern Association-New England League merger proposal, Phenomenal Smith indicated that if Manchester were dropped, local investors would have to be paid. Murnane again assured the local owners that stockholders' interests would be given "every consideration."[31]

By December, however, despite Murnane's repeated assurances, local owners seemed on the verge of losing their investment. New England League owners including Louis Pieper, Portland's Hugh Duffy, and Worcester's Jesse Burkett favored taking the team away from Manchester without remuneration to local investors. In several columns, Finn reminded his readers of the owners' $3,000 outlay to save the team and implied that Kiernan, Keady, and James Smith had paid virtually nothing into the team. After Christmas, Spaulding finally wrote to Murnane—still considered Manchester's strongest advocate—formally requesting protection of their investment and implied that if their rights were not respected, the local owners would take the New England League to court. Nevertheless, when the league voted at its December meeting to proceed with merger negotiations and reimburse Kiernan, Keady, and James Smith for the Manchester team, Spaulding claimed that he had "been informed of no such proposal and that he would endeavor to protect the local stockholders of the club."[32]

In early January, about a week after the league meeting, Jack Kiernan finally emerged to discuss the situation with Manchester's neglected local owners. Although Manchester citizens had offered to pay $3,000 toward the team, Kiernan claimed, they "did not make good their offer and have therefore lost their standing." The local owners paid player salaries to the amount of $1,600 or $1,700, he said, but they did not pay the full amount owed for the team "and have lost out" on their claim. He also told reporters that he had never been paid for his work as the team's manager.

Jack Finn took issue with Kiernan's account and went through all of the expenses paid by the local owners: salaries, uniforms, and other payments totaling $2,700, with another $300 in reserve to be used for other bills that came in. Kiernan had received $200 per month, Finn told his readers, though not for the final three weeks of the season. Moreover, the out-of-town owners had not put much of their own money into the team, he claimed. In fact, they still owed money on the club, as a result of which the team deducted $20 from gate receipts after every road game to pay the Textiles' previous owners.[33] Thus, as far as Finn was concerned, the local owners *had* paid the money owed for purchase of one-half of the club.

To argue this point as well as the case for compensation to the local owners, Finn, Spaulding, and Postmaster John R. Willis attended another league meeting on January 5, 1916. The league merely referred the Manchester representatives to Kiernan, Keady, and Smith, telling them to work out compensation on their own. Spaulding again threatened legal action against the New England League. Three days later, however, the *Leader* reported that Spaulding might not have a case: although the stockholders in the Manchester Baseball Association had drawn up papers for the transfer of the franchise, Kiernan, Keady, and Smith had never signed them. Legally, the local "owners" did not own the team after all.[34]

The end of the New England League—and of the Manchester Textiles—officially arrived in February, when a new ten-team Eastern League was announced representing five cities each from the New England League and the Eastern Association. Mayor Spaulding again suggested the Manchester owners would take the league to court, but by then it was too late.[35] Although he shared the *Mirror's* position that the New England League owners had not dealt with local stockholders fairly, ultimately Finn blamed the local owners:

> When the purchase of stock was made last summer, the first move should have been a transfer of the franchise to the local men but this detail was put off and let drift till the season had ended and then again it dragged along with the result that the local investors were not possessed of any particular standing in the league and Messrs. Smith, Keady and Kiernan

were the whole works as far as the Manchester club was concerned. Had the franchise been transferred such would not have been the case and rather than be dealing with the out-of-town men interested in the local team, the dickering for the past several months would have been done with the Manchester men. They permitted the needed credentials to slip along, to remain in the possession of others and the serious error committed is now manifest.[36]

A few people held out hope that Manchester might become part of a new league. After the merger, Fred Lake proposed a circuit consisting of Manchester, Haverhill, Brockton, Pawtucket, Fitchburg, Fall River, New Bedford, and Newport, with each team operating under local ownership. About Manchester, Lake told Jack Finn, "Once you get the Amoskeag corporation and its employes [sic] interested in a baseball franchise, you'll find Manchester is a grand ball town.... Without this support local interest in the team is lacking. When independent baseball draws 3,000 people on Saturdays, league baseball in Manchester would draw more if under local direction."[37] Nothing came of Lake's proposal. Professional baseball would not return to Textile Field until 1926.

As for the Textiles, league magnates eventually agreed that Tom Keady, Jack Kiernan, and James Smith never signed any papers formally turning over one-half of the team to local shareholders. Without written evidence of the transaction, Mayor Harry Spaulding—a lawyer by trade—was unable to assemble a legal case against the New England League. They were never reimbursed, though in October 1916, the Amoskeag Textile Club finally recouped the remaining $650 owed it for use of Textile Field in 1915.[38]

Although the Amoskeag Textile Club's gamble on the Manchester Textiles failed, its previous warnings about the New England League's instability and its ability to distance itself from the league at an early point in the season allowed the ATC to appear to have won. Amoskeag demonstrated to Manchester's business leaders—the people actually pushing for a New England League team—that an outside league not under Amoskeag's control would fail, even in Textile Field. Admittedly, the club also lost badly with its failed amateur team. However, unlike the Textiles, which disgraced the entire city through the Manchester Publicity Association and the business community generally, Amoskeag's failure was perceived to be purely financial. So far as the public was concerned, Amoskeag's benevolence programs were not designed to improve the company's profits, a fact which only brought positive media coverage to the textile corporation. The $30,000 spent on Textile Field was a case in point. Similarly, the public could write off the failure of the Merrimack Valley League as just another attempt to improve the lives of Amoskeag Manufacturing Company workers at any cost, regardless of the baseball program's actual goal of promoting corporate loyalty, Americanizing immigrants, and fighting unionization.

Epilogue:
The Great Strike of 1922

In 1912, in the wake of the Bread and Roses Strike in Lawrence, the Amoskeag Manufacturing Company set out to ward off radical labor movements in Manchester, encourage employee loyalty, and regain control over its state and city in the face of Progressive-era reforms. To help accomplish these goals, Amoskeag joined other companies across the United States that expanded their corporate-benevolence programs, while also participating in a national movement to Americanize foreign-born workers. Textile Field was among the most tangible and symbolic of its efforts in both areas. The grandstand allowed Amoskeag to demonstrate, in a very public way, that it had the best interests of its workforce at heart, while theoretically promoting American values through the game of baseball. As such, control over Textile Field, and of Manchester's baseball scene in general, became of paramount importance to Amoskeag.

With the exception of the brief 1914 work stoppage in Mill No. 11 and a five-day strike staged by a group of employees in 1918, Amoskeag remained strike-free until 1922. Unlike in Lawrence and Lowell, Amoskeag could point to the fact that radical syndicalism in the form of the Industrial Workers of the World never infiltrated its ranks. But did baseball, and the ballpark built to serve as the game's local stage, actually play a significant role in keeping the labor peace?

Despite Amoskeag's efforts in this area, baseball was not responsible for the relative peace. With the possible exception of school-aged boys, Manchester's foreign-born residents did not take a strong interest in baseball at any level. But media outlets that emerged in 1912, particularly the two newspapers that used baseball to establish themselves among local readers—the *Amoskeag*

Bulletin and the *Manchester Leader*—probably did help to reduce employer-employee tensions. In a period of pre-war job scarcity and economic uncertainty, Amoskeag management employed these media to clearly articulate its view of what was causing the problems. Understanding that southern competition and war conditions limited jobs and kept wages low, combined with industry-wide wage increases in the spring of 1912, may have helped to dissuade workers from taking radical action against the corporation.

That situation changed in 1917 when a sudden increase in the demand for cotton textiles led to a period of war-related prosperity for Amoskeag. In response, operatives organized a chapter of the United Textile Workers, which was affiliated with the American Federation of Labor, and in 1918 the union successfully negotiated a wage increase of fifteen percent. The following year, the UTW pressured Amoskeag to adopt the 48-hour workweek for which American workers had been pressing since before the Haymarket Affair. Workers received another fifteen-percent wage increase in 1920, after the war's end.[1]

Aside from Amoskeag's use of media, another factor that kept labor radicalism out of the company was the poor state of the Industrial Workers of the World in New England. In 1917, the IWW claimed between 100,000 and 250,000 members, and according to Melvyn Dubofsky "seemed to pose a distinct threat to the established order in America."[2] Yet after the Paterson Silk Strike four years earlier, the Wobblies never regained the influence they had had in the industrial Northeast. By 1917, several of the group's most prominent members, including Lawrence strike leaders Joseph Ettor, Arturo Giovannitti, and Elizabeth Gurley Flynn, either had left the IWW or assumed a reduced role. Moreover, the organization's anti-war activities, some of which ran afoul of federal sedition laws, and a series of violent Western strikes in which it participated, led the federal government to raid 48 IWW offices and indict 166 actual and alleged members. Of those, 113—including Big Bill Haywood—faced trial.[3]

The United States of America v. William D. Haywood, et al took place in Chicago before the same judge, Kenesaw Mountain Landis, who had heard—and refused to rule on—the antitrust suit brought by the Federal League against organized baseball. Unlike the relatively short Federal League trial, however, this one lasted five months, ending in August 1918. And though Landis was widely praised for being fair and impartial during the trial, when the IWW members were found guilty he sentenced them to anywhere from 10 days to 20 years in prison, with some receiving fines of up to $30,000. Many of the defendants later had their sentences reduced or commuted. Haywood, however, did not. While appealing his case to the Supreme Court, the IWW leader jumped bail and fled to the Soviet Union. He died in Moscow in 1928. At the time of his death, a photograph of Landis reportedly hung on his apartment wall.[4]

Pearl McGill did not face prosecution. In 1917, four years after leaving the IWW, she met and married Edward Vance, and the two settled in Buffalo, Iowa, where she was a popular schoolteacher and church member. Soon, her husband began to show signs of mental illness, for which he blamed Pearl. As his condition worsened, Pearl Vance began to fear for her life. The two divorced in 1923 while Edward was confined to the state hospital. In April 1924, four months after his release, Edward Vance returned to Buffalo, hid in his ex-wife's house, and surprised her when she returned home from visiting a sick friend. He chased her into the street and shot her, instantly killing her.[5]

During this time, perhaps for symbolic reasons, baseball remained important to the Amoskeag Textile Club. The game endured despite the fact that its popularity dropped off considerably in Manchester after 1913, as evidenced by the various attempts to create new leagues and teams between 1916 and 1921. In 1916 the club sponsored a "yard league" consisting of six teams for which only Amoskeag employees were eligible to play. But it was poorly promoted even in the *Amoskeag Bulletin*, whose editor, William McKay, admitted that he did not particularly support the venture. The following year, Amoskeag and McElwain formed the Manchester City Baseball League, which operated for two seasons. The two companies then revived a four-team Manufacturers League from 1919 to 1921. None of these ventures proved as successful as Amoskeag had hoped. Even when the Textile Club was able to bring a major-league team to Textile Field—the Boston Braves in April 1919—attendance was disappointing, nothing like what the Red Sox or even the Athletics had attracted in Textile Field's first years of existence. Additionally, newspaper coverage of these leagues was sporadic, and crowds at baseball games still did not include significant numbers of European immigrants.[6]

Prospects for baseball were not great in the early 1920s, either. In 1920 a scandal erupted in professional baseball in which eight members of the Chicago White Sox were alleged to have thrown the 1919 World Series in favor of the Cincinnati Reds. In response, Major League Baseball hired Kenesaw Mountain Landis as its first commissioner. Landis banned all eight players from professional baseball for life. Meanwhile, the Boston Red Sox had sent most of their best players, including Babe Ruth, to the New York Yankees, as a result of which the team would not finish above .500 again until 1935. The Braves were nearly as bad, finishing with a winning record only once between 1917 and 1932. Though local interest in major-league baseball did persist, these problems may have dampened local enthusiasm for professional baseball, particularly among more casual fans.

In the late 1910s and early 1920s, no minor-league teams announced plans to move to Manchester, and many people who had promoted the game before World War I no longer showed any interest in supporting a local team. William McKay concentrated his efforts on the Amoskeag Print Works and on improving the *Amoskeag Bulletin,* eventually settling on a monthly magazine-style publication that the Textile Club introduced in January 1922. Though the *Bulletin* covered some Amoskeag-related baseball news, McKay himself generally stayed out of local baseball matters, particularly ones relating to Textile Field. John Carney spent his off-seasons on his farm in Litchfield, a few miles outside of Manchester, but otherwise concentrated on his coaching duties at Cornell University in Ithaca, New York. Arthur B. Jenks was engaged in banking by this time, and he no longer involved himself significantly in the Manchester Publicity Association or its successor organization. (He would later serve as a United States Congressman in the late 1930s and early 1940s.) Harry Spaulding likewise stayed out of baseball, and throughout the 1920s concentrated his efforts on his legal career. In 1927, upon being accused of stealing $3,000 as executor of a will, Spaulding and his wife disappeared into New York City, though the former mayor continued to practice law there under his real name. Police arrested Spaulding in 1930 when he returned to Manchester for his wife's funeral.[7]

Although McKay, Spaulding, and Jenks no longer actively promoted baseball, some familiar names still could be spotted at Textile Field, including John "Phenomenal" Smith, Amoskeag pitcher and coach Jack Fraser, and catcher Eddie Flanagan, whose play for the Beacons had attracted the attention of the New England League's Portland franchise in 1913. Smith, whose nickname appears to have been forgotten by the general public by this time, lost interest in the Manufacturers League prior to the 1921 season when the Amoskeag Textile Club refused to grant him control over Textile Field concessions.[8] In 1922 he managed the Manchester Police Department team, taking Flanagan and other local baseball stars with him.

With a formidable team emerging under Smith, a logical move for Fraser and the Amoskeag Textile Club seemed to be to field an independent club in 1922, which the *Amoskeag Bulletin* confirmed they would do on page six of its February 1922 issue. But another development, covered on page ten, threatened to cancel the team's season even before it started. Amoskeag announced that effective February 13, the company would reduce wages by 20 percent and increase the workweek from 48 hours to 54. William Parker Straw, who took over as company agent after his father's retirement less than two years earlier, did his best to blame the move on competition from the South where, he noted, wages were roughly half those in the North and the workweek was 55 to 60 hours.[9]

John F. "Phenomenal" Smith, manager of the Manchester Police Department team, at Textile Field circa 1922 (courtesy Manchester [New Hampshire] Historic Association).

The *Amoskeag Bulletin*'s February 1922 issue would be the last one published. On Friday, February 10, the United Textile Workers announced that its members had voted overwhelmingly—12,032 to 116—to reject Straw's proposal. Workers went on strike three days later. With a few exceptions, most strikers remained away from their jobs over the next nine months. Baseball and corporate benevolence had failed to keep the labor peace.[10]

The New England Textile Strike of 1922 lasted more than nine months at Amoskeag and in many other New Hampshire towns and cities. Manchester residents of a decade or more could be forgiven if events, personalities, and situations that occurred during the strike seemed vaguely familiar. In 1922, former Governor Robert Bass appeared in Manchester to survey the strike, eventually announcing that he would form the New Hampshire Civic Association to investigate New Hampshire's social and economic problems. The *Leader* speculated that the statewide textile strike and the 48-hour law might be among the first issues the new group would consider.[11] In Lawrence, rumors persisted that elements of the strike were being led by Ben Legere, a former Wobbly who had helped to found a new IWW-style labor movement called the One Big Union.[12] Even former United States Senator Henry Hollis found himself in the news over questions surrounding his divorce, a case that caused political and religious leaders to reconsider the state's complicated divorce laws.[13]

In Manchester, Police Chief Michael J. Healy reacted no differently to the strike than he had with the IWW and Free Speech Alliance in 1912. Pressured to protect scabs from intimidation, Healy limited the number of picketers at each mill gate to two, refused to allow strikers to photograph anyone entering or exiting the mills, and at various points rejected parade and demonstration permits. In cases in which mass meetings were allowed in front of the library on Concord Common, Healy refused to permit anyone who was not a Manchester citizen to speak, including strike leaders representing the United Textile Workers. He announced that in accordance with a Supreme Court ruling, the police would consider twelve or more people when at least one is armed, or thirty or more even when no weapons are present, to constitute a mob. Later in the work stoppage, Healy allegedly ordered strikers to remain in their homes while scabs left the mills, a charge he later denied in court. By mid-summer, he also refused to allow the sale of flowers or tags on Elm Street to support the strikers, claiming—despite evidence suggesting otherwise—that Elm Street business owners had complained about the presence of strike supporters in the business district.

By early June, strikers called for Healy's removal, to which the 65-year-old Chief of Police responded, "I shall continue to do my duty as I see it, without fear or favor." He did just that, successfully lobbying city government for additional resources and hiring 35 new police officers in late July.[14] Healy did suffer one setback when, in the wake of Prohibition and his apparently reduced ability to collect money through the so-called Healy Method, he unsuccessfully pressed the city to force "bars that serve everything but booze" to be licensed for their supposed threat to dry laws.[15] But the chief had the *Union-Leader*'s unwavering support; at one point the newspaper called him "the BEST FRIEND the men and women of Manchester who have been on strike for the past sixteen weeks have."[16] Michael Healy remained in charge of the Manchester Police Department until his death on March 8, 1937.

L'Avenir National strongly opposed the work stoppage in several front-page editorials, arguing in one that out-of-town organizers had not been transparent in their tallying and reporting of workers' votes to strike, rendering the validity of the work stoppage questionable.[17] But the *Manchester Leader and Evening Union* generally remained neutral throughout the nine-month ordeal. The only exceptions came with reports of violence on the part of strikers, occasional expressions of support for Chief Healy, and one instance in which the newspaper, claiming to be "spokesman for the community of Manchester," urged workers to accept an offer by Amoskeag's management to work a 54-hour week at their pre-strike wages.[18]

Just how much Frank Knox involved himself in his newspapers' day-to-day operations at that time is unknown. He had spent the war years in Europe as an Army major, leaving the Union-Leader Corporation in the hands of his longtime business partner John Muehling. Muehling continued to run the paper for long stretches over the next two-and-a-half decades, a period that at various times saw Knox run unsuccessfully for governor of New Hampshire, leave Manchester to manage William Randolph Hearst's newspaper holdings in Chicago, run unsuccessfully for Vice President of the United States in 1936, and work as Secretary of the Navy under President Franklin D. Roosevelt. It also saw the Union-Leader Corporation purchase and close the *Manchester Mirror*, the only English-language daily newspaper that remained to compete with the *Union-Leader*. After both Muehling and Knox died in 1944, Knox's widow sold the company to William Loeb, who transformed the *Union-Leader* into a nationally known—and at times, highly controversial—conservative newspaper.

Although radical labor movements did not figure in the strike, Ben Legere and the One Big Union movement did make appearances in Manchester in early fall. In September, a panicked *Leader* exclaimed that a "wave of Communist literature" had hit the city, literature that later was traced to the One Big Union. According to *L'Avenir National*, books and pamphlets of a radical nature found their way into the UTW's reading room. Then in mid–October, Legere himself arrived in Manchester to survey the situation, and "announced his intentions to 'advance on Manchester.'" The One Big Union never did gain a foothold there, however. A half-century later, one Amoskeag clerk claimed that Healy kept Legere's group out of Manchester through the intimidation of its operatives, refusing them permits to organize rallies and physically forcing them onto trains out of town. The clerk's memory of long-past events seems to combine aspects of Healy's 1912 campaign against the Free Speech Alliance and IWW and his work restricting the activities of the UTW in 1922. Healy may have run radicals out of town, but more than likely, Legere's group simply ran out of time.[19]

By the time of the One Big Union's appearance in Manchester in October, Amoskeag already had reopened several of its mills and raised the pay of those who returned to work, straining the strikers' ranks. Roman Catholic Bishop George Albert Guertin intervened, convincing workers to accept a 51-hour workweek in return for the wage scale that existed before the strike—a scale that Amoskeag had restored in September regardless. But Amoskeag's management rejected the compromise. Perhaps coincidentally, two days after Amoskeag's rejection, Bishop Guertin donated church-owned land to the city so that a bridge could be constructed over the Merrimack River. The Queen City Bridge would open in 1923, finally connecting McElwain's central plant to the West Side and opening southwest Manchester to additional development. It was the same bridge supported by Gustav Wenzel in 1914 to benefit McElwain and the Eighth Ward, and the same one that Amoskeag had opposed.[20] Between the devastating strike and the battle over the Queen City Bridge, Amoskeag's control over its workers and the politics of the city had eroded precipitously.

Despite Amoskeag's intransience, the strike did end. As in 1912, labor problems and the Republican-dominated state government's refusal to address those problems—the Governor and Executive Council would not call a special legislative session to consider passage of a 48-hour law—led to the election of a Democratic majority in the legislature. Thanks to his support for the 48-hour movement, Democrat and former major-league baseball player Fred H. Brown was elected Governor. Even the Republican-leaning *Union-Leader* viewed the election as a public endorsement of the 48-hour movement: "the vote can be construed in no other way by any man who does not intentionally blind himself to palpable FACTS." Despite the GOP's continued control over the Senate and Executive Council, strikers were so heartened by the election that they ended their walkout before the end of November.[21] Even so, they would have to wait until 1937 before the General Court passed a 48-hour workweek for women and children. The Legislature passed the measure on March 10—coincidentally, the day Chief Michael Healy was buried.[22]

Epilogue: The Great Strike of 1922

As for baseball, Amoskeag never did field a team in 1922. Tired of waiting for an end to the strike, most members of the ATC team joined other ball clubs around the city. Then in mid–August, when an opportunity arose to play against the well-known House of David traveling baseball team from Michigan, Jack Fraser created "Fraser's All Stars," and claimed that attendance at the game would determine whether or not Connie Mack might bring his Philadelphia Athletics back to Textile Field in early September. A reported 2,500 fans watched Fraser's team defeat the House of David, 5–4, but immediately afterward Connie Mack telegraphed the *Union-Leader* offices to state that the Athletics would be unable to return to Manchester. Fraser kept his team together over the next month for a series of games against out-of-town clubs.[23]

After the strike, the Amoskeag Textile Club did reinstate the baseball team with Fraser as its manager and pitcher, and Eddie Flanagan returned to catch. In September 1923, Fraser arranged a game with the National League's Brooklyn Robins, sometimes called the Dodgers, at Textile Field. The ATC engaged longtime Manchester umpire Barney McLaughlin to serve as one of two umpires in the exhibition, and Brooklyn guaranteed appearances by star outfielder Zack Wheat and first baseman Jack Fournier, the latter a favorite among French Canadian fans.

The Brooklyn-Amoskeag game was a disappointment in most respects. Only about 1,000 fans attended, and a promised minor-league battery never arrived, forcing the aging and unprepared Fraser and Flanagan into the game. Fraser only lasted four innings, giving up twelve hits—but he was the best of Amoskeag's three pitchers, who combined to give up thirteen runs. Flanagan was knocked unconscious when a thrown ball hit him in the head as he tried to score. Near the end of the game, Brooklyn's outfielders and infielders switched places, and Fournier came in to pitch, turning the contest into what the *Leader* called a "Comedy Game." "Amoskeag was greatly outclassed," reported the newspaper, and "the fans ... thought there should have been stronger opposition displayed against big time boys by the Amoskeag management."[24]

Local disappointment in Amoskeag such as that expressed after the 1923 Brooklyn game never dissipated, and on Christmas Eve in 1935, after two more major strikes, the Amoskeag Manufacturing Company closed forever. Textile Field still stands, however. Now called Gill Stadium—renamed for Ignace Gill, Manchester Parks and Recreation director from 1935 to 1967—it has seen many changes since Amoskeag donated the stadium to the city of Manchester in 1927. Flagpoles along the façade have disappeared, the giant scoreboard is gone, an elevator and press box have been constructed, and the original wooden chairs and deck have been replaced with molded plastic seats and a metal deck.

Perhaps most jarringly, huge new dugouts were built in the former dirt track at the front of the grandstand, and an artificial playing surface replaced the natural grass-and-dirt field. But although the grounds have changed, Gill Stadium remains, a forgotten relic of early 20th-century social and political movements in New England.

Conclusion: Textile Field and the Progressive Movement in Manchester

Cultural landscapes reveal much about the values and events of our past. Textile Field was built in a particular time and place by a group of people representing the Amoskeag Manufacturing Company. To truly understand why the grandstand exists, one must consider the spatial and temporal contexts of its construction—in other words, the political, social, cultural, and economic situation that existed in Manchester, New Hampshire in the Progressive Era.

Between 1912 and 1916, the Amoskeag Manufacturing Company employed baseball, as well as the American flag, welfare work programs generally, conservative media outlets, and city police and government officials to control labor in Manchester and maintain an acceptable profit margin for the company's investors. Over the long term, Amoskeag's efforts did not work, as the 1922 strike and the eventual failure of the company proved. Even in the short term, minor strikes and the disappointing crowd that attended the Philadelphia Athletics game in 1914 indicate that baseball and other programs did not have their intended effect on a majority of Amoskeag's workforce. Amoskeag managers knew their company could not compete with Southern textile corporations if they did not take radical measures to control workers and wages, and the 1912 Lawrence Bread and Roses Strike was an important event in the evolution of their thinking.

In her groundbreaking 1982 book, *Family Time and Industrial Time*, Tamara Hareven writes that the after the Lawrence strike, the threat of work stoppages "provided a convenient explanation to stockholders who viewed the welfare program as a luxury." For instance, when a stockholder confronted Agent Herman Straw and Treasurer Frederic Dumaine about the cost of Textile Field's construction, they could respond that the alternative would be to allow the Industrial Workers of the World into Manchester.[1] But the Wobblies provided more than a convenient excuse; to many Amoskeag managers, including Dumaine and Straw, the threat posed by Big Bill Haywood and the IWW was very real. If they thought otherwise, the Manchester Police Department would not have spent so much time keeping Haywood and other IWW leaders out of Manchester, nor would the department have provoked the city's Socialists and IWW sympathizers into creating the Free Speech Alliance and attempting to remove Chief Michael Healy from his job.

Beyond its benevolence programs, Amoskeag managers sought to control the company's workforce by any means possible. Its authority over Manchester's city government—as demonstrated in the Queen City Bridge episode—remained secure until 1922, and its command over the police force persisted until Amoskeag closed permanently at the end of 1935. Its widely acknowledged role in state government weakened after the 1912 elections, when the company lost its ability to influence the selection of United States senators and to control the appointment of the Manchester police chief. The election of a Republican Governor and Executive Council in 1914 solved the latter problem, as long as Amoskeag managers could continue to influence mainstream members of the New Hampshire Republican Party. Subsequent Republican majorities probably allowed the company to control debates over the reduction of the workweek, which was not reduced to 48 hours until 1937, a year after Amoskeag's formal dissolution. But passage of the Seventeenth Amendment to the Constitution in 1913 permanently removed Amoskeag's direct influence over the election of senators.

Amoskeag also became skilled at controlling its public image through local media. With the help of the *Manchester Daily Mirror and American, L'Avenir National,* and *Manchester Union,* the company extended its messages of corporate benevolence, patriotism, and anti-unionism to the public. Newspapers underreported some events that might have sparked solidarity among laborers, such as the police activities and hearings surrounding the Free Speech Alliance. Alternatively, newspapers reported other events with such bias as to signal their own solidarity with Manchester's businesses and police chief, as when they published the addresses of the city's IWW sympathizers. The *Amoskeag Bulletin* only cemented the company's ability to control its message to its workers. Established to "keep the workers posted on all the events of the mill and to serve as a liaison between the workers and the management," in the words of Daniel Creamer and Charles Coulter, the penny newspaper proved so adept at representing Amoskeag management that the city's newspapers routinely quoted from it, and even reprinted entire articles.[2]

Of course, Amoskeag's interest in controlling Manchester sometimes meant opposing, or at least not supporting, efforts to improve the city. Company management lacked enthusiasm for a playground in the Eighth Ward in part because Amoskeag owned almost no property there. Its use of city government to reject the Queen City Bridge proposal—a widely popular proposition that would have benefitted the ward as well as the city—may best be seen as a way by which to keep Manchester's second-largest employer, the W.H. McElwain Company, from growing into a serious threat to Amoskeag's control.

Amoskeag's need to control its workers and Manchester in general relates directly to the Progressive Era. The pro-union movement as represented by Jesse Markee's American Federation of Labor mouthpiece, the *Manchester Advocate,* as well as the arrival of the Industrial Workers of the World and the development of other unionizing efforts, may be the most obvious examples of the public's changed attitudes toward labor and corporations during this period. Demands for shorter working hours, a living wage, an end to child labor, and overall better living conditions further threatened Amoskeag's profitability as well as the company's image as a benevolent employer, particularly once the *Manchester Leader* opened for business.

Hareven suggests that by Frederic Dumaine's design, the Amoskeag Manufacturing Company's benevolence programs were intended to improve conditions for workers, assimilate them into American culture, and allow Amoskeag—rather than civic organizations–to take credit for those efforts. If the programs seemed progressive, Hareven writes, that is because they were inspired by the progressive movement and by the fact that some of management's goals for employees overlapped with those of the era's liberal reformers.[3] While that is true, we suggest that Dumaine was wary not only of civic organizations, but also of the intervention of the Democratic and Progressive Parties in Amoskeag's affairs. In fact, Amoskeag managers were highly partisan, partly because of their ability to influence some elements of the New Hampshire Republican Party and partly because of that party's history of support for the textile industry. They had no wish to allow worker loyalties to be diverted by interests antithetical to those of the Amoskeag Manufacturing Company. What better way to subvert the progressive reform movement than by making those reforms appear to have originated with the company itself?

Not surprisingly, citizens met Amoskeag's—and, more generally, corporate America's—attempts to control the workforce with public pressure, new media outlets, new legislation, and new government officials. Neither Manchester's Free Speech protests, which originated with Belgian cigarmakers and local

Socialists who were well informed about IWW movements and tactics in the American West, nor the less radical grassroots playground movement that began with the Eighth Ward's German and Irish families, would have been thought possible in Manchester before the start of the Progressive Era. Jesse Markee's *Manchester Advocate*, likewise, represented a new—and to Amoskeag, potentially dangerous—perspective on employer-employee relations in the city as it promised power to the city's working class. Some of that power would be found in the local labor movement, but some could also be found at the ballot box. There, voters were urged to elect anyone who would support Manchester's workers—whether those men were Republicans like Thomas Chalmers or Democrats who might support Henry Hollis for United States Senator. The *Manchester Leader*'s origins were less rooted in the working class, given Robert Bass's intentions in financing the newspaper, but Frank Knox and John Muehling definitely aimed to educate the reading public about progressivism in an effort to eliminate social ills, even if they eventually came to serve the city's business interests as well.

As awareness of the city's social problems grew, critics blamed corporations and their tendency to attract and recruit immigrant laborers and to pay them poorly for their work. At the same time, some observers blamed immigrants themselves—particularly those from Eastern and Southern Europe—for a lack of patience and a penchant for anarchism, violence, and terrorism. Thus, in addition to Amoskeag's efforts to improve immigrant lives through social programs (not to mention the Manchester Police Department's surveillance of the city's Greek community), the company focused on Americanization programs. Flag Day and the giant flag sewn by operatives in Mill No. 11 in 1914, and the earlier decision to fly American flags on all Amoskeag buildings (as well as in the company playground) are just three examples of Amoskeag's use of the American flag to promote patriotism and otherwise assimilate immigrant workers. Other efforts included the ATC's English classes, bowling and basketball leagues, cooking classes, the Manufacturers League, and the construction or renovation of the Rock Rimmon and Textile Field baseball grounds.

Baseball was especially important to Amoskeag managers. It was a popular game in Manchester in 1912 and 1913, thanks in no small measure to the success of the Boston Red Sox. It was thought to be an "Americanizing" game, not only for the players, but for those who watched it as well. Amoskeag employees who watched the games would automatically take a rooting interest in their own team, management believed, thereby strengthening their ties to the corporation. Besides, baseball represented a diversion that kept workers from spending free time in less productive pursuits, such as joining radical political parties and labor unions. Together, these facts—along with the threat of the IWW and

Conclusion: Textile Field and the Progressive Movement

Amoskeag's ability to publicize its progressive benevolence—seemingly made the $30,000 investment in Textile Field's construction worthwhile.

For the Amoskeag Manufacturing Company to ensure loyalty among its employees, company managers had to remain in control of baseball, particularly Textile Field. Local media depicted Textile Field as a professional-caliber stadium, more impressive than anything in New England outside of the Boston area. Games against the regular lineups of the Boston Red Sox and Philadelphia Athletics were meant to reinforce that professionalism, as were the efforts of league teams to hire ringers for their rosters and, in Amoskeag's case, to attract other major-league, minor-league, and top-tier independent teams for exhibitions. In the eyes of Amoskeag's William McKay and W. Parker Straw, only two factors threatened to undermine the game in Manchester: the constant bickering among players and umpires—contrary to the spirit of the baseball creed—and the coming of the New England League to Manchester.

The New England League was the greater of these two problems. Admittedly, the league appealed to the city's merchants and professionals as opposed to its blue-collar workers, and in that way does not appear to have been a threat to Amoskeag. But if the minor league were allowed a foothold in Manchester, the Amoskeag Manufacturing Company's control over baseball was not assured. Amoskeag's efforts to control the league can be interpreted in two ways: a sincere, paternalistic desire to protect Manchester residents from what management

Gill Stadium, formerly Textile Field, in 2016 (Scott Roper).

thought was a corrupt, unstable baseball league; or, as with other benevolence programs, a need for the company to take credit for the game's continued existence in the city. In all likelihood, both were true. Amoskeag management's rejection of the league in favor of the failed Northeastern League in 1913, its rejection and eventual quasi-acceptance (though not on Saturdays) of Fred Lake's team in Textile Field in 1914, its attempt to forge a relationship with the Federal League in 1915, and its efforts to work with Tom Keady and Jack Kiernan later that year suggest both motivations.

Unfortunately for the Amoskeag Manufacturing Company, baseball did not have the desired effect. Economic problems that emerged with the start of World War I, coupled with immigrant concerns about the effects of the war on their countries of origin, made baseball nothing more than an unnecessary diversion. Besides, most adult immigrants do not seem to have cared about the game, many preferring soccer instead. Their children were more likely to enjoy baseball, even if economic conditions prevented them from attending many local games. Among this group, though, baseball failed to prevent labor discord. In fact, many who had picked up the game before and during the 1912–1916 period entered the local factories in the 1920s. Most of those workers participated in or supported the strikes of 1922 and the early- and mid–1930s.

Many of the problems faced by Manchester residents and corporations in the Progressive Era echo today in the United States. As union representation declines and wealth disparity expands, the working and middle classes increasingly are faced with a possibility of living in poverty without the protection of a social safety net. Politicians wearing American flag lapel pins use conservative and liberal media to spread time-worn arguments about immigration, free trade, minimum wage, the need to expand or scale back Social Security, and even the supposed benefits of repealing the Seventeenth Amendment to the Constitution.[4] Like the most affluent companies and individual "titans of industry" in the early 1900s, today's corporations and the super-rich have an inordinate say in American politics. National obsessions with entertainment, sports, and celebrity culture may serve in the role that Amoskeag managers had hoped for baseball, while grassroots political movements have managed to tap into voter discontent with the country's current social, political, and economic situation.

In short, we seem to have forgotten about the poor social and economic conditions that existed prior to the Progressive Era, conditions that nearly resulted in class revolution in the early twentieth century. By reflecting on the causes and effects of the Lawrence Bread and Roses Strike and the relationship between labor and capital in Manchester, perhaps we can re-learn the lessons of the past to help us better understand the problems of the contemporary United States.

Chapter Notes

Preface

1. Daniel Creamer and Charles W. Coulter, *Labor and the Shut Down of the Amoskeag Textile Mills* (Philadelphia: Works Projects Administration, National Research Project, 1939); Tamara K. Hareven, *Family Time and Industrial Time: The Relationship Between the Family and Work in a New England Industrial Community* (Lanham, MD: University Press of America, 1993); Hareven and Randolph Langenbach, *Amoskeag: Life and Work in an American Factory-City* (Hanover, NH: University Press of New England, 1978); Arthur M. Kenison, *Dumaine's Amoskeag: Let the Record Speak* (Manchester, NH: Saint Anselm College Press, 1997); Andrea Tone, *The Business of Benevolence: Industrial Paternalism in Progressive America* (Ithaca, NY: Cornell University Press, 1997).

2. Joseph A. Conforti, *Imagining New England: Explorations of Regional Identity from the Pilgrims to the Mid–Twentieth Century* (Chapel Hill: The University of North Carolina Press, 2001), 316.

3. Ardis Cameron, *Radicals of the Worst Sort: Laboring Women in Lawrence, Massachusetts, 1860–1912* (Urbana: University of Illinois Press, 1993); Philip S. Foner, *History of the Labor Movement in the United States, vol. IV: The Industrial Workers of the World 1905–1917* (New York: International Publishers, 1965); Robert Paul McCaffery, *Islands of Deutschtum: German-Americans in Manchester, New Hampshire and Lawrence, Massachusetts, 1870–1942* (New York: Peter Lang, Inc., 1997); Patrick Renshaw, *The Wobblies: The Story of the IWW and Syndicalism in the United States*, updated edition (Chicago: Ivan R. Dee, Publisher, 1999; originally published 1967); Gary Samson, *A World Within a World: Manchester, the Mills, and the Immigrant Experience* (Dover, NH: Arcadia Publishing, 1995); Bruce Watson, *Bread and Roses: Mills, Migrants, and the Struggle for the American Dream* (New York: Viking, 2005).

4. Nancy Coffey Heffernan and Ann Page Stecker, *New Hampshire: Crosscurrents in Its Development*, updated edition (Hanover, NH: University Press of New England, 1996); Ronald Jager and Grace Jager, *New Hampshire: An Illustrated History of the Granite State* (Woodland Hills, CA: Windsor Publications, Inc., 1983); James Wright, *The Progressive Yankees: Republican Reformers in New Hampshire, 1906–1916* (Hanover, NH: University Press of New England, 1987).

5. Steven A. Riess, *Touching Base: Professional Baseball and American Culture in the Progressive Era*, Revised Edition (Urbana,: University of Illinois Press, 1999); Roy Rosenzweig, *Eight Hours for What We Will: Workers and Leisure in an Industrial City, 1870–1920* (New York: Cambridge University Press, 1983); Dorothy Seymour Mills and Harold Seymour, *Baseball: The People's Game* (New York: Oxford University Press, 1990), 213–57.

6. Michael Gershman, *Diamonds: The Evolution of the Ballpark* (Boston: Houghton Mifflin Company, 1993); Bruce Kuklick, *To Every Thing a Season: Shibe Park and Urban Philadelphia, 1909–1976* (Princeton, NJ: Princeton University Press, 1991); Neil J. Sullivan, *The Diamond in the Bronx: Yankee Stadium and the Politics of New York* (New York: Oxford University Press, 2001).

7. Charlie Bevis, *The New England League: A Baseball History, 1885–1949* (Jefferson, NC: McFarland, 2008), 140–168; Neil J. Sullivan,

The Minors: The Struggles and the Triumph of Baseball's Poor Relation from 1876 to the Present (New York: St. Martin's Press, 1990), 57–65; Harold Seymour and Dorothy Seymour Mills, *Baseball: The Golden Age* (New York: Oxford University Press, 1971), 196–213.

Introduction

1. *Amoskeag Bulletin*, April 15, 1913, May 1, 1913; *Manchester Daily Mirror and American*, April 3, 1913.
2. George Waldo Browne, *The Amoskeag Manufacturing Company of Manchester, New Hampshire: A History* (Manchester, NH: Amoskeag Manufacturing Company, 1915), 168; *Manchester Daily Mirror and American* April 3, 1913.
3. Tone, *The Business of Benevolence*, 6–9, 17.
4. Hareven, *Family Time and Industrial Time*, 12; Hareven and Langenbach, *Amoskeag*, 10.
5. Hareven and Langenbach, *Amoskeag*, 9–10 (quoted). See also Hareven, *Family Time and Industrial Time*, 12–13; Langenbach, "Amoskeag Millyard Remembered," *Historic Preservation* 27:3 (1975), 36–29; Langenbach, "The Amoskeag Millyard, An Epic in Urban Design," *Harvard Alumni Bulletin* 70 (April 13, 1968), 21–28, via Conservationtech.com, http://www.conservationtech.com/RL's%20resume&%20pub's/RL-publications/Milltowns/1968-HARVbulletin/HarvBulletin.htm, last accessed July 13, 2008; Langenbach, "Lost City on the Merrimack," *The Boston Globe Sunday Magazine* March 9, 1969, via Conservationtech.com, http://www.conservationtech.com/RL's%20resume&%20pub's/RL-publications/Milltowns/1969-AMOSKEAG(Globe).htm, last accessed July 13, 2008.
6. Samson, *A World Within a World*, 38–39; Hareven and Langenbach, *Amoskeag*, 15; Hareven, *Family Time and Industrial Time*, 10.
7. Grace Holbrook Blood, *Manchester on the Merrimack: The Story of a City*, revised edition (Manchester, NH: Manchester Historic Association, 1975), 111–12; Samson, *A World Within a World*, 38–39; Hareven, *Family Time and Industrial Time*, 13–14.
8. Browne, *The Amoskeag Manufacturing Company*, 140; Hareven, *Family Time and Industrial Time*, 9–10, 15–20, 120–22; Samson, *A World Within a World*, 37, 51–54; Creamer and Coulter, 154–63; Paul E. Rivard, *A New Order of Things: How the Textile Industry Transformed New England* (Hanover: University Press of New England, 2002), 122.
9. Hareven, *Family Time and Industrial Time*, 14.
10. Robert P. Bass, letter to Joseph M. Dixon, October 3, 1912 (Bass Papers, Dartmouth College).
11. Robert Macieski, "'Before Their Time': Lewis W. Hine and the New Hampshire Crusade gainst Child Labor," *Historical New Hampshire* 55 (2000), 94 (quoted), 96–97, 101–03; Macieski, *Picturing Class: Lewis W. Hine Photographs Child Labor in New England* (Amherst: University of Massachusetts Press, 2015), 66–74; J. Wright, *The Progressive Yankees*, xv.
12. "New England Conferences to Promote Rural Progress," *The Survey* 30 (April 1913), 55–56 (55 quoted); Riess, *Touching Base*, 6–7.
13. Tone, *The Business of Benevolence*, 6, 17.
14. J. Wright, *The Progressive Yankees*, 86.
15. J. Wright, *The Progressive Yankees*, 94, 112–15; Heffernan and Stecker, *New Hampshire*, 165; Jager and Jager, *New Hampshire*, 63.
16. Creamer and Coulter, *Labor and the Shut Down of the Amoskeag Textile Mills*, 8.
17. Kenison, *Dumaine's Amoskeag*, 6, 17, 33; Samson, *A World Within a World*, 26.
18. Kenison, *Dumaine's Amoskeag*, 31–32; Creamer and Coulter, *Labor*, 16–23, 39, 43–44.
19. Browne, *The Amoskeag Manufacturing Company*, 130–31; Creamer and Coulter, *Labor*, 172; Hareven, *Family Time and Industrial Time*, 40–43.
20. Quoted in Foner, *History of the Labor Movement in the United States*, 33.
21. Roy Rosenzweig, , *Eight Hours for What We Will*, 148, 160; Dorothy Seymour Mills and Harold Seymour, *Baseball: The People's Game*, 213–35; Tone, *The Business of Benevolence*, 66–98.
22. "The Finest Answer to I.W.W.-ism," *The Square Deal* 17 (December 1915), 139–41; see also *The Sunday Standard* July 5, 1914.
23. Tone, *The Business of Benevolence*, 3.

Chapter 1

1. Watson, *Bread and Roses*, 12–17; 50–51; 73.
2. See, for example, *Manchester Daily Mirror and American* January 13, 1912, January 30, 1912; *Manchester Union* January 13, 1912, January 15, 1912.
3. *L'Avenir National* January 19, 1912.
4. *L'Avenir National* January 20, 1912.
5. *Manchester Union* January 30, 1912; *Manchester Daily Mirror and American* January 30, 1912; Watson, *Bread and Roses*, 106–15.
6. *Manchester Daily Mirror and American* January 31, 1912; *Manchester Union* January 15, 1912.

7. See, for example, *L'Avenir National* January 31, 1912, February 27, 1912, February 28, 1912, March 27, 1912, April 3, 1912. For the Clergy's position, see *Manchester Daily Mirror and American* March 14, 1912.

8. *Manchester Daily Mirror and American* January 30, 1912.

9. *Manchester Union* January 30, 1912.

10. Creamer and Coulter, *Labor*, 173; *Manchester Daily Mirror and American* January 25, 1912, January 30, 1912. The number of unions operating in Manchester in 1912 is taken from a list in *The Manchester City Directory* (1912).

11. *Manchester Daily Mirror and American* February 1, 1912.

12. *Manchester Union* January 26, 1912.

13. *Manchester Daily Mirror and American* January 27, 1912.

14. *L'Avenir National* January 30, 1912.

15. *L'Avenir National* January 31, 1912; *Manchester Daily Mirror and American* January 31, 1912.

16. Renshaw, *The Wobblies*, 105.

17. Hareven and Langenbach, *Amoskeag*, 78–79, 133.

18. *Manchester City Directory* 1888–1937; *Manchester Leader and Evening Union* March 8, 1937 (evening edition), March 9, 1937 (morning edition).

19. *Manchester Union* September 8, 1899; *Manchester Leader and Evening Union* March 8, 1937 (evening edition).

20. Creamer and Coulter, *Labor*, 172–75, 181–89; Hareven, *Family Time and Industrial Time*, 46–47; The Police Record (Complaint Books), 1868–1925, of the Police Department, City of Manchester, New Hampshire, Volume 6 (October 4, 1910–July 1, 1912), see July 1, 1911 through June 30, 1912; Mark Kelleher, "'The Efficiency Expert as Corporate Father': Mismanagement of the Amoskeag Manufacturing Company, 1906–1935" (Unpublished manuscript, Saint Anselm College, 1984), 27.

21. United States Department of Labor, *Report on the Strike of Textile Workers in Lawrence, Mass. In 1912* (Washington: Government Printing Office, 1912) 189–201.

22. Creamer and Coulter, *Labor*, 168.

23. *Manchester Union* July 12, 1905.

24. *Manchester Union* July 12, 1905, July 13, 1905.

25. *Manchester Union* July 13, 1905.

Chapter 2

1. Ora Pearl McGill, letter to Eliza and James McGill, January 6, 1912.

2. Kate Rousmaniere, "The Short, Radical Life of Pearl McGill." *Labor: Studies in Working-Class History of the Americas* 6:3 (2009), 9–19, 11–16; McGill, letter to Eliza and James McGill, March 5, 1912.

3. Elizabeth Gurley Flynn, *The Rebel Girl—An Autobiography: My First Life (1906–1926)* (New York: International Publishers, 1994; originally published 1955), 132; McGill, letters to Eliza and James McGill, January 11, 1912, March 5, 1912; Rousmaniere, "The Short, Radical Life of Pearl McGill," 11–16.

4. Flynn, *The Rebel Girl*, 127; Renshaw, *The Wobblies*, 99; Cameron, *Radicals of the Worst Sort*, 121–22.

5. *Manchester Daily Mirror and American* April 30, 1912, October 31, 1912; *Boston Daily Globe* October 31, 1912.

6. *Manchester Union* February 2, 1912; *L'Avenir National* February 1–2, 1912; *Manchester Daily Mirror and American* February 2, 1912.

7. *L'Avenir National* February 1–2, 1912; *Manchester Union* February 2, 1912; *Manchester Daily Mirror and American* February 2, 1912, February 19, 1912.

8. *Manchester Union* February 2–3, 1912; *L'Avenir National* February 2, 1912; *Manchester Daily Mirror and American* February 2, 1912.

9. Melvyn Dubofsky, *We Shall Be All: A History of the Industrial Workers of the World*, ed. Joseph A. McCartin (Chicago: University of Illinois Press, 2000), 98–113; Renshaw, *The Wobblies*, 84–95.

10. Dubofsky, *We Shall Be All*, 102–03.

11. *The Industrial Worker* March 21, 1912.

12. Dubofsky, *We Shall Be All*, 137–140; Renshaw, *The Wobblies*, 43–74; Watson, *Bread and Roses*, 91–96.

13. *L'Avenir National* February 1, 1912; *Manchester Daily Mirror and American* February 2, 1912; *Manchester Union* February 5, 1912; Watson, *Bread and Roses*, 91.

14. *Manchester Daily Mirror and American* April 30, 1912.

15. *Manchester Daily Mirror and American* February 2, 1912; *Manchester Union* February 3, 1912.

16. *Manchester Union* February 5, 1912.

17. McGill, letter to Eliza McGill and "Home Folks," March 5, 1912.

18. *Manchester Daily Mirror and American* February 15, 1912.

19. *Manchester Daily Mirror and American* February 2, 1912; *Manchester Union* February 3, 1912, February 5, 1912. In his autobiography, Bill Haywood noted that he traveled throughout New England during the Bread and Roses

Strike in an effort to raise money and awareness, and in some cases he was forced to travel incognito to avoid arrest by police who feared his influence. However, he did not mention specifically to which cities he traveled during the strike. William D. Haywood, *Bill Haywood's Book: The Autobiography of William D. Haywood* (New York: International Publishers, 1958 [1929]), 253.

20. *The Industrial Worker* July 25, 1912.
21. *Manchester Daily Mirror and American* February 19, 1912.
22. *Manchester Union* February 19, 1912; *Manchester Daily Mirror and American* February 19, 1912; *The Industrial Worker* February 29, 1912.
23. *Manchester Daily Mirror and American* February 19, 1912.
24. *Manchester Union* February 19, 1912; *Manchester Daily Mirror and American* February 19, 1912.
25. *Manchester Union* February 20, 1912.
26. *The Industrial Worker* February 29, 1912.
27. *Manchester Union* February 20, 1912.
28. *L'Avenir National* February 10, 1912.
29. *Nashua Telegraph* February 8, 1912.
30. The Police Record (Complaint Books), 1868–1925, of the Police Department, City of Manchester, New Hampshire, Volume 6 (October 4, 1910–July 1, 1912), see February 23, 1912.
31. *Manchester Union* February 21, 1912, February 24, 1912; *Manchester Daily Mirror and American* February 24, 1912.
32. *The Industrial Worker* March 7, 1912.

Chapter 3

1. *The Industrial Worker* February 29, 1912, March 7, 1912.
2. *Manchester Daily Mirror and American* February 9, 1912.
3. *Le Canado-Americain* March 4, 1912.
4. See, for example, *Manchester Daily Mirror and American* February 12, 1912, February 15, 1912 (quoted); *Le Canado-Americain* February 19, 1912, March 4, 1912.
5. David J. Goldberg, *A Tale of Three Cities: Labor Organization and Protest in Paterson, Passaic, and Lawrence, 1916–1921* (New Brunswick, NJ: Rutgers University Press, 1989), 92.
6. Cameron, *Radicals of the Worst Sort*, 121.
7. *Manchester Daily Mirror and American* February 19, 1912.
8. Cameron, *Radicals of the Worst Sort*, 120.

9. See Chalmers's letter to the editor in the *Manchester Advocate*, October 15, 1914.
10. *L'Avenir National* March 9, 1912; *Manchester Daily Mirror and American* March 13, 1912; Dubofsky, *We Shall Be All*, 147; Watson, *Bread and Roses*, 143–45, 159, 201; Flynn, *The Rebel Girl*, 136–137.
11. Cameron, *Radicals of the Worst Sort*, 143.
12. Dubofsky, *We Shall Be All*, 148–49; *Manchester Daily Mirror and American* February 23, 1912 (quoted).
13. Samuel Evans, ed., *History of Wapello County, Iowa, Volume One* (Chicago: SJ Clarke Publishing Company, 1914), 229; Evans, *History of Wapello County, Iowa, and Representative Citizens* (Chicago: Biographical Publishing Company, 1901), 140; United States Department of Commerce, Bureau of the Census, Census manuscript sheets for Toledo, OH (1900), ProQuest, *HeritageQuest Online*, http://heritagequestonline.com, last accessed April 26, 2013; Iowa GenWeb Project, "Wilton History 1854–1947: Wilton Press," http://iagenweb.org/muscatine/wiltonhistory/wiltonpress.htm, last accessed September 24, 2012; Jennings/Gray Genealogy, "Jesse Markee Mattie J. Hicks," http://royandsharon.lifegrid.com/MARKEE,%20Jesse.htm, last accessed September 24, 2012.
14. *Manchester City Directory* (1909), 426; *The Typographical Journal* 39 (July 1911), 71.
15. *The Typographical Journal* 40 (May 1912), 611.
16. J. Wright, *The Progressive Yankees*, 130.
17. Robert P. Bass, letter to Frank Knox, January 16, 1912.
18. J. Wright, *The Progressive Yankees*, 59–60, 70, 74, 180–81; Blood, 304–05.
19. Robert P. Bass, letter to Frank Knox, January 16, 1912; Knox, letters to Bass, January 9, 1923 and January 23, 1912; John F. Bass, telegraph to Robert P. Bass, August 15, 1912; Blood, *Manchester on the Merrimack*, 301–05; Kevin Cash, *Who the Hell Is William Loeb?* (Manchester, NH: Amoskeag Press, 1975), 23–25.
20. George Remick, letter to Robert P. Bass, September 9, 1912.
21. Hareven and Langenbach, *Amoskeag*, 295.
22. Coulter and Creamer, *Labor*, 173.
23. The Police Record (Complaint Books), 1868–1925, of the Police Department, City of Manchester, New Hampshire, Volume 6 (October 4, 1910–July 1, 1912), see March 5, 1912; *Manchester Daily Mirror and American* March 6, 1912.
24. *Manchester Daily Mirror and American* February 19, 1912.

25. Watson, *Bread and Roses*, 159, 201; *Manchester Daily Mirror and American* March 9, 1912.
26. *Manchester Daily Mirror and American* February 3, 1912.
27. *The Typographical Journal* 40 (May 1912), 611 (quoted); Coulter and Creamer, *Labor*, 173–74; *Manchester Daily Mirror and American* April 2, 1912.
28. *Manchester Union* April 3, 1912.
29. *Manchester Daily Mirror and American* March 19, 1912 (quoted); *L'Avenir National* March 19, 1912, April 1, 1912; Hareven, *Family Time and Industrial Time*, 48.
30. *Manchester Daily Mirror and American* April 30, 1912; *Manchester Union* February 20, 1912, April 29, 1912, April 30, 1912.

Chapter 4

1. *Manchester Daily Mirror and American* April 12, 1912, May 1, 1912.
2. Gershman, *Diamonds*, 85–104; Kuklick, *To Every Thing a Season*, 25–26; Glenn Stout, *Fenway 1912: The Birth of a Ballpark, a Championship Season, and Fenway's Remarkable First Year* (Boston: Houghton Mifflin Hardcourt, 2011), 29–30.
3. Pete Palmer and Gary Gillette, editors, *The Baseball Encyclopedia* (New York: Barnes and Noble Books, 2004), 1189; Marshall D. Wright, *Nineteenth Century Baseball: Year-by-Year Statistics for the Major League Teams, 1871 through 1900* (Jefferson, NC: McFarland, 1996), 109.
4. *Manchester Daily Mirror and American* April 11, 1912.
5. Palmer and Gillette, eds., *The Baseball Encyclopedia*, 1189; David Nemec, *The Beer and Whiskey League: The Illustrated History of the American Association—Baseball's Renegade Major League* (Guilford, CT: The Lyon Press, 2004), 102; M. Wright, *Nineteenth Century Baseball*, 109.
6. *Manchester Union* September 1–7, 1899 (quoted); *Manchester Mirror and Daily American* September 1–7, 1899.
7. Bevis, *The New England League*, 108.
8. Ray Robinson, *Matty: An American Hero* (New York: Oxford University Press, 1993), 23–24; Philip Seib, *The Player: Christy Mathewson, Baseball, and the American Century* (New York: Four Walls Eight Windows, 2003), 15–16.
9. *Manchester Daily Mirror and American* April 12–27, 1901.
10. *Manchester Daily Mirror and American* September 8, 1902; Lloyd Johnson and Miles Wolff, eds., *The Encyclopedia of Minor League Baseball: The Official Record of Minor League Baseball* (Durham, NC: Baseball America, Inc., 1993), 104.
11. *Manchester Daily Mirror and American* September 11, 1903, July 20, 1905.
12. *Manchester Daily Mirror and American* July 19, 1905; *Manchester Union* September 6, 1899.
13. For more on the seasons of the Manchester, Goffstown, and Exeter teams, see *Manchester Union* April 1–June 15, 1912; *Manchester Daily Mirror and American* April 1–June 15, 1912.
14. Riess, *Touching Base*, 7; see also Mitchell Nathanson, "Gatekeepers of Americana: Ownership's Never-Ending Quest for Control of the Baseball Creed," *NINE: A Journal of Baseball History and Culture* 15 (Fall 2006), 68–87, 73.
15. Clarence Jenkins, "America's Game: A Study of Baseball Fiction from the Gilded Age Through the Progressive Era," *NINE: A Journal of Baseball History and Social Policy Perspectives* 6 (1998), 49–60.
16. Albert G. Spalding, *America's National Game* (San Francisco: Halo Books, 1991; originally published New York: American Sports Publishing Company, 1911), 3, 6–7.
17. *L'Avenir National* April 22, 1912.
18. The Police Record (Complaint Books), 1868–1925, of the Police Department, City of Manchester, New Hampshire, Volume 6 (October 4, 1910–July 1, 1912), see January 1, 1912, through June 30, 1912.
19. *Manchester Daily Mirror and American* May 16, 1912.
20. *Manchester Daily Mirror and American* May 23, 1912, May 28, 1912; *L'Avenir National* May 28, 1912.
21. *Manchester Daily Mirror and American* May 31, 1912.
22. *Manchester Daily Mirror and American* June 3, 1912, June 6–8, 1912; *L'Avenir National* June 6, 1912.
23. Amoskeag Manufacturing Company Employee Records for Ernest Bond, Bill Donovan, Albert Greager, and Willard Taber, Manchester Historic Association, Manchester, New Hampshire; United States Department of Commerce, Bureau of the Census, Census manuscript sheets for Manchester, NH, Ward Nine (1910), ProQuest, *HeritageQuest Online*, http://heritagequestonline.com, last accessed April 26, 2013.
24. *Manchester Daily Mirror and American* June 17, 1912.

25. *L'Avenir National* June 15, 1912, June 17, 1912; *Manchester Daily Mirror and American* June 17, 1912.
26. *Manchester Daily Mirror and American* June 11, 1912.
27. Coulter and Creamer, *Labor*, 174; Browne, *The Amoskeag Manufacturing Company*, 163–166 (quoted); *Manchester Daily Mirror and American* August 9, 1912; *Boston Globe* August 13, 1912.
28. Browne, *The Amoskeag Manufacturing Company*, 169–70.
29. Coulter and Creamer, *Labor*, 179.
30. Browne, *The Amoskeag Manufacturing Company*, 166–70.
31. *Manchester Daily Mirror and American* September 21, 1912.
32. *Manchester Union* July 9, 1912; *Manchester Daily Mirror and American* July 1, 1912, July 8, 1912, July 15, 1912, July 22, 1912.
33. *Manchester Daily Mirror and American* September 3, 1912, September 9, 1913, September 16, 1912.
34. *Manchester Daily Mirror and American* June 12, 1912, September 21, 1912, September 23, 1912.

Chapter 5

1. *Boston Globe* October 9, 1912.
2. Glenn Stout and Richard A. Johnson, *Red Sox Century: One Hundred Years of Red Sox Baseball* (Boston: Houghton Mifflin Company, 2000), 85.
3. *New York Times* October 10, 1912.
4. *Boston Globe* October 10, 1912, *New York Times* October 10, 1912.
5. *New York Times* October 10, 1912.
6. *Manchester Leader* October 10, 1912.
7. *L'Avenir National* October 9, 1912.
8. J. Wright, *The Progressive Yankees*, 136.
9. *Manchester Leader* October 10, 1912.
10. *Manchester Advocate* October 25, 1912.
11. *Manchester Leader* October 31, 1912; *Boston Journal* October 31, 1912, clipping in the "Free Speech" file, Robert P. Bass Papers.
12. *Boston Journal* October 31, 1912.
13. *Manchester Leader* October 31, 1912.
14. *Boston Journal* October 31, 1912; *Boston Globe* October 31, 1912; *Boston Herald*, date unknown, clipping in the "Free Speech" file, Robert P. Bass Papers.
15. *Manchester Daily Mirror and American* October 28, 1912.
16. *Manchester Daily Mirror and American* November 1, 1912.
17. *Manchester Daily Mirror and American* October 28, 1912.
18. *Manchester Leader* October 31, 1912.
19. *Manchester Advocate* October 25, 1912, November 1, 1912.
20. J. Wright, *The Progressive Yankees*, 143–44; *Manual for the General Court 1913* (State of New Hampshire: Concord, NH, 1913), 100–03; Thomas Chalmers, "The Influence of the Revolution of the Religious Life of America, *The Granite Monthly* 48 (July 1916), 193–96 (196 quoted).

Chapter 6

1. Dubofsky, *We Shall Be All*, 148–149.
2. Ibid., 60.
3. Rousmaniere, "The Short, Radical Life of Pearl McGill," 16.
4. *Nashua Telegraph* June 18, 1913.
5. Creamer and Coulter, *Labor*, 182.
6. *L'Avenir National* November 8, 1912.
7. *Manchester Leader* November 11, 1912.
8. *Manchester Daily Mirror and American* June 11, 1880, March 28–April 22, 1891, May 4, 1891, May 30, 1894.
9. *Manchester Daily Mirror and American* October 18, 1912; *Manchester Union* June 11, 1912.
10. *Manchester Daily Mirror and American* November 15, 1912.
11. *Manchester Daily Mirror and American* November 14, 1912.
12. *Manchester Daily Mirror and American* November 15, 1912.
13. *Manchester Daily Mirror and American* November 21–22, 1912.
14. *Manchester Daily Mirror and American* November 15, 1912.
15. *Manchester Daily Mirror and American* November 22, 1912.
16. *Manchester Advocate* November 22, 1912. *Manchester Leader*, December 24, 1912.
17. *Manual for the General Court 1913*, 77.
18. *Amoskeag Bulletin* December 2, 1912.
19. Coulter and Creamer, *Labor*, 181.
20. *Amoskeag Bulletin* December 2, 1912.
21. *Manchester Daily Mirror and American* December 6, 1912.
22. *Manchester Daily Mirror and American* December 10, 1912.
23. *L'Avenir National* December 4, 1912.
24. *Manchester Advocate* December 20, 1912.
25. *L'Avenir National* December 10, 1912; *Manchester Daily Mirror and American* December 10, 1912.

26. *Amoskeag Bulletin* December 6, 1912.
27. *Manchester Daily Mirror and American* December 17, 1912, December 21, 1912; *Manchester Leader* December 20, 1912.
28. *Manchester Daily Mirror and American* December 27, 1912.
29. *Manchester Daily Mirror and American* December 28, 1912 (quoted); *Manchester Leader* December 30, 1912.
30. *Manchester Leader* December 30, 1912; *Manchester Daily Mirror and American* December 30, 1912; *L'Avenir National* December 31, 1912.
31. *Manchester Daily Mirror and American* December 30, 1912.
32. *Manchester Leader* December 30, 1912.
33. *Manchester Daily Mirror and American* December 30, 1912; *L'Avenir National* December 31, 1912; *Manchester Leader* December 30, 1912.
34. United States Department of Commerce, Bureau of the Census, *Thirteenth Census of the United States: Population—General Report and Analysis* (Washington, D.C.: Government Printing Office, 1913) 1282.
35. *Amoskeag Bulletin* January 1, 1913.
36. *Manchester Daily Mirror and American* January 18, 1913.
37. *Manchester Daily Mirror and American* January 9, 1913.
38. *Manchester Daily Mirror and American* January 13, 1913, January 17, 1913.
39. *L'Avenir National* January 22–24, 1913; *Manchester Daily Mirror and American* January 21, 1913; January 24, 1913; *Amoskeag Bulletin* February 1, 1913.
40. *Manchester Daily Mirror and American* January 3, 1913, January 9, 1913, January 27, 1913.
41. *L'Avenir National* February 1, 1913; *Manchester Daily Mirror and American* January 29, 1913, January 30, 1913.
42. *Amoskeag Bulletin* February 1, 1913. For more on the Northeastern League and its battle with the New England League, see Bevis, *The New England League*, 142–43.

Chapter 7

1. *Manchester Daily Mirror and American* January 28, 1913; J. Wright, *The Progressive Yankees*, 144–45.
2. J. Wright, *The Progressive Yankees*, 45.
3. *Manchester Advocate* October 25, 1912.
4. *Nashua Telegraph* March 18, 1913; United States Department of Commerce, Bureau of the Census, Census manuscript sheets for Manchester, NH, Ward Three (1910), ProQuest, *HeritageQuest Online*, http://heritagequestonline.com, last accessed April 26, 2013.
5. J. Wright, *The Progressive Yankees*, 144.
6. Creamer and Coulter, *Labor*, 43–45; Kenison, *Dumaine's Amoskeag*, 32–33.
7. *Manual for the General Court 1897* (Concord, NH: Edward N. Pearson, Public Printer, 1897), 40–41; *Manual for the General Court 1913*; *Journal of the House of Representatives of the State of New Hampshire* (Concord, NH: The Rumford Printing Company, 1913); John A. Riddle, William M. Patten, Quincy Barnard, Arthur W. Holbrook, and Gordon Woodbury, *History of the Town of Bedford, New Hampshire, from 1737* (Concord, NH: The Rumford Printing Company, 1903), 1120–21; *Nashua Telegraph* March 18, 1913; Blood, *Manchester on the Merrimack*, 304.
8. *Manchester Advocate* March 24, 1913.
9. *Manchester Advocate* March 24, 1913; *Manchester Daily Mirror and American* April 10, 1913; State of New Hampshire, *Journal...*, 910.
10. Charlie Bevis, *Sunday Baseball: The Major Leagues' Struggles to Play Baseball on the Lord's Day, 1876–1934* (Jefferson, NC: McFarland, 2003), 149.
11. *Manchester Daily Mirror and American* February 27, 1913.
12. *Manchester Daily Mirror and American* February 24, 1913; April 1, 1913; April 7, 1913.
13. *L'Avenir National* February 12, 1913; *Amoskeag Bulletin* February 15, 1913.
14. *Manchester Daily Mirror and American* February 6, 1913; *Amoskeag Bulletin* February 15, 1913; *L'Avenir National* February 18, 1913.
15. Amoskeag Manufacturing Company Employee Record for Willard G. Taber.
16. *L'Avenir National* February 14, 1913.
17. Amoskeag Manufacturing Company Employee Record for Emil Pernod.
18. *L'Avenir National* February 21, 1913, February 26, 1913.
19. *Manchester Daily Mirror and American* February 10, 1913, February 25, 1913.
20. *Manchester Leader* May 13, 1913.
21. Thomas Chalmers, writing in the *Manchester Advocate*, December 26, 1913.
22. *Manchester Daily Mirror and American* November 21, 1912; December 17, 1912 (quoted).
23. *Portsmouth Herald* December 18, 1912.
24. *Supplement to the Public Statutes and Session Laws of New Hampshire* (Concord, NH: Arthur H. Chase, William D. Chandler, 1914), 553.
25. *Manchester Leader* May 13, 1913.
26. *Manchester Leader* May 23, 1913.

27. *Manchester Leader* June 5, 1913.
28. *Manchester Advocate* August 29, 1913.
29. *Manchester Daily Mirror and American* April 10, 1913; *Journal of the House of Representatives...*, 911–12.
30. *Journal of the House of Representatives...*, 939.
31. *Nashua Telegraph* March 18, 1913.
32. *Manchester Daily Mirror and American* April 14, 1913.
33. *Manchester Daily Mirror and American* April 14, 1913; *Manchester Daily Mirror and American* April 17, 1913.
34. *Manchester Daily Mirror and American* April 17, 1913; *Nashua Telegraph* March 18, 1913.
35. *Manchester Daily Mirror and American* April 18, 1913.
36. "Editor and Publisher's Notes," *The Granite Monthly* 48 (August 1916), 256.
37. United States Department of Commerce, Bureau of the Census, Census manuscript sheets for Manchester, NH, Ward Three (1920), ProQuest, *HeritageQuest Online*, http://heritagequestonline.com, last accessed April 26, 2013.

Chapter 8

1. *Amoskeag Bulletin* March 1, 1913.
2. Gershman, *Diamonds*, 55–59, 109.
3. Kuklick, *To Every Thing a Season*, 25; Riess, *Touching Base*, 114–17; Harold Seymour and Dorothy Seymour Mills, *Baseball: The Golden Age*, 49–51.
4. The Police Record (Complaint Books), 1868–1925, of the Police Department, City of Manchester, New Hampshire, Volume 6 (October 4, 1910–July 1, 1912), see July 1, 1911–June 30, 1912.
5. Gershman, *Diamonds*, 85–92; Kuklick, *To Every Thing a Season* 25–26; Riess, *Touching Base*, 114–17; Harold Seymour and Dorothy Seymour Mills, *Baseball: The Golden Age*, 49–51.
6. *Manchester Daily Mirror and American* April 3, 1913 (quoted); *L'Avenir National* April 4, 1913.
7. Sanborn-Perris Map Company, Ltd., *Atlas of Manchester, New Hampshire* (New York: Sanborn Fire Insurance Company, 1915); *Manchester Daily Mirror and American* April 3, 1913.
8. *Amoskeag Bulletin* April 15, 1913, May 15, 1913 (quoted).
9. *Manchester Daily Mirror and American* April 19, 1913, April 26, 1913; *Manchester Leader* May 8, 1913; *L'Avenir National* April 25–26, 1913; *Amoskeag Bulletin* May 1, 1913.
10. *Manchester Leader* May 6, 1913.
11. See, for example, Rosenzweig, *Eight Hours for What We Will*, 127–152; Joe L. Frost, *A History of Children's Play and Play Environments: Toward a Contemporary Child-Saving Movement* (New York: Routledge, 2010) 62–69, 84–110; Melissa R. Klapper, *Small Strangers: The Experiences of Immigrant Children in America, 1880–1925* (Chicago: Ivan R. Dee, 2007) 14–17; Reuben M. Rainey, "Hallowed Grounds and Rituals of Remembrance: Union Regimental Monuments at Gettysburg," in in Paul Groth and Todd W. Bressi, eds., *Understanding Ordinary Landscapes* (New Haven: Yale University Press, 1997) 67–80.
12. J. Wright, *The Progressive Yankees*, 47; *Manchester Leader* May 6, 1913.
13. *L'Avenir National* May 12, 1913; *Manchester Daily Mirror and American* May 12, 1913; *Amoskeag Bulletin* May 15, 1913.
14. *Amoskeag Bulletin* May 15, 1913; *Manchester Daily Mirror and American* May 9, 1913, May 12, 1913; *Manchester Leader* May 9, 1913, May 12, 1913.
15. *Manchester Leader* May 31, 1913.
16. *L'Avenir National* June 6, 1913, June 14, 1913, July 10, 1913; *Manchester Leader* May 19, 1913.
17. "Textile Club is Doing Much for Manchester, N.H.," circa 1915 newspaper article in Gill Stadium subject file, Manchester Historic Association, Manchester, NH.
18. Langenbach 1968, 19; 1975, 27; Hareven and Langenbach, *Amoskeag*, 15; Hareven, *Family Time and Industrial Time*, 10; Heffernan and Stecker, *New Hampshire*, 147; Amoskeag Manufacturing Company Mechanical Department Building and Machinery Work Orders, 1908–1934, "Textile Field Work Orders, Sketches, 1913–1916."
19. *Amoskeag Bulletin* June 15, 1913.
20. *Manchester Leader* June 28, 1913; *Manchester Union* July 1, 1913.
21. *Manchester Union* July 1, 1913.
22. *Manchester Leader* July 1, 1913; J. Wright, *The Progressive Yankees*, 147.
23. *Manchester Advocate* July 4, 1913.
24. *The Typographical Journal* 44 (January 1914), 777.
25. *Amoskeag Bulletin* July 1, 1913.
26. *Manchester Leader* May 13, 1913.
27. *Manchester Daily Mirror and American* July 14, 1913; *Manchester Leader* May 13, 1913; *Amoskeag Bulletin* June 1, 1913.
28. *Manchester Leader* June 3, 1913.

29. *Manchester Daily Mirror and American* July 8, 1913.
30. *Manchester Daily Mirror and American* July 14, 1913.
31. *L'Avenir National* July 15, 1913; *Manchester Daily Mirror and American* June 17, 1913.
32. *Manchester Daily Mirror and American* July 14, 1913, July 17, 1913; *L'Avenir National* July 17, 1913.
33. *Manchester Daily Mirror and American* July 17, 1913, July 19, 1913, July 31, 1913.
34. *Manchester Daily Mirror and American* July 24, 1913; *Manchester Leader* July 24, 1913.
35. *Manchester Daily Mirror and American* July 24, 1913.

Chapter 9

1. *Manchester Daily Mirror and American* November 23, 1912; *Manchester Union* January 1, 1913.
2. *Manchester Daily Mirror and American* November 6, 1912.
3. *Manchester Advocate* February 14, 1913; March 7, 1913.
4. *Manchester Advocate* March 24, 1913.
5. Frost, *A History of Children's Play and Play Environments*, 62, 69–73, 89; Klapper, *Small Strangers*, 88–90; Rosenzweig, *Eight Hours for What We Will*, 127–152; H. S. Braucher, "Tendencies and Developments in the Field of Public Recreation," *The Playground* 5 (1911) 126–43.
6. *Manchester Union* July 14, 1911.
7. *Manchester Union* May 2, 1913; *Manchester Leader* May 3, 1913; *Manchester Daily Mirror and American* May 3, 1911.
8. *Manchester Union* May 6, 1913.
9. *Manchester Daily Mirror and American* May 6, 1913.
10. *Manchester Daily Mirror and American* May 6, 1913, *Manchester Union* May 5, 1913, *L'Avenir National* May 7, 1913, *Manchester Leader* May 7, 1913.
11. *Manchester Union* May 6, 1913.
12. *Manchester Daily Mirror and American* April 7, 1913.
13. *Manchester Daily Mirror and American* May 10, 1913.
14. *Manchester Daily Mirror and American* May 13, 1913.
15. *Manchester Daily Mirror and American* May 13, 1913 (quoted); *Manchester Union* May 14, 1913; *L'Avenir National* May 13, 1913.
16. *Manchester Daily Mirror and American* May 13, 1913; May 15, 1913; May 17, 1913 (quoted); *Manchester Union* May 14, 1913; May 15, 1913; May 16, 1913; *L'Avenir National* May 13, 1913.
17. *Manchester Daily Mirror and American* May 19, 1913; May 22, 1913; May 27, 1913; *Manchester Union* July 8, 1913; August 12, 1913.
18. *Manchester Daily Mirror and American* May 17, 1913; *Manchester Leader* May 17, 1913; *Manchester Union* May 19, 1913.
19. *Manchester Union* May 19, 1913.
20. *Manchester Daily Mirror and American* May 17, 1913.
21. *Manchester Daily Mirror and American* May 17, 1913; *Manchester Leader* May 17, 1913; *Manchester Union* May 19, 1913.
22. *Manchester Mirror and Daily American* May 27, 1913.
23. *Manchester Union* May 28, 1913.
24. Janice Brown, "Manchester NH's First Casualty of WW1: Pvt. Henry John Sweeney (1897–1918)," *Cow Hampshire: New Hampshire's History Blog*, http://www.cowhampshireblog.com/2014/05/24/manchester-nhs-first-casualty-of-ww1-pvt-henry-john-sweeney-1897-1918/, posted May 24, 2014; accessed February 15, 2016.

Chapter 10

1. *Manchester Daily Mirror and American* July 22, 1875, July 23, 1875, June 22, 1877, June 8, 1878, September 19, 1877, September 20, 1877, April 11, 1888, August 17, 1912; *Manchester Union* July 23, 1875, April 11, 1838; *New York Clipper* September 29, 1877; *The Sporting Life* April 11, 1888, April 18, 1888; *Amoskeag Bulletin* June 15, 1913, October 1, 1914, February 15, 1915, August 2, 1915.
2. Sampson, Davenport and Company, *The Manchester Directory* (Manchester, NH: Temple and Farrington, 1880 and 1884); *Amoskeag Bulletin* October 1, 1914; *Manchester Daily Mirror and American* June 17–27, 1885; April 11, 1888; *Manchester Union*, April 11, 1888. We found no mention of the West End (or "Squog") Grounds in the *Manchester Daily Mirror and American* after May 29, 1890.
3. Bob Klapisch and Pete Van Wieren, *The Braves: An Illustrated History of America's Team* (Atlanta: Turner Publishing, Inc., 1995), 27–30; Stout and Johnson, *Red Sox Century*, 3–20.
4. *Manchester Union* October 3, 1901; Stout and Johnson, *Red Sox Century*, 13–14; Bill Nowlin, "The Boston Pilgrims Never Existed," *The National Pastime* 23 (2003), 71–76.
5. *Manchester Union* October 3, 1901

(quoted); Marc Okkonen, *Baseball Uniforms of the 20th Century: The Official Major League Baseball Guide* (New York: Sterling Publishing Company, Inc., 1991), 90.

6. On October 3, 1901, the *Boston Globe* reported an attendance of 600, the *Manchester Union* reported "between 600 and 700," and the *Manchester Daily Mirror and American* reported 1,000. The *Mirror*'s figure matches that of *L'Avenir National*, October 2, 1901.

7. *L'Avenir National* October 2, 1901; *Manchester Daily Mirror and American* April 17, 1901, October 3, 1901; *Manchester Union* October 3, 1901.

8. *Boston Globe* October 3, 1901; for a description of uniforms, see *Manchester Daily Mirror and American* April 29, 1901.

9. *Manchester Union* October 3, 1901.

10. *Manchester Daily Mirror and American* October 3, 1901.

11. Stout and Johnson, *Red Sox Century*, 95–96.

12. *Manchester Daily Mirror and American* July 31, 1913.

13. *Manchester Leader and Evening Union* July 30, 1913.

14. *Manchester Daily Mirror and American* July 31, 1913; August 1, 1913; *Manchester Leader and Evening Union* July 31, 1913.

15. *Manchester Leader and Evening Union* July 31, 1913.

16. *Amoskeag Bulletin* June 15, 1913.

17. *Amoskeag Bulletin* August 1, 1913; *Manchester Daily Mirror and American* August 1, 1913

18. *Amoskeag Bulletin* August 1, 1913.

19. *Manchester Daily Mirror and American* August 1, 1913; *Amoskeag Bulletin* August 1, 1913.

20. *Amoskeag Bulletin* August 15, 1913. Although Manchester newspapers typically referred to the catcher as "Tragressor," the spelling utilized here is that used by Gary Caruso, *The Braves Encyclopedia* (Philadelphia: Temple University Press, 1995), 280.

21. *Amoskeag Bulletin* August 15, 1913.

22. *Amoskeag Bulletin* September 4, 1913; *Manchester Leader and Evening Union* September 3, 1913.

23. *Amoskeag Bulletin* September 4, 1913.

24. *L'Avenir National* September 2, 1913; *Amoskeag Bulletin* September 4, 1913.

25. *Manchester Leader* September 6, 1913. For more on the Royal Rooters, particularly on their influence over the 1903 World Series between Boston and Pittsburgh, see Roger I. Abrams, *The First World Series and the Baseball Fanatics of 1903* (Boston: Northeastern University Press, 2003), especially pages 82–103.

26. Translated as "Boston Red Sox, Champions of the World, vs. The Best Players of the Manufacturers League. The Local League Team will be Aided by a Battery from the Boston Nationals." *L'Avenir National* September 4, 1913; see also *Manchester Daily Mirror and American* August 30, 1913.

27. *Amoskeag Bulletin* September 4, 1913.

28. Harold Kase, *The Boston Braves, 1871–1953* (Boston: Northeastern University Press, 2004; originally published New York: G. P. Putnam and Sons, 1948), 86.

29. *Amoskeag Bulletin* September 15, 1913.

30. Paul J. Zingg, *Harry Hooper: An American Baseball Life* (Urbana: University of Illinois Press, 1993), 120–22 (quoted); Stout and Johnson, *Red Sox Century*, 87, 95–96.

31. *L'Avenir National*, September 8, 1913, September 9, 1913; *Manchester Daily Mirror and American*, September 8, 1913; *Manchester Leader and Evening Union* September 8–9, 1913; *Amoskeag Bulletin* September 4, 1913, September 15, 1913; *Boston Daily Globe* September 9, 1913; *Nashua Telegraph* September 8–9, 1913; Okkonen, *Baseball Uniforms...*, 114.

32. *Manchester Daily Mirror and American* September 8, 1913.

Chapter 11

1. *Amoskeag Bulletin* October 1, 1913; *Manchester Daily Mirror and American* September 29, 1913.

2. *Manchester Daily Mirror and American* April 11, 1908; August 2, 1913; *Amoskeag Bulletin* October 1, 1914; William Parker Straw, letters to John J. Carney, September 27, 1913, and October 7, 1913; "John Carney," Baseball-Reference.com, http://www.baseball-reference.com/c/carfnejo01.shtml, last accessed July 25, 2008; David Pietrusza, *Major Leagues: The Formation, Sometimes Absorption and Mostly Inevitable Demise of 18 Professional Baseball Organizations, 1871 to Present* (Jefferson, NC: McFarland, 1991), 333–34; J. Wright, *The Progressive Yankees*, 185, 199, 226–28; Bevis, *The New England League*, 115.

3. *Amoskeag Bulletin* November 15, 1913, December 1, 1913; Amoskeag Manufacturing Company Employee Record for John Carney, Manchester Historic Association, Manchester, New Hampshire.

4. *Amoskeag Bulletin* December 15, 1913;

L'Avenir National December 5, 1913, December 11, 1913.

5. William Parker Straw, letter to F. C. Dumaine, December 5, 1913.

6. "Fred Lake Stats," *Baseball Almanac*, http://www.baseball-almanac.com/players/player.php?p=lakefr01, last accessed July 13, 2008; Don Hyslop, "Fred Lake," *Society for American Baseball Research Baseball Biography Project*, http://bioproj.sabr.org/bioproj.cfm?a=v&v=1&bid=1408&pid=7876, last accessed July 30, 2008.

7. *Manchester Leader and Evening Union* January 1, 1914; *Amoskeag Bulletin* December 15, 1913, January 1, 1914.

8. Klapper, *Small Strangers*, 15; *L'Avenir National* December 9, 1913; *Nashua Telegraph* August 27, 1913; *Manchester Daily Mirror and American* January 1, 1914, February 14, 1914, April 8, 1914; *Manchester Leader and Evening Union* October 2, 1914, December 2, 1914.

9. The Police Record (Complaint Books), 1868–1925, of the Police Department, City of Manchester, New Hampshire, Volume 7 (January 1, 1914–August 9, 1915), see March 14, 1914, March 20, 1914, April 16, 1914, April 18, 1914, April 21, 1914, May 19, 1914, June 15, 1914, June 18, 1914; *Manchester Leader and Evening Union* June 18, 1914.

10. *Manchester Leader and Evening Union* January 1, 1914, January 5, 1914, January 7, 1914.

11. *Manchester Leader and Evening Union* January 15, 1914, January 23, 1914, January 29, 1914; *Manchester Daily Mirror and American* January 8, 1914.

12. *Manchester Daily Mirror and American* February 18, 1914, February 20, 1914; *Amoskeag Bulletin* February 1, 1914, February 15, 1914, March 2, 1914; *Manchester Leader and Evening Union* February 19, 1914.

13. *Manchester Leader and Evening Union* January 3, 1914, January 9, 1914.

14. *Manchester Leader and Evening Union* February 16, 1914, February 20, 1914; *Manchester Daily Mirror and American* February 14, 1914, February 21, 1914.

15. *L'Avenir National* March 4, 1914; *Manchester Leader and Evening Union* March 4, 1914; *Manchester Daily Mirror and American* March 10, 1914.

16. *Manchester Daily Mirror and American* March 7, 1914; *Amoskeag Bulletin* March 16, 1914.

17. *Amoskeag Bulletin* March 16, 1914.

18. *Manchester Leader and Evening Union* March 17, 1914.

19. *Manchester Leader and Evening Union* March 27, 1914; *Sporting Life* August 15, 1914.

20. James A. Riley, *The Biographical Encyclopedia of the Negro Baseball Leagues* (New York: Carroll and Graf Publishers, Inc., 1994), 111 (quoted); *Manchester Daily Mirror and American* April 20, 1914, May 28–29, 1914, June 15, 1914; *Manchester Leader and Evening Union* June 26–27, 1914, June 30, 1914, July 1–3, 1914; *Amoskeag Bulletin* July 1, 1914.

21. *Manchester Daily Mirror and American* March 23, 1914, April 7, 1914; *Manchester Leader and Evening Union* March 25, 1914, April 2–3, 1914, May 9, 1913, May 18, 1913; Hareven, *Family Time and Industrial Time*, 44. In all likelihood, Fraser is the same individual mentioned by an interviewee in Hareven as "Jack Howard." Like Fraser, Howard was described as a former Philadelphia Athletics pitcher who previously had pitched for Holy Cross. In Palmer and Gillette, neither name is listed as ever having played baseball at the major-league level.

22. *Manchester Leader and Evening Union* April 17, 1914 (quoted); *Amoskeag Bulletin* May 1, 1914.

23. *Amoskeag Bulletin* May 1, 1914; *Manchester Leader and Evening Union* April 10, 1914.

24. Daniel R. Levitt, *The Battle that Forged Modern Baseball: The Federal League Challenge and Its Legacy* (Lanham, MD: Ivan R. Dee, 2012), 50.

25. *Manchester Leader and Evening Union* April 21, 1914 (quoted); *Amoskeag Bulletin* May 1, 1914.

26. *Manchester Leader and Evening Union* May 9, 1914 (quoted); *Amoskeag Bulletin* May 1, 1914.

Chapter 12

1. *Manchester Leader and Evening Union* March 13–14, 1914; *Amoskeag Bulletin* December 15, 1914, March 16, 1914.

2. *Manchester Advocate* August 22, 1913.

3. *Manchester Advocate* March 25, 1914.

4. Brian O'Donnell, "From a Trade to a Science: Progressive Management of the McElwain Shoe Manufacturing and Retailing Empire," *Historical New Hampshire* 55 (Fall/Winter 2000), 108–123: 115.

5. *Manchester Union* March 7, 1913.

6. *Manchester Union* March 6, 1913.

7. *Manchester Daily Mirror and American* March 6, 1913.

8. *Manchester Union* March 8, 1937.

9. *Manchester Advocate* March 7, 1913.

10. *Manchester Advocate* March 6, 1914.

11. Creamer and Coulter, *Labor*, 167.

12. Ibid., 169.
13. *Manchester Advocate* April 8, 1914; April 22, 1914.
14. *Manchester Daily Mirror and American* June 6, 1914.
15. Blood, *Manchester on the Merrimack*, 326; *Manchester Leader and Evening Union* June 29, 1914; *Manchester Daily Mirror and American* June 6, 1914, June 20, 1914; *Manchester Advocate* July 1, 1914; January 21, 1915.

Chapter 13

1. *Manchester Leader and Evening Union* May 4, 1914; *Amoskeag Bulletin* May 1, 1914, May 15, 1914 (quoted).
2. *Manchester Leader and Evening Union* April 27, 1914, May 9, 1914.
3. *Amoskeag Bulletin* May 1, 1914, May 15, 1914 (quoted).
4. *Amoskeag Bulletin* May 15, 1914.
5. *Amoskeag Bulletin* June 15, 1914 (quoted); *Manchester Daily Mirror and American* June 6, 1914; *Manchester Leader and Evening Union* June 11, 1914.
6. The Police Record (Complaint Books), 1868–1925, of the Police Department, City of Manchester, New Hampshire, Volume 7 (January 1, 1914–August 31, 1915), see June 15, 1914.
7. *Amoskeag Bulletin* March 16, 1914.
8. Haywood, *Bill Haywood's Book*, 252.
9. *Manchester Leader and Evening Union* June 1, 1914 (emphasis original).
10. *Manchester Daily Mirror and American* June 6, 1914.
11. *Manchester Daily Mirror and American* June 1–16, 1914; *Amoskeag Bulletin* June 15, 1914; *Manchester Leader and Evening Union* June 9, 1914; *The Sunday Standard* July 5, 1914.
12. *Manchester Leader and Evening Union* May 28, 1914; *Manchester Daily Mirror and American* June 9, 1914 (quoted).
13. *Manchester Daily Mirror and American* June 16, 1914.
14. *Manchester Leader and Evening Union* June 13, 1914 (quoted), June 15, 1914.
15. *Manchester Daily Mirror and American* June 13, 1914 (quoted), June 16, 1914.
16. *Amoskeag Bulletin* July 1, 1915, July 15, 1915.
17. *Manchester Leader and Evening Union* June 26–27, 1914, July 1–3, 1914; *Amoskeag Bulletin* July 1, 1914.
18. *Manchester Daily Mirror and American* July 28, 1914.
19. The *Union-Leader* reported that the parties had been negotiating for about three weeks. *Manchester Leader and Evening Union* July 28, 1914.
20. *L'Avenir National* July 28, 1914; *Manchester Leader and Evening Union* July 28, 1914.
21. *Manchester Daily Mirror and American* July 28, 1914.
22. *Manchester Leader and Evening Union* July 29, 1914.
23. *Manchester Leader and Evening Union* July 28, 1914, July 29, 1914; *L'Avenir National* July 28–29, 1914, July 31, 1914 *Manchester Daily Mirror and American* July 28, 1914.
24. *L'Avenir National* July 30, 1914; *Amoskeag Bulletin* August 1, 1914 (quoted).
25. Kerry Keene, Raymond Sinibaldi, and David Hickey, *The Babe in Red Stockings: An In-Depth Chronicle of Babe Ruth with the Boston Red Sox, 1914–1919* (Champaign, IL: Sagamore Publishing, 1997), 19; Robert W. Creamer, *Babe: The Legend Comes to Life* (Norwalk, CT: The Easton Press, 1998 [originally published by Simon and Schuster, Inc., 1974]), 89–92.
26. *L'Avenir National* August 18, 1914; *Manchester Leader and Evening Union* August 18, 1914; Keene et al, *The Babe in Red Stockings*, 19.
27. *Amoskeag Bulletin* August 15, 1914.
28. *The Sunday Standard* July 5, 1914.
29. *Manchester Advocate* July 29, 1914; *The Typographical Journal* 45 (September 1914), 411.
30. *Manchester Advocate* October 15, 1914.

Chapter 14

1. Ring Lardner, "The Cost of Baseball," in Lardner, *Ring Around the Bases: The Complete Baseball Stories of Ring Lardner*, edited by Matthew J. Bruccoli (Norwalk, CT: The Easton Press, 1996 [originally published by Simon and Schuster, Inc., 1992]), 569–75; Kuklick, *To Every Thing a Season*, 48–51; "Oakland Athletics Attendance," *Baseball Almanac*, http://www.baseball-almanac.com/teams/athlatte.shtml, last accessed July 23, 2008.
2. Marc Okkonen, *The Federal League of 1914–1915: Baseball's Third Major League* (Garrett Park, MD: Society for the American Baseball Research, 1989), 6–16; Harold Seymour and Dorothy Seymour Mills, *Baseball: The Golden Age*, 196–213; James E. Elfers, *The Tour to End All Tours: The Story of Major League Baseball's 1913–1914 World Tour* (Lincoln: University of Nebraska Press, 2003), 228–29; 237–42; Norman L. Macht, *Connie Mack and the Early Years of Baseball* (Lincoln: University of Nebraska Press, 2007), 621.
3. Harold Seymour and Dorothy Seymour

Mills, *Baseball: The Early Years* (New York: Oxford University Press, 1960), 221–39; see also Geoffrey C. Ward and Ken Burns, *Baseball: An Illustrated History* (New York: Alfred A. Knopf, 1994), 39–40.

4. Connie Mack, *My 66 Years in the Big Leagues* (Mineola, NY: Dover Publications, Inc., 2009; originally published Philadelphia: The John C. Winston Company, 1950), 26; "John Carney," Baseball-Reference.com, www.baseball-reference.com/c/carfnejo01.shtml, last accessed July 25, 2008; "1889 Washington Nationals," Baseball-Reference.com, www.baseball-reference.com/teams/WHS/1889.shtml, last accessed July 25, 2008; "1890 Buffalo Bisons," Baseball-Reference.com, www.baseball-reference.com/teams/BUF/1890.shtml, last accessed July 25, 2008; Richard Adler, *Mack, McGraw, and the 1913 Baseball Season* (Jefferson, NC: McFarland, 2008), 7; Pietrusza, *Major Leagues*, 99–126; Macht, *Connie Mack and the Early Years of Baseball* 71–83.

5. *Manchester Leader and Evening Union* August 31, 1914, September 2, 1914, September 3, 1914 (quoted); *The Emerald and Catholic Opinion* August 27, 1914, September 3, 1914; *L'Avenir National* September 3, 1914; *Amoskeag Bulletin* August 15, 1914, September 15, 1914; The Police Record (Complaint Books), 1868–1925, of the Police Department, City of Manchester, New Hampshire, Volume 7 (January 1, 1914–August 9, 1915), August 26, 1914; Okkonen, *Baseball Uniforms...* , 116.

6. *Manchester Leader and Evening Union* September 3, 1914.

7. *The Emerald and Catholic Opinion* September 3, 1914; *Manchester Leader and Evening Union* September 3, 1914.

8. *Amoskeag Bulletin* September 15, 1914. The September 3, 1914 edition of *L'Avenir National* claimed that the two events together attracted 20,000. The *Union-Leader* estimated crowds of 4,000 for the game, and 12,000 for the fireworks.

9. *Amoskeag Bulletin* July 1, 1914.

10. *Amoskeag Bulletin* August 15, 1914.

11. McCaffery, *Islands of Deutschtum*, 101.

12. *Manchester Advocate* August 19, 1914.

13. *Manchester Leader and Evening Union* September 8–10, 1914; *Amoskeag Bulletin* September 15, 1914.

14. *Manchester Leader and Evening Union* September 5, 1914 (quoted), September 14, 1914, October 20, 1914.

15. *Manchester Leader and Evening Union* September 22, 1914, December 2, 1914, December 3, 1914.

16. *Manchester Leader and Evening Union* October 10, 1914.

17. *Manchester Advocate* November 19, 1914.

18. *Manchester Leader and Evening Union* October 1–2, 1914, October 28, 1914, November 4–5, 1914; J. Wright, *The Progressive Yankees*, 148, 151–52.

19. Troy Soos, *Before the Curse: The Glory Days of New England Baseball, 1858–1918* (Hyannis, MA: Parnassus Imprints, 1997), 150; David M. Jordan, *The Athletics of Philadelphia: Connie Mack's White Elephants, 1901–1954* (Jefferson, NC: McFarland, 1999), 64.

20. *Manchester Leader and Evening Union* October 5, 1914.

21. *Manchester Leader and Evening Union* October 13, 1914; Jordan, 66–67.

22. Philip J. Lowry, *Green Cathedrals: The Ultimate Celebration of Major League and Negro League Ballparks*, updated edition (New York: Walker and Company, 2006), 26; Jordan, 66–69; Soos, 150.

23. *Manchester Leader and Evening Union* October 9, 1914, October 10, 1914, October 12, 1914, October 13, 1914.

24. *Manchester Leader and Evening Union* October 26, 1914.

25. *Manchester Leader and Evening Union* October 21, 1914.

26. *Manchester Leader and Evening Union* November 10–11, 1914, *Amoskeag Bulletin* November 16, 1914.

27. *Amoskeag Bulletin* November 16, 1914.

28. *Manchester Daily Mirror and American* November 13, 1914.

29. *Manchester Leader and Evening Union* November 10–11, 1914, November 15, 1914, November 17, 1914; *Amoskeag Bulletin* November 16, 1914.

30. *Amoskeag Bulletin* November 16, 1914.

31. For comparisons between Herman F. and William Parker Straw and first-hand reflections on the latter's unpopularity, see Hareven and Langenbach, *Amoskeag*, especially pages 75–76, 94, 101–02, 108–09.

32. *Amoskeag Bulletin* January 15, 1915; *Manchester Leader and Evening Union* January 4, 1915.

Chapter 15

1. *Manchester Leader and Evening Union* December 10, 1914, December 17, 1914; *Manchester Daily Mirror and American* December 10, 1914.

2. *L'Avenir National* January 8, 1915; *Manchester Leader and Evening Union* January 5–8, 1915, January 11, 1915, January 13–14, 1915; *Manchester Daily Mirror and American* January 8, 1915, January 13, 1915.

3. Sullivan, *The Minors*, 59–63; *Boston Globe* January 15, 1915; *Manchester Leader and Evening Union* December 18, 1914, January 16, 1915; *Manchester Daily Mirror and American* January 16, 1915.

4. Levitt, *The Battle that Forged Modern Baseball*, 180–187.

5. David Pietrusza, *Judge and Jury: The Life and Times of Judge Kenesaw Mountain Landis* (South Bend, IN: Diamond Communications, Inc., 1998), 153–157.

6. *L'Avenir National* January 11, 1915.

7. *Manchester Daily Mirror and American* January 16, 1915 (quoted); *Manchester Leader and Daily American* January 19, 1915.

8. *L'Avenir National* January 21, 1915; *Manchester Leader and Evening Union* January 21, 1915 (quoted).

9. *L'Avenir National* January 22, 1915; *Manchester Leader and Evening Union* January 22, 1915.

10. *Manchester Leader and Evening Union* January 23, 1915.

11. *Boston Globe* January 29–31, 1915; *L'Avenir National* January 30, 1915; *New York Times* January 31, 1915 (quoted); *Manchester Leader and Evening Union* February 1, 1915.

12. *L'Avenir National* February 1, 1915; *Manchester Daily Mirror and American* February 1, 1915; *Manchester Advocate* February 4, 1915.

13. *Boston Globe* February 1, 1915; *L'Avenir National* February 3, 1915; *Manchester Leader and Evening Union* January 30, 1915, February 3, 1915; *Manchester Daily Mirror and American* February 3, 1915; *New York Times* February 5, 1915; see also Bevis, *The New England League*, 153–54.

14. *New York Times* February 5, 1915; *Manchester Leader and Evening Union* February 5–9, 1915; *L'Avenir National* February 5–10, 1915; *Manchester Daily Mirror and American* February 5, 1915 (quoted).

15. *Manchester Leader and Evening Union* February 9, 1915 (quoted); *L'Avenir National* February 9, 1915.

16. *Manchester Leader and Evening Union* February 11, 1915.

17. *Manchester Leader and Evening Union* February 12, 1915, February 15–17, 1915.

18. *Manchester Daily Mirror and American* February 16, 1915.

19. *Manchester Daily Mirror and American* February 17, 1915; *Manchester Leader and Evening Union* February 17, 1915, February 23, 1915; *Boston Globe* February 17, 1915; Bevis, *The New England League*, 154–55.

20. *Manchester Leader and Evening Union* February 17, 1915.

21. *Manchester Leader and Evening Union* February 23–24, 1915.

22. *Manchester Daily Mirror and American* February 25, 1915.

23. *Manchester Daily Mirror and American* February 26, 1915; March 1, 1915; *L'Avenir National* February 26, 1915; *Manchester Leader and Evening Union* February 26, 1915.

24. *Manchester Daily Mirror and American* February 27, 1915; see also *Amoskeag Bulletin* March 1, 1915.

25. *Manchester Leader and Evening Union* March 1, 1915; *Manchester Daily Mirror and American* February 26, 1915 (quoted).

26. *Manchester Daily Mirror and American* March 2, 1915 (quoted), March 3, 1915.

27. *Manchester Daily Mirror and American* March 2, 1915; for other examples, see also March 12, 1915; *Manchester Leader and Evening Union* March 3, 1915.

28. *Manchester Leader and Evening Union* March 6, 1915, March 11, 1915; *Manchester Daily Mirror and American* March 12, 1915.

29. *Manchester Daily Mirror and American* March 12, 1915; *Manchester Leader and Evening Union* March 12, 1915; *Amoskeag Bulletin* March 15, 1915.

30. *Manchester Leader and Evening Union* March 19, 1915.

31. *Manchester Leader and Evening Union* April 8, 1915 (quoted), April 3, 1915; April 7, 1915; April 10, 1915; April 12, 1915.

32. *Manchester Daily Mirror and American* April 15, 1915, April 20, 1915; Amoskeag Manufacturing Company Employee Record for Emil Pernod, Manchester Historic Association, Manchester, New Hampshire.

33. *Manchester Leader and Evening Union* March 8, 1915, March 23, 1915, April 2, 1915 (quoted).

34. *Manchester Leader and Evening Union* April 13, 1915, April 15, 1915.

35. *Manchester Leader and Evening Union* April 17, 1915, April 30, 1915, May 1, 1915 (quoted).

Chapter 16

1. *Manchester Leader and Evening Union* April 29, 1915.

2. *Manchester Daily Mirror and American* April 26, 1915.
3. *Amoskeag Bulletin* May 1, 1915, May 15, 1915.
4. James Green, *Death in the Haymarket: A Story of Chicago, the First Labor Movement and the Bombing that Divided Gilded Age America* (New York: Anchor Books, 2007), 174–91; Sindey Lens, "The Bomb at Haymarket," in Franklin Rosemont and David Roediger, eds., *Haymarket Scrapbook* (Chicago: AK Press/ Charles H. Kerr Publishing Company, 2012 [1986]), 11–18; Fred Thompson, "The Facts on May Day," in Rosemont and Roediger, 175.
5. Thompson, "The Facts on May Day," 175.
6. Haywood, *Bill Haywood's Book*, 31 (quoted); Green, *Death in the Haymarket*, 277–78; Sal Salerno, "The Impact of Haymarket on the Founding of the IWW: The Anarchism of Thomas J. Hagerty," in Rosemont and Roediger, 189–91.
7. *Manchester Leader and Evening Union* May 4, 1915.
8. Creamer and Coulter, *Labor*, 184.
9. *Manchester Daily Mirror and American* July 24, 1915, August 10, 1915.
10. *Manchester Leader and Evening Union* May 5, 1915.
11. *Manchester Leader and Evening Union* February 9, 1915.
12. *Manchester Leader and Evening Union* May 6, 1915.
13. John Patrick Jordan, *Saints and Sinners: The Pioneer Irish of Manchester, New Hampshire, 1835–1900* (Manchester, NH: n.pub., 2014), 40.
14. *Manchester Leader and Evening Union* May 27, 1914; see also May 26, 1914, May 28, 1914, May 29, 1914.
15. *Manchester Leader and Evening Union* September 3, 1914.
16. *Amoskeag Bulletin* March 15, 1915.
17. *Manchester Leader and Evening Union* March 8, 1915, April 30, 1915.
18. *Manchester Leader and Evening Union* April 12, 1915.
19. Roberta Edwards Lenkeit, *Introducing Cultural Anthropology*, third edition (Boston: McGraw-Hill, 2007), 216.
20. Randy Roberts, *Papa Jack: Jack Johnson and the Era of White Hopes* (New York: The Free Press, 1983); Dan Streible, *Fight Pictures: A History of Boxing and Early Cinema* (Berkeley: University of California Press, 2008), 195–281.
21. *Amoskeag Bulletin* May 1, 1915; *Manchester Leader and Evening Union* April 25–27, 1915; *Manchester Daily Mirror and American* April 26, 1915.
22. *Manchester Leader and Evening Union* April 27, 1915.
23. *Manchester Leader and Evening Union* May 4, 1915.
24. *Manchester Leader and Evening Union* February 9, 1915; *Manchester Daily Mirror and American* July 24, 1915.
25. *Manchester Leader and Evening Union* May 3, 1915.
26. *Manchester Leader and Evening Union* May 1, 1915; *L'Avenir National* May 1, 1915.

Chapter 17

1. *L'Avenir National* May 3, 1915; *Manchester Leader and Evening Union* May 3–4, 1915, December 9, 1914; *Manchester Daily Mirror and American* May 1, 1915; *Amoskeag Bulletin* May 1, 1915; *Manchester Advocate* November 19, 1914, January 25, 1915.
2. *Manchester Leader and Evening Union* May 3, 1915.
3. *Manchester Daily Mirror and American* May 12, 1915; *Amoskeag Bulletin* May 15, 1915.
4. *Manchester Daily Mirror and American* May 12, 1915, May 19, 1915.
5. In his history of the New England League, Charles Bevis writes that attendance suffered in the New England League because of "jitneys," forerunners to large buses that could transport fans around New England to major-league games in Boston, and the August, 1915 opening of Braves Field in Boston, which made the wooden grandstands of the New England League seem obsolete. If these factors pertained to any New England League city, their effects were minimal in Manchester. Economic conditions and the lack of free time granted by the city's employers made travel to Boston infrequent among the predominantly working-class population. Moreover, despite its wooden seating deck, Textile Field was compared favorably with big-league grandstands. Manchester's attendance suffered for at least three months before Braves Field's opening—besides which attendance at local games increased after the opening of Fenway Park—so Braves Field seems not to have factored in the Textiles' attendance problems. See Bevis, *The New England League*, 156–57.
6. *L'Avenir National* May 8, 1915.
7. *Manchester Leader and Evening Union* May 14, 1915; see also *L'Avenir National* May

14, 1915; *Manchester Daily Mirror and American* May 15, 1915.

8. *Manchester Leader and Evening Union* June 2, 1915; *Amoskeag Bulletin* June 15, 1915.

9. *Manchester Daily Mirror and American* June 25, 1915, June 28, 1915.

10. *Amoskeag Bulletin* June 15, 1915.

11. *L'Avenir National* June 25, 1915; *Manchester Mirror and Daily American* June 25, 1915; *Manchester Leader and Evening Union* June 24, 1915.

12. *L'Avenir National* June 25, 1915; *Manchester Mirror and Daily American* June 25, 1915; *Manchester Leader and Evening Union* June 24, 1915; Bevis, *The New England League*, 155–56.

13. *L'Avenir National* June 26, 1915 (quoted), June 29, 1915; *Manchester Daily Mirror and American* June 28–29, 1915.

14. *Manchester Leader and Evening Union* July 2, 1915.

15. *Manchester Daily Mirror and American* July 1, 1915.

16. *L'Avenir National* July 1, 1915; *Manchester Leader and Evening Union* July 3, 1915, July 8, 1915.

17. *Manchester Leader* July 8, 1915, January 5, 1916.

18. *Amoskeag Bulletin* May 15, 1915.

19. *Manchester Leader and Evening Union* May 22, 1915; *L'Avenir National* May 22, 1915.

20. *Manchester Daily Mirror and American* June 21, 1915, September 27, 1915; *Manchester Leader and Evening Union* July 6, 1915; *Amoskeag Bulletin* July 15, 1915, August 2, 1915, August 13, 1915; *L'Avenir National* August 2, 1915, August 30, 1915, September 13, 1915.

21. *Amoskeag Bulletin* August 13, 1915; *L'Avenir National* August 6, 1915; August 27–28, 1915, September 13, 1915, September 20, 1915; *Nashua Telegraph* July 27, 1915.

22. *Amoskeag Bulletin* January 17, 1916.

23. *Manchester Leader and Evening Union* July 3, 1915 (quoted), July 7, 1915, July 15, 1915; July 19, 1915; *Manchester Daily Mirror and American* July 7, 1915, July 13, 1915.

24. *Manchester Leader and Evening Union* August 4–5, 1915, August 14, 1915, August 25, 1915, August 27, 1915; *L'Avenir National* August 14, 1915.

25. *Manchester Leader and Evening Union* August 28, 1915, August 30, 1915 (quoted), September 1, 1915, September 8–9, 1915, September 15, 1915.

26. *Manchester Leader and Evening Union* September 11, 1915, September 15, 1915, September 18–21, 1915, September 23–24, 1915, September 27–28, 1915; *L'Avenir National* September 20, 1915.

27. *L'Avenir National* September 28, 1911; *Manchester Leader and Evening Union* September 27, 1915 (Finn quote); September 28, 1911 (Lake quote).

28. *Manchester Daily Mirror and American* October 13, 1915.

29. RF Potts, "A Baseball Outing," *Baseball Magazine* 16 (January 1916), 104–08.

30. *Manchester Leader and Evening Union* October 27, 1915.

31. *Manchester Leader and Evening Union* October 29, 1915; *L'Avenir National* October 29, 1915.

32. *Manchester Leader and Evening Union* December 7, 1915, December 13, 1915, December 24, 1915, December 27, 1915, December 29, 1915, December 31, 1915, January 3, 1916, January 6, 1916; *L'Avenir National* December 31, 1916. *Manchester Daily Mirror and American* December 31, 1915 (quoted).

33. *Manchester Leader and Evening Union* January 5, 1916; *L'Avenir National* January 5, 1916.

34. *Manchester Leader and Evening Union* January 6, 1916, January 8, 1916.

35. *L'Avenir National* February 1, 1916, February 18, 1916; *Manchester Daily Mirror and American* February 15, 1916; *Manchester Leader and Evening Union* February 1, 1916, February 15, 1916.

36. *Manchester Leader and Evening Union* February 18, 1916; *Manchester Daily Mirror and American* February 2, 1916.

37. *Manchester Leader and Evening Union* February 18, 1916, February 25, 1916 (quoted); *L'Avenir National* February 18, 1916.

38. *Amokeag Bulletin* October 16, 1916.

Epilogue

1. *Amoskeag Bulletin* July 15, 1918, February 17, 1919, May 29, 1920.

2. Dubofsky, *We Shall Be All*, 255; Foner, *History of the Labor Movement in the United States*, 551.

3. Dubofsky, *We Shall Be All*, 233–36; Foner, *History of the Labor Movement in the United States*, 553–58; Pietrusza, *Judge and Jury*, 118–21.

4. Pietrusza, *Judge and Jury*, 116–37; Dubofsky, *We Shall Be All*, 258–63.

5. "The Murder of Ora Pearl Vance," *Scott County Iowa Genealogy*, http://www.celticcousins.net/scott/orapearlvancemurder.htm,

last accessed November 21, 2012 (reprint of "Teacher Is Murdered," *Davenport Democrat and Leader* May 1, 1924).

6. *Manchester Leader and Evening Union* March 15, 1916; *Amoskeag Bulletin* April 1, 1916, April 15, 1916, May 15, 1916, June 15, 1916, July 1, 1918, February 17, 1919, May 2, 1921; *Rules of the City Baseball League, 1917* (Manchester, NH: The Mirror Press, 1917), 3.

7. *Manchester Leader* August 23, 1922; *Nashua Telegraph* July 26, 1930.

8. *Amoskeag Bulletin* May 2, 1921, May 16, 1921.

9. *Amoskeag Bulletin* May 19, 1920; *Amoskeag Bulletin* (magazine), January 1922, 26 and February 1922, 6, 10.

10. *Manchester Leader and Evening Union* February 10, 1922; *L'Avenir National* February 10, 1922.

11. *Manchester Leader* March 16, 1922, July 5, 1922.

12. *Manchester Leader* June 28, 1922, September 22, 1922, October 17, 1922; *L'Avenir National* April 22, 1922.

13. *Manchester Leader* April 19, 1922.

14. *Manchester Leader* June 1, 1922, June 3, 1922, June 6, 1922 (quoted), June 9, 1922, June 10, 1922, June 26–27, 1922, July 7, 1922, July 17, 1922, July 20, 1922, August 4, 1922; *L'Avenir National* August 4, 1922.

15. *Manchester Leader* August 14, 1922.

16. *Manchester Leader* June 7, 1922.

17. *L'Avenir National* February 11, 1922.

18. *Manchester Leader* September 11, 1922.

19. *Manchester Leader* September 23, 1922, October 17, 1922; *L'Avenir National* September 23, 1922, October 17–18, 1922; Hareven and Langenbach, *Amoskeag*, 78, 325.

20. *Manchester Leader* September 11, 1922, October 25, 1922, October 30, 1922, November 1, 1922, November 3, 1922; *L'Avenir National* September 11, 1922, October 25, 1922, October 30, 1922, November 1, 1922; *Nashua Telegraph* October 30, 1922, November 1, 1922.

21. *Manchester Leader* February 23, 1922, May 17, 1922, November 8, 1922 (quoted), November 26–27, 1922; *L'Avenir National* November 8, 1922, November 26–27, 1922; *Nashua Telegraph* November 25, 1922, November 27, 1922.

22. *Manchester Union* March 11, 1937.

23. *Manchester Leader* April 10, 1922, August 18–19, 1922, August 21–22, 1922; *L'Avenir National* August 18–19, 1922.

24. *Manchester Leader* September 4–6, 1923.

Conclusion

1. Hareven, *Family Time and Industrial Time*, 58–59.

2. Creamer and Coulter, *Labor*, 181.

3. Hareven, *Family Time and Industrial Time*, 61.

4. Alan Greenblatt, "Rethinking the 17th Amendment: An Old Idea Gets Fresh Opposition," http://www.npr.org/sections/itsallpolitics/2014/02/05/271937304/rethinking-the-17th-amendment-an-old-idea-gets-fresh-opposition, posted February 5, 2014, last accessed April 1, 2016.

Bibliography

Abrams, Roger I. *The First World Series and the Baseball Fanatics of 1903*. Boston: Northeastern University Press, 2003.

Adler, Richard. *Mack, McGraw, and the 1913 Baseball Season*. Jefferson, NC: McFarland, 2008.

Amoskeag Manufacturing Company. Employee Records. Manchester Historic Association, Manchester, NH.

Amoskeag Manufacturing Company. Mechanical Department Building and Machinery Work Orders, 1908–1934. Manchester Historic Association, Manchester, NH.

Amoskeag Textile Club. Records. Manchester Historic Association, Manchester, NH.

Bass, Robert P. Papers, 1849–1954. Dartmouth College, Hanover, NH.

Bevis, Charlie. *The New England League: A Baseball History, 1885–1949*. Jefferson, NC: McFarland, 2008.

_____. *Sunday Baseball: The Major Leagues' Struggles to Play Baseball on the Lord's Day, 1876–1934*. Jefferson, NC: McFarland, 2003.

Blood, Grace Holbrook. *Manchester on the Merrimack: The Story of a City*, revised edition. Manchester, NH: Manchester Historic Association, 1975.

Braucher, H.S. "Tendencies and Developments in the Field of Public Recreation," *The Playground* 5:126–43, 1911.

Brown, Janice. "Manchester NH's First Casualty of WW1: Pvt. Henry John Sweeney (1897–1918)." *Cow Hampshire: New Hampshire's History Blog*, 2014. http://www.cowhampshireblog.com/2014/05/24/manchester-nhs-first-casualty-of-ww1-pvt-henry-john-sweeney-1897-1918/, last accessed February 15, 2016.

Browne, George Waldo. *The Amoskeag Manufacturing Company of Manchester, New Hampshire: A History*. Manchester, NH: Amoskeag Manufacturing Company, 1915.

Cameron, Ardis. *Radicals of the Worst Sort: Laboring Women in Lawrence, Massachusetts, 1860–1912*. Urbana: University of Illinois Press, 1993.

Caruso, Gary. *The Braves Encyclopedia*. Philadelphia: Temple University Press, 1995.

Cash, Kevin. *Who the Hell Is William Loeb?* Manchester, NH: Amoskeag Press, 1975.

Chalmers, Thomas. "The Influence of the Revolution of the Religious Life of America," *The Granite Monthly* 48:193–96, 1916.

Conforti, Joseph A. *Imagining New England: Explorations of Regional Identity from the Pilgrims to the Mid-Twentieth Century*. Chapel Hill: The University of North Carolina Press, 2001.

Creamer, Daniel, and Charles W. Coulter. *Labor and the Shut Down of the Amoskeag Textile Mills*. Philadelphia: Works Projects Administration, National Research Project, 1939.

Creamer, Robert W. 1998. *Babe: The Legend Comes to Life*. Norwalk, CT: The Easton Press, 1998; originally published New York: Simon & Schuster, Inc., 1974.

Dubofsky, Melvyn. *We Shall Be All: A History of the Industrial Workers of the World*, ed. Joseph A. McCartin. Chicago: University of Illinois Press, 2000.

"1889 Washington Nationals." n.d. Baseball-Reference.com, www.baseball-reference.com/teams/WHS/1889.shtml, last accessed July 25, 2008.

"1890 Buffalo Bisons." n.d. Baseball-Reference.com, www.baseball-reference.com/teams/BUF/1890.shtml, last accessed July 25, 2008.

Elfers, James E. *The Tour to End All Tours: The Story of Major League Baseball's 1913–1914 World Tour*. Lincoln: University of Nebraska Press, 2003.

Evans, Samuel, ed. *History of Wapello County, Iowa, Volume One*. Chicago: SJ Clarke Publishing Company, 1914.

———. *History of Wapello County, Iowa, and Representative Citizens*. Chicago: Biographical Publishing Company, 1901.

"The Finest Answer to I.W.W.-ism." 1915. *The Square Deal* 17:139–41

Flynn, Elizabeth Gurley. *The Rebel Girl—An Autobiography: My First Life (1906–1926)*. New York: International Publishers; originally published 1955, 1994.

Foner, Philip S. *History of the Labor Movement in the United States, vol. IV: The Industrial Workers of the World 1905–1917*. New York: International Publishers, 1965.

"Fred Lake Stats." n.d. *Baseball Almanac*, http://www.baseball-almanac.com/players/player.php?p=lakefr01, last accessed July 13, 2008.

Frost, Joe L. *A History of Children's Play and Play Environments: Toward a Contemporary Child-Saving Movement*. New York: Routledge, 2010.

Gershman, Michael. *Diamonds: The Evolution of the Ballpark*. Boston: Houghton Mifflin Company, 1993.

Gill Stadium Subject File. 1913–present. Manchester Historic Association, Manchester, NH.

Goldberg, David J. *A Tale of Three Cities: Labor Organization and Protest in Paterson, Passaic, and Lawrence, 1916–1921*. New Brunswick, NJ: Rutgers University Press, 1989.

Green, James. *Death in the Haymarket: A Story of Chicago, the First Labor Movement and the Bombing that Divided Gilded Age America*. New York: Anchor Books, 2007.

Greenblatt, Alan. "Rethinking the 17th Amendment: An Old Idea Gets Fresh Opposition," 2014. http://www.npr.org/sections/itsallpolitics/2014/02/05/271937304/rethinking-the-17th-amendment-an-old-idea-gets-fresh-opposition, last accessed April 1, 2016.

Hareven, Tamara K. *Family Time and Industrial Time: The Relationship between the Family and Work in a New England Industrial Community*. Lanham, MD: University Press of America, 1993.

———, and Randolph Langenbach. *Amoskeag: Life and Work in an American Factory-City*. Hanover, NH: University Press of New England, 1978.

Haywood, William D.. *Bill Haywood's Book: The Autobiography of William D. Haywood*. New York: International Publishers; originally published 1929, 1958.

Heffernan, Nancy Coffey, and Ann Page Stecker. *New Hampshire: Crosscurrents in Its Development*, updated edition. Hanover, NH: University Press of New England, 1996.

Hyslop, Don. n.d. "Fred Lake." *Society for American Baseball Research Baseball Biography Project*, http://bioproj.sabr.org/bioproj.cfm?a=v&v=1&bid=1408&pid=7876, last accessed July 30, 2008.

Iowa GenWeb Project. n.d. "Wilton History 1854–1947: Wilton Press," http://iagenweb.org/muscatine/wiltonhistory/wiltonpress.htm, last accessed September 24, 2012.

Jager, Ronald, and Grace Jager. *New Hampshire: An Illustrated History of the Granite State*. Woodland Hills, CA: Windsor Publications, Inc, 1983.

Jenkins, Clarence. "America's Game: A Study of Baseball Fiction from the Gilded Age Through the Progressive Era." *NINE: A Journal of Baseball History and Social Policy Perspectives* 6:49–60, 1998.

Jennings/Gray Genealogy. n.d. "Jesse Markee Mattie J. Hicks," http://royandsharon.lifegrid.com/MARKEE,%20Jesse.htm, last accessed September 24, 2012.

"John Carney." n.d. Baseball-Reference.com, http://www.baseball-reference.com/c/carfnejo01.shtml, last accessed July 25, 2008.

Johnson, Lloyd, and Miles Wolff, eds. *The Encyclopedia of Minor League Baseball: The Official Record of Minor League Baseball*. Durham, NC: Baseball America, Inc, 1993.

Jordan, David M. *The Athletics of Philadelphia: Connie Mack's White Elephants, 1901–1954*. Jefferson, NC: McFarland, 1999.

Jordan, John Patrick. *Saints and Sinners: The Pioneer Irish of Manchester, New Hampshire, 1835–1900*. Manchester, NH: n.pub, 2014.

Journal of the House of Representatives of the State of New Hampshire. Concord, NH: The Rumford Printing Company, 1913.

Kase, Harold. *The Boston Braves, 1871–1953*. Boston: Northeastern University Press, 2004; originally published New York: G. P. Putnam and Sons, 1948.

Keene, Kerry, Raymond Sinibaldi, and David Hickey. *The Babe in Red Stockings: An In-Depth Chronicle of Babe Ruth with the Boston Red Sox, 1914–1919*. Champaign, IL: Sagamore Publishing, 1997.

Kelleher, Mark. "'The Efficiency Expert as Corporate Father:' Mismanagement of the Amoskeag Manufacturing Company, 1906–1935."

Unpublished manuscript, Saint Anselm College, 1984.

Kenison, Arthur M. *Dumaine's Amoskeag: Let the Record Speak.* Manchester, NH: Saint Anselm College Press, 1997.

Klapisch, Bob, and Pete Van Wieren. 1995. *The Braves: An Illustrated History of America's Team.* Atlanta: Turner Publishing, Inc.

Klapper, Melissa R. *Small Strangers: The Experiences of Immigrant Children in America, 1880–1925.* Chicago: Ivan R. Dee, 2007.

Kuklick, Bruce. *To Every Thing a Season: Shibe Park and Urban Philadelphia, 1909–1976.* Princeton, NJ: Princeton University Press, 1991.

Langenbach, Randolph. "Amoskeag Millyard Remembered," *Historic Preservation* 27:26–29, 1975.

_____. "The Amoskeag Millyard, An Epic in Urban Design," *Harvard Alumni Bulletin* 70 (April 13, 1968), 21–28, via Conservationtech.com, http://www.conservationtech.com/RL's%20resume&%20pub's/RL-publications/Milltowns/1968-HARVbulletin/Harv Bulletin.htm, last accessed July 13, 2008.

_____. "Lost City on the Merrimack." *The Boston Globe Sunday Magazine,* March 9, 1969, via Conservationtech.com, http://www.conservationtech.com/RL's%20resume&%20pub's/RL-publications/Milltowns/1969-AMOSKEAG(Globe).htm, last accessed July 13, 2008.

Lardner, Ring. "The Cost of Baseball" in Matthew J. Bruccoi, ed., *Ring Around the Bases: The Complete Baseball Stories of Ring Lardner.* Norwalk, CT: The Easton Press, 1996, 569–75; originally published by Simon & Schuster, Inc., 1992.

Lenkeit, Roberta Edwards. *Introducing Cultural Anthropology,* third edition. Boston: McGraw-Hill, 2007.

Lens, Sindey. "The Bomb at Haymarket." In Franklin Rosemont and David Roediger, eds., *Haymarket Scrapbook.* Chicago: AK Press/Charles H. Kerr Publishing Company, 2012, 11–18; originally published 1986.

Levitt, Daniel R. *The Battle that Forged Modern Baseball: The Federal League Challenge and Its Legacy.* Lanham, MD: Ivan R. Dee, 2012.

Lowry, Philip J. *Green Cathedrals: The Ultimate Celebration of Major League and Negro League Ballparks,* updated edition. New York: Walker and Company, 2006.

Macht, Norman L. *Connie Mack and the Early Years of Baseball.* Lincoln: University of Nebraska Press, 2007.

Macieski, Robert. "'Before Their Time': Lewis W. Hine and the New Hampshire Crusade against Child Labor." *Historical New Hampshire* 55:90–107, 2000.

_____. *Picturing Class: Lewis W. Hine Photographs Child Labor in New England.* Amherst: University of Massachusetts Press, 2015.

Mack, Connie. *My 66 Years in the Big Leagues.* Mineola, NY: Dover Publications, Inc., 2009; originally published Philadelphia: The John C. Winston Company, 1950.

Manual for the General Court 1897. Concord, NH: Edward N. Pearson, Public Printer, 1897.

Manual for the General Court 1913. State of New Hampshire: Concord, NH, 1913.

McCaffery, Robert Paul. *Islands of Deutschtum: German-Americans in Manchester, New Hampshire and Lawrence, Massachusetts, 1870–1942.* New York: Peter Lang, Inc., 1997.

McGill Family Papers, 1885–2005. Iowa Women's Archives, University of Iowa, Iowa City IA.

"The Murder of Ora Pearl Vance." *Scott County Iowa Genealogy,* http://www.celticcousins.net/scott/orapearlvancemurder.htm, last accessed November 21, 2012; reprint of "Teacher Is Murdered," *Davenport Democrat and Leader* May 1, 1924.

Nathanson, Mitchell. "Gatekeepers of Americana: Ownership's Never-Ending Quest for Control of the Baseball Creed." *NINE: A Journal of Baseball History and Culture* 15:68–87, 2006.

Nemec, David. *The Beer and Whiskey League: The Illustrated History of the American Association—Baseball's Renegade Major League.* Guilford, CT: The Lyon Press, 2004.

"New England Conferences to Promote Rural Progress." *The Survey* 30:55–56, 1913.

Nowlin, Bill. "The Boston Pilgrims Never Existed." *The National Pastime* 23:71–76, 2003.

"Oakland Athletics Attendance." n.d. *Baseball Almanac,* http://www.baseball-almanac.com/teams/athlatte.shtml, last accessed July 23, 2008.

O'Donnell, Brian. "From a Trade to a Science: Progressive Management of the McElwain Shoe Manufacturing and Retailing Empire." *Historical New Hampshire* 55:108–23, 2000.

Okkonen, Marc. *Baseball Uniforms of the 20th Century: The Official Major League Baseball Guide.* New York: Sterling Publishing Company, Inc., 1991.

_____. *The Federal League of 1914–1915: Baseball's Third Major League.* Garrett Park, MD: Society for the American Baseball Research, 1989.

Palmer, Pete, and Gary Gillette, eds. *The Baseball Encyclopedia*. New York: Barnes and Noble Books, 2004.

Pietrusza, David. *Judge and Jury: The Life and Times of Judge Kenesaw Mountain Landis*. South Bend, IN: Diamond Communications, Inc., 1998.

_____. *Major Leagues: the Formation, Sometimes Absorption and Mostly Inevitable Demise of 18 Professional Baseball Organizations, 1871 to Present*. Jefferson, NC: McFarland, 1991.

The Police Record (Complaint Books), 1868–1925, of the Police Department, City of Manchester, New Hampshire, Volumes 6–8. 1910–1915. Office of the City Clerk, Manchester, NH.

Potts, R.F. "A Baseball Outing." *Baseball Magazine* 16:104–08, 1916.

Rainey, Reuben M. "Hallowed Grounds and Rituals of Remembrance: Union Regimental Monuments at Gettysburg." In Paul Groth and Todd W. Bressi, eds., *Understanding Ordinary Landscapes*. New Haven: Yale University Press, 1997, 67–80.

Renshaw, Patrick. *The Wobblies: The Story of the IWW and Syndicalism in the United States*, updated edition. Chicago: Ivan R. Dee, Publisher, 1999.

Riddle, John A., William M. Patten, Quincy Barnard, Arthur W. Holbrook, and Gordon Woodbury. *History of the Town of Bedford, New Hampshire, from 1737*. Concord, NH: The Rumford Printing Company, 1903.

Riess, Steven A. *Touching Base: Professional Baseball and American Culture in the Progressive Era*, revised edition. Urbana: University of Illinois Press, 1999.

Riley, James A. *The Biographical Encyclopedia of the Negro Baseball Leagues*. New York: Carroll and Graf Publishers, Inc., 1994.

Rivard, Paul E. *A New Order of Things: How the Textile Industry Transformed New England*. Hanover: University Press of New England, 2002.

Robinson, Ray. *Matty: An American Hero*. New York: Oxford University Press, 1993.

Roberts, Randy. *Papa Jack: Jack Johnson and the Era of White Hopes*. New York: The Free Press, 1983.

Rosenzweig, Roy. *Eight Hours for What We Will: Workers and Leisure in an Industrial City, 1870–1920*. New York: Cambridge University Press, 1983.

Rousmaniere, Kate. "The Short, Radical Life of Pearl McGill." *Labor: Studies in Working-Class History of the Americas* 6:9–19, 2009.

Rules of the City Baseball League. Manchester, NH: The Mirror Press, 1917.

Salerno, Sal. "The Impact of Haymarket on the Founding of the IWW: The Anarchism of Thomas J. Hagerty." In Franklin Rosemont and David Roediger, eds., *Haymarket Scrapbook*. Chicago: AK Press/Charles H. Kerr Publishing Company, 2012, 189–191 ; originally published 1986.

Sampson, Davenport and Company. *The Manchester Directory, 1880–1884*. Manchester, NH: Temple and Farrington.

Sampson, Murdock and Company. *Manchester City Directory, 1887–1921*. Boston: Sampson, Murdock and Company.

Samson, Gary. *A World Within a World: Manchester, the Mills, and the Immigrant Experience*. Dover, NH: Arcadia Publishing, 1995.

Sanborn-Perris Map Company, Ltd. *Atlas of Manchester, New Hampshire*. New York: Sanborn Fire Insurance Company, 1915.

Seib, Philip. *The Player: Christy Mathewson, Baseball, and the American Century*. New York: Four Walls Eight Windows, 2003.

Seymour, Harold, and Dorothy Seymour Mills. *Baseball: The Early Years*. New York: Oxford University Press, 1960.

_____, and _____. *Baseball: The Golden Age*. New York: Oxford University Press, 1971.

Seymour Mills, Dorothy and Harold Seymour. *Baseball: The People's Game*. New York: Oxford University Press, 1990.

Soos, Troy. *Before the Curse: The Glory Days of New England Baseball, 1858–1918*. Hyannis, MA: Parnassus Imprints, 1997.

Spalding, Albert G. *America's National Game*. San Francisco: Halo Books, 1997.; originally published New York: American Sports Publishing Company, 1911.

Stout, Glenn. *Fenway 1912: The Birth of a Ballpark, a Championship Season, and Fenway's Remarkable First Year*. Boston: Houghton Mifflin Harcourt, 2011.

_____, and Richard A. Johnson. *Red Sox Century: One Hundred Years of Red Sox Baseball*. Boston: Houghton Mifflin Company, 2000.

Streible, Dan. *Fight Pictures: A History of Boxing and Early Cinema*. Berkeley: University of California Press, 2008.

Sullivan, Neil. *The Diamond in the Bronx: Yankee Stadium and the Politics of New York*. New York: Oxford University Press, 2001.

_____. *The Minors: The Struggles and the Triumph of Baseball's Poor Relation from 1876 to the Present*. New York: St. Martin's Press, 1990.

Supplement to the Public Statutes and Session

Laws of New Hampshire. Concord, NH: Arthur H. Chase, William D. Chandler, 1914.

Thompson, Fred. "The Facts on May Day." In Franklin Rosemont and David Roediger, eds., *Haymarket Scrapbook.* Chicago: AK Press/Charles H. Kerr Publishing Company, 2012, 175; originally published 1986.

Tone, Andrea. *The Business of Benevolence: Industrial Paternalism in Progressive America.* Ithaca, NY: Cornell University Press, 1997.

United States Department of Commerce, Bureau of the Census. Census manuscript sheets for Toledo, OH and Manchester, NH, 1900. Via ProQuest, *HeritageQuest Online,* http://heritagequestonline.com, last accessed April 26, 2013.

_____. Census manuscript sheets for Manchester, NH, 1910. Via ProQuest, *HeritageQuest Online,* http://heritagequestonline.com, last accessed April 26, 2013.

_____. Census manuscript sheets for Manchester, NH, 1920. Via ProQuest, *HeritageQuest Online,* http://heritagequestonline.com, last accessed April 26, 2013.

_____. *Thirteenth Census of the United States: Population—General Report and Analysis,* 1913. Washington, D.C.: Government Printing Office.

United States Department of Labor. *Report on the Strike of Textile Workers in Lawrence, Mass. in 1912.* Washington, D.C.: Government Printing Office.

Ward, Geoffrey C., and Ken Burns. *Baseball: An Illustrated History.* New York: Alfred A. Knopf, 1994.

Watson, Bruce. *Bread and Roses: Mills, Migrants, and the Struggle for the American Dream.* New York: Viking, 2005.

Wright, James. *The Progressive Yankees: Republican Reformers in New Hampshire, 1906–1916.* Hanover, NH: University Press of New England, 1987.

Wright, Marshall D. *Nineteenth Century Baseball: Year-by-Year Statistics for the Major League Teams, 1871 through 1900.* Jefferson, NC: McFarland, 1996.

Zingg, Paul J. *Harry Hooper: An American Baseball Life.* Urbana: University of Illinois Press, 1993.

Newspapers

Amoskeag Bulletin (Manchester, NH), 1912–1922.
L'Avenir National (Manchester, NH), 1911–1916, 1922.
Boston Globe, 1901–1902, 1912–1916.
Boston Herald, 1912.
Boston Journal, 1912.
Le Canado-Americain (Manchester, NH), 1912–1914.
The Granite Monthly 48:256, 1916.
The Emerald and Catholic Opinion (Manchester, NH), 1914–1915.
The Industrial Worker (Spokane, WA), 1912.
Manchester Advocate, 1912–1914.
Manchester Daily Mirror and American, 1875–1922.
Manchester Leader, 1912–1913.
Manchester Leader and Evening Union, 1913–1923.
Manchester Union, 1876–1913.
Nashua Telegraph (Nashua, NH), 1912–1916, 1922.
New York Times, 1912–1916.
Portsmouth Herald (Portsmouth, NH), 1912.
The Sporting Life (Philadelphia, PA), 1914.
The Sunday Standard (New Bedford, MA), July 5, 1914.
The Typographical Journal (Indianapolis, IN), 1911–1914.

Index

Numbers in ***bold italics*** indicate pages with illustrations

alcohol and alcoholism 23, 125, 136–37
American Federation of Labor 15, 28, 38, 40, 41, 42, 62, 65, 137, 179, 180, 200, 211
American Woolen Company 3, 16, 19, 41, 124
Amoskeag Bank Building 186
Amoskeag Bulletin 7, 9, 16, 69–72, 74, 76, 80, 88, 90–91, 94, 96, 114–16, 118, 123, 128–130, 142–43, 147, 149, 150, 158, 159, 160, 163, 164, 178, 183, 185, 189, 190, 192, 193, 200, 201, 202, 204, 210
Amoskeag Great Flag ***146***, 147, 212
Amoskeag Millyard 10, ***11***, 13, 14, 21, 44 53, ***72***, 94, 100, ***102***, 104 137, 139, 142
Amoskeag Playground 17, 102, ***103***, 104, 146, 150, 212
Amoskeag Textile Club 7, 8, 9, 16–17, 55–58, 64, 67–76, 80, 88, 90–97, 98–99, 113–19, 122–24, ***126***, 127–31, 133, 141–43, 146–53, ***155***, 156–60, 163–65, 167–77, 178, 180, 184–87, 190–94, 198, 201, 202, 207
Amoskeag Village 105
L'Avenir National 12, 20, 29, 43, 53, 70, 71, 73, 80, 81, 116, 123, 147, 148, 149, 157, 158, 159, 169, 177, 183, 189, 191, 193, 205, 210
Baker, Frank "Home Run" 158
Balkan War 138, 145
Barry, Jack 158
Barry, John 108
Barry Playground 55, 103
baseball creed 3, 5, 49, 52–55, 97, 141, 144, 177, 179, 195, 213
Baseball Riot of 1905 24–26, 53
Bass, John F. 43

Bass, Robert P. 14, 34, 38, 42–44, 47, 61–63, 65, 77–78, 81–82, 85, 92, 95, 160, 204, 212
Beacon Shoe Factory 54, 55, 56, 57, 75, 91, 92, 93, 96, 97, 121, 142, 160, 202; *see also* F.M. Hoyt Shoe Company
Bedford, New Hampshire 79
benevolence programs 2, 4, 5, 9, 10, 16, 17, 64, 70, 92, 94, 101, 124, 129, 133, 138–40, 150, 151, 180, 186, 198, 199, 204, 209, 210, 211, 213, 214
Bingham, Henry S. 53, 54, 56
Bond, Ernest 54
Boston Athletic Club Pilgrims 130
Boston Beaneaters *see* Boston Braves
Boston Braves 48, 57, 80, 90, 110, 111, 114, 119, ***123***, 124, 161–62, 194, 201
Boston Doves *see* Boston Braves
Boston Globe 111, 115, 170
Boston Journal 12
Boston, Massachusetts 1, 3, 9, 22, 27, 28, 43, 44, 48, 58, 59, 60, 66, 82, 90, 91, 94, 110, 111, 113–15, 120, 122, 124, 134, 140, 143, 148, 152, 156–57, 161, 162, 167, 171, 173, 183, 190, 191, 195, 196, 213
Boston Red Sox 3, 5, 7, 10, 43, 57, 58, 59–62, 80, 90, 91, 94, 98, 109, 110–20, 121, 124, 127, 130, 133, 142, 147, 149, 152, 154, 156, 157, 158, 162, 194, 195, 196, 201, 212, 213
Boston Red Stockings *see* Boston Braves
Boston Royal Rooters *see* Royal Rooters
Boulanger, Nazaire 79
boxing 179, 183–85
Bread and Roses Strike *see* Lawrence Textile Strike

237

Brice, Fred 80–81, 122
Britton, William 64, 77, 78
Brooklyn Dodgers 89, 207
Brooklyn Robins *see* Brooklyn Dodgers
Brooklyn Royal Giants 130, 147, 183
Brotherhood of Professional Baseball Players 156
Brown, Fred 206
Burke, John P. 33, 35
Burkett, Jesse 130, 196
Burns Detective Agency 44

Le Canado-Americain 38
Carey, James F. 35
Carlisle Indian Training School 127, 157, 162, 163, 164
Carney, John 7, 52, 115, 121, 122, 124, **126**, 127, 128, 130, 147, 148, 149, 156, 157, 162, 164, 165, 202
Carpenter, Frank 79
Carpenter, George 77
Carrigan, Bill 118, 149
Carroll, William C. 191
Caruso, Joseph 21, 65
Cassidy, George M. 48, 68
Challis, Frank H. 63
Chalmers, Thomas **39**, 40, 44, 64, 81, 85, 151, 212
Chamber of Commerce *see* Manchester Chamber of Commerce
Chicago Cubs 110, 127, 130, 133
Chicago White Sox 75, 147, 148
Chicago White Stockings *see* Chicago Cubs
children's march 103–105
Chinese University 147
Cigarmakers Union Local 192 21, 29, 32, 40, 44, 46, 82
Clarke, Frank L. 143
Club Jolliet 21, 46, 82
College of the Holy Cross 22, 127, 157, 162, 163, 164
Collins, Betsy 97
Collins, Eddie 158
Collins, Jimmy 111, 112
Collins, Ray 59
Comiskey Park 94
Concord Common 204
Concord Monitor 78
Conlon, Arthur 97
Coombs, Jack 158
Copley Plaza Hotel 122, 124, 128

Darrow, Clarence 32
Dartmouth College 119, 122, 163, 171, 178

Debs, Eugene 15, 180
Demerritt, Albert 79
Democratic Party 63, 64, 77, 84, 85, 86, 95, 103, 125, 151, 181, 211
Derry, New Hampshire 127, 161, 162
Derryfield Club 117, 119, 154, 156, 157, 196
Derryfield Park 52
Dionne, Alma 94–95
Donovan, Bill 54
Dow, Perry 94, 113, 115, 118
Draper-Maynard Sporting Goods Company 196
Duffy, Hugh 175, 196
Dumaine, Frederick C. 22, 124, 140, 210, 211
Dunbar, Frank 124
Dunn, James 182
Duval, William 104

Eastern Association 6, 168, 169, 171, 195, 196, 197
Eastern League 6, 195–97
Ebbets Field 89
Eighth Ward 98, 99–109, 110, 133, 139, 140, 159, 206, 211, 212
elections 5, 7, 14, 44, 60, 61, 63, 64, 66, 68, 76, 101, 153, 160, 161, 206, 210; of United States Senator 78–87, 210
Engel, George 180
ethnicity *see* race
Ettor, Joseph 19–21, 26, 29, 33, 38, 65, 200
Executive Council 47, 62, 63, 64, 81, 82, 83, 125, 206, 210

Farrell, Peter A. 22
Federal League 6, 8, 131, 155, 157, 164, 167, 168–74, 175, 183, 200, 214
Felker, Samuel 64, 80, 81, 125
Fenway Park 3, 9, 48, 59, **60**, 90, 91, 94, **112**, 162
Fielden, Samuel 179–80
Fifth Ward 55, 64
Finn, Jack 96, 113, 127, 129, 130, 131, 142, 147, 158, 160, 163, 167, 169 170, 171, 172, 173, 174, 175, 176, 186, 190, 191, 194, 195, 196, 197, 198
fire coverage 7, 100, 103, 105–7, 109
Fisher, Adolph 180
Fitchburg, Massachusetts 73, 74, 75, 122, 123, 124, 127, 128, 147, 148, 171, 172, 173, 175, 178, 188, 189, 194, 195, 198
Fitzgerald, John "Honey Fitz" 82, 115, 117
flag 55, 69, **102**, 104, 117, 133, 140, 144–47, 150, 157, 188, 193, 209, 212, 214; *see also* Amoskeag Great Flag

Flag Day 144–146, 150
Flanagan, Eddie 91, 202, 207
Floyd, Charles 117
Flynn, Elizabeth Gurley 28, 200
F.M. Hoyt Shoe Company 54, 55, 63, 81, 127, 134, 125, 187
football 8, 67, 119, 122, 127, 128, 143, 157, 162, 163, 164, 171, 172
Forbes Field 90
48-hour workweek 69, 161, 200, 202, 204, 206, 210
Fournier, Jack 207
Fraser, Jack 130, 185, 202, 207
Free Speech Hearings 61–63, 210
Free Speech movement 7, 26, 27–36, 44, 46, 47, 61, 63, 65, 82, 84, 101, 117, 204, 206, 210, 211; *see also* New Hampshire Free Speech Alliance
Freeman, William 67, 111

Gagnon, Grant 106
Gardner, Larry 118, 149
Gill, Ignace 207
Gill Stadium *see* Textile Field
Gilmore, James A. 170, 171
Giovannitti, Arturo 20, 21, 29, 65, 200
Gray, Jimmy 98
Greager, Albert 54
Greenfield, Massachusetts 190–92
Gregg, Vean 118
Guertin, Bishop George Albert 206
Guilbeault, Mederic 45–47, 82

Halliday, Thomas 29, 33
Hampton Beach, New Hampshire 55
Harvard Stadium 9
Harvard University 12, 79, 151, 163
Hayes, Charles 100, 104, 106, 107, 108, 109, 117, 161, 188
Haymarket Affair 179–80, 200
Haywood, William D. "Big Bill" 32, 33, 35, 38, 46, 65, 82, **83**, 144, 180, 200, 210
H.B. Reed Company 21, 54, 55, 57, 75, 93, 97, 127
Healy, Michael J. 5, 21–26, **28**, 29–30, 32–35, 37, 38, 44, 45, 46, 47, 48, **51**, 60–65, 82, **83**, 84, 90, 101, 117, 125, 126, 136, 182, 204–6, 210
Healy Method 22–23, 125, 136, 205
Hine, Lewis 12, **13**
Holcomb, Joe 175
Hollis, Henry 77–79, 85–86, 145, 204, 212
Holy Cross College *see* College of the Holy Cross

Hooper, Harry 59, 118, 149
Horne, Herman 110
House of David 207
Howie, George 33
Hurley, Francis 57

immigration 2, 4–7, 12, 14, 16, 20, 21, 23, 24, 25, 29, 35, 38, 49, 54. 56. 74, 92, 105, 110, 119, 125, 135–139, 144, 159, 183, 198, 201, 212, 214
The Industrial Worker 33, 34, 36, 37
Industrial Workers of the World 3, 4, 5, 6, 7, 10, 15, 16, 17, 19–21, 24, 26, 28–35, 37, 38, 40, 41, 44, 45, 38, 62, 63, 65, 82, **83**, 144, 150, 151, 152, 180, 199, 200, 201, 204, 206, 210, 211, 212
International League 53, 127, 149, 172

Jeanette, Joe 183
Jenks, Arthur B. 145, 187, 190, 191, 192, 202
Johnson, Albert 136
Johnson, Jack 184
Johnson, Walter 91, 118, 169
Jolliet Hall *see* Club Jolliet
Joseph A. Brown Picnic 181

Kane, Joe 175
Keady, Tom 171–75, 177, 190–92, 196–98, 214
Kelly, John 130
Kelly, Mike "King" 111
Kiernan, Jack 174–76, 178, 188, 190–92, 196–98, 214
Knowlton, E. J. 75
Knox, Frank 9, 43, 58, 60–62, 83–84, 91, 92, 95, 96, 136, 139, 140, 148, 161, 178–80, **181**, 182–89, 191, 205, 212
Konopka, Anthony 137
Kubilia, John 29, 46

Lake, Fred 7, 49–50, **51**, 121, 122, **123**, 124, 127, 128, 131, 141, 147–50, 157, 158, 160, 163, 164, 167, 169–72, 173, 174, 189, 195, 198, 214
Landis, Kenesaw Mountain 169, 200, 201
Lane, Thomas 106
Langford, Sam 183
Lardner, Ring 154
Laurence, Robert 29–30
Lavigne, Narcisse 171
Lawrence, Massachusetts 3, 4, 6, 7, 16, 19, 20, 21, 24, 25, 26, 28, 29, 30, 31, 32, 33, 34, 35, 37, 38, **39**, 40, 41, 42, 44, 45, 47, 51, 52, 55, 66, 82, **83**, 90, 101, 113, 114, 124, 127, 144,

Index

149, 151, 160, 170, 175, 179, 189, 190, 194, 199, 200, 204, 209, 214
Lawrence Textile Strike 3, 4, 7, 16, 19, 20–21, 24, 26, 28–35, 37–47, 65, 82, **83**, 90, 101, 124, 137, 144, 151, 179, 199, 200, 209
Leach, James 106
Leader Publishing Company 44
Legere, Ben 204–6
Leonard, Dutch 118
Leonard, Frank 66, 67, 68, 72, 75, 86, 118–19, 149
Levesque, Billy 113, 130
Lewis, Duffy 118
Lingg, Louis 180
Loeb, William 205
LoPizzo, Anna 20, 21, 29
Lowell, Massachusetts 11, 19, 25, **28**, 45, 52, 65, 66, 75, **83**, 98, 124, 128, 160, 169, 170, 171, 175, 199
Lyons, Frank 9, 118, 119

Mack, Connie 130, 154, **155**, 156, 158, 159, 161, 207
Main Street School 104
Manchester Advocate 60, 62–64, 69, 79, 84, 101, 132, 133–38, 151, 161, 170, 211, 212
Manchester Atlantics 110
Manchester Chamber of Commerce 47, 186; *see also* Manchester Publicity Association
Manchester Daily Mirror and American 9, 12, 19, 20, 21, 32, 42–44, 45, 50, 52, 54, 55, 57, 61, 63, 67, 68, 70, 71, 72, 73, 74, 75, 76, 80, 81, 82, 86, 90, 96, 97, 98, 99, 103, 105, 106, 112, 117, 119, 121, 125, 127, 128, 130, 136, 139, 144, 145, 147, 148, 151, 159, 162, 163, 164, 167, 169, 170, 172, 174, 176, 177, 178, 181, 189, 190, 191, 192, 195, 197, 205, 206
Manchester High School 22, 52, 80, 128, 152
Manchester Lands and Buildings Committee 106–107
Manchester Leader 7, 43–44, 60–63, 66, 69, 72, 74, 80, 83–84, 91–93, 95, 96, 98, 114, 131, 136, 139, 140, 144, 145, 147, 148, 151, 158, 162, 167, 168, 171, 175, 187, 190, 194, 195, 197, 200, 204, 205, 211, 212
Manchester Manchesters (baseball team) 111–12, 49, 50, **51**, 52
Manchester Police Commission 7, 12, 22, 32, 34, 45, 47, 62, 63, 65, 82, 84
Manchester Police Department 12, 22–26, 29–35, 37, 44, 48, **51**, 52, 53, 60, 63, 64, 82, 83, 90, 94, 95, 97, 100, 104, 119, 125, 136, 143, 181, 182, 183, 202, 204, 205, **203**, 209, 210, 212

Manchester Publicity Association 139, 145, 179, 186, 187, 188, 190, 191, 198
Manchester Textiles (baseball team) 122–24, 127–28, 147–50, 157, 158, 160, 163–64, 167–68, 171–77, 185–87, 188–98
Manchester Union 18, 19, 20, 23, 25, 32, 33, 34, 43, 49, 50, 52, 56, 61, 62, 63, 70, 79, 80, 92, 95, 96, 103, 105, 111, 112, 135, 136, 163
Manchester Union-Leader 113, 125, 127–31, 139, 148, 149, 151, 158, 159, 161, 163, 168, 170, 172, 174, 176, 179, 180, 181, 182, 183, 184, 186, 205, 206, 207, 210
Mann Act 95, 184
Manning, John 71, 73, 74 75, 80
Manufacturers League 3, 53–57, 61, 64, 66–70, 74, 75–76, 78, 80, 81, 88–93, 96–98, 113–15, **116**, 117, 121, 126–31, 133, 142–43, 148, 149, 150, 152, 153, 156, 157, 158, 160, 162, 164, 166, 167, 170, 172–73, 176, 185, 186, 201, 202, 212
Markee, Jesse 27, 38, 41, 42, 44, 45, 50, 52, 63, 65, 71, 84, 96, 101, 136–38, 151, 211, 212
Marrow, Charles 134
Mathewson, Christy 49, 50, 51, 59, 169
McAleer, James 114, 115, 118, 119
McCarthy, Chucky 91
McCarthy, George 176
McCarthy, John 93
McGill, Ora Pearl 6, 27–30, 32–33 35, 65, 201
McGreevy, Michael "Nuf Ced" 115
McGregorville 105
McInnis, Stuffy 156
McKay, William B. 54, 57, 69, 70, 71, 97, 98, 121, 127, 147, 157, 169, 170–74, 176, 178, **185**, 189, 192, 193, 201, 202, 213
McKean, Charles 104
McKean, Clarence 104
McKinnon, Hugh **168**, 169–72
McLaughlin, Barney 93, 97, 207
McLaughlin, Charles 103, 104, 106, 108
McLaughlin, Jim 96
McLaughlin, Mike 96
Merkle, Fred 59
Merrimack Valley League 115, 185, 186, 193, 194, 198
Milford, New Hampshire 193
Moore, John 170
Moquin, Arthur 106
Moses, George 78
Muehling, John 43, 60, 61, 205, 212
Murnane, Tim 50, 76, 115, 121, 170, 171, 173, 195, 196

Index

Murphy, Eddie 158

Nashua Telegraph 85
National Agreement 93, 129, 131, 141, 155, 168
National Association 121, 131, 169
National Association of Base Ball Players 110
New Bedford, Massachusetts 16, 68, 72, 93, 113, 114, 122, 124, 127, 130, 168, 198
New Bedford Sunday Standard 150
New England League 3, 6, 7, 8, 17, 49, 50, **51**, 54, 55, 64, 65–68, 70–73, 75–76, 80, 88, 90, 91, 93, 98, 111, 113, 115, 119, 120, 121, 122, **123**, 124, 128–32, 133, 141, 142, 147–50, 152–53, 156, 157, 160, 164, 167–77, 178, 185, 187, 188, 191, 192, 194–98, 200, 202, 213
New Hampshire Free Speech Alliance 7, 29, 31–36, 38, 45–47, 62, 65, 82, 117, 204, 206, 210
New Hampshire National Guard 35, 145
New York Giants 48, 51, 58, 59, 61, 62, 89, 121
Noonan, Dan 175
Northeastern League 71, 73–76, 77, 80, 88, 90, 214
Nunamaker, Les 118

O'Donnell, John 175
Oldring, Rube 158
O'Loughlin, Silk 59
One Big Union 204–6
O'Neil, Charles J. 86, 87
O'Rourke, Jim 93

Page, Calvin 77
Park Common 25
Parker, Jack 93
Parker, Perham 79
Parker School 104
Parsons, Albert 179–80
Parsons, Lucy 180
Paterson Silk Strike 200
Pellens, Gerard 29, 46
Pernod, Emil 81, 96, 175, 176
Peterborough, New Hampshire 14, 79
Philadelphia Athletics 48, 49, 90, 121, 127, 130, 133, 147, 150, 153, 154, **155**, 156, 157, 158, 161, 162, 163, 207, 209, 213
Philadelphia Phillies 48, 89, 195
Phillips Andover Academy 52
Phillips Exeter Academy 52, 79, 122
Pieper, Louis 66, 171, 173, 175, 194, 195, 196
Pillsbury, Hobart 80, 87

Pillsbury, Rosecrans 43, 79, 92, 95
Pine Island Park 181
Piscataquog River 99, 100, 106, 107
Piscataquog Village 104–5
Pittsburgh Pirates 48, 90
"The Plains" 66–67
playgrounds 5, 17, 44, 55, 92, 100–5, 107–9, 146, 150, 211, 212
Plymouth, New Hampshire 196
Polish Club 21, 29–30, 44, 46, 62, 63, 82
Polo Grounds 58, 89, 121
Portland, Maine 49, 50, **51**, 52, 66, 68 71, 72, 73, 74, 75, 76, 91, 138, 148, 168, 170, 174, 175, 195, 196, 202
Portland Press 138
Portsmouth, New Hampshire 77, 193
poverty 2, 12, 19, 23–24, 40, 101–2, 108, 133, 138, 177–81, 214
Progressive Era *see* Progressive Movement
Progressive Movement 2, 4, 5, 6, 7, 10, 12–14, 16, 37, 38, **39**, 41, 42, 43 45, 47, 64, 78, 92, 100, 177, 181, 187, 199, 209, 211–14
Progressive Party 5, 39, 43, 60, 61, 63, 64, 66, 76, 77, 79, 82, 85, 86, 87, 90, 92, 95, 125, 160, 161

Queen City Bridge 99, 100, 105, 109, 133, 139, 140, 141, 151, 152, 186, 206, 210, 211
Quinby, Henry 78

race and racism 3, 4, 6, 12, 20 21, **22**, 23–26, 34, 35, 38, 40, 43, 44, 53–55, 65, 100, 103–5, 115–16, 126, 130, 135–36 138, 144–45, 147, 150, 152, 159, 174, 177, 182–84, 187, 189, 190, 207, 212
Rami, John 20, 29
Recreation Club 21, 46
Recreation Grounds *see* Rock Rimmon
Redmond, James 135–36, 137
Republican Party 5, 12, 14, 35, 43, 61, 63, 64, 69, 77, 78, 79, 85, 87, 92, 95 96, 161, 180, **181**, 188, 206, 210, 211, 212
reserve clause 131, 155, 156, 157, 164
Ricord, Joe 162
Roach, Andy 175
Robbins, Horace 76
Rock Rimmon 44, 45, 55, 88, 93, 103, 142, 143, 148–49, 192, 193, 212
Rodelsperger, Herman 104
Roosevelt, Franklin D. 205
Roosevelt, Theodore 43, 62
Roy, Victor 100
Royal Rooters 59, 115, 117, 119, 162, 196
Ruth, George "Babe" 149, 201

Sacred Heart of Jesus School 104
Saint Anselm College 48, 52, 68, 91, 119, 128, 152, 163
St. Denis murder 182–83
St. Joseph's High School 52
St. Raphael School 104
Sakarikos, Demetrios 126
Sanger, Margaret 40
Savory, Charles 78
Schwab, Michael 180
7-20-4 Cigar Factory *see* Sullivan 7-20-4 Cigar Factory
Seventeenth Amendment to the Constitution 80, 210, 214
Shea, John 108
Shibe Park 5, 90, 154, **155**, 162
Slayton, Hovey 63
Smith, Albert 94–95
Smith, E.C. 32
Smith, Ezra 79, 85
Smith, James 191, 192, 196, 197, 198
Smith, John F. "Phenomenal" 7, 48–50, **51**, 52, 59, 61, 91, 93, 111–12, 115, **123**, 196, 124–26, 128, 178, 202, **203**
Smith-Webster Report 85
Snow, Caddie 78
Snow, Clifford L. 64, 77–80, 85–88, 95
Snow, Ellen 87
soccer 68, 115, 119, 214
socialism 7, 15, 24, 27, 28, 40. 41, 180
Socialist Party 21, 30, 35, 38, 46, 63, 65, 101, 210, 211–12
South End Grounds 162
Spalding, Albert G. 53, 110
Spaulding, Harold 161, 188, 191 192, 195–98, 202
Speaker, Tris 15, 118, 169, 196
Spies, August 179–80
'Squog Grounds 110, 111, 122
'Squog Village *see* Piscataquog Village
Stahl, Jake 118
Stallings, George 162
Stark Club 21, 29, 30, 40, 44, 46, 62, 82
Stark Hall *see* Stark Club
Stark Hotel 136
Stark Manufacturing Company 54, 55, 75, 81, 93, 96–97, 121, 127, 130, 142, 175–76
Stearns, Fred 85
Steele, Thomas 33
Stevens, Raymond 78
Strand, Paul 114, 118–19
Straw, Ezekiel 11, 165
Straw, Herman 63, 67, 104, 107, 110, 165, 210
Straw, William Parker 56, 73, 92, 97, 107, 122, 128, 134, 135, 141, **146**, 165, 167, 177, 193, 202, 213
strikes in Manchester 21, 24, 34–35, 44–45, 49, 65, 82, 133–35, 152, 199, 204–7, 209, 214
Sullivan 7-20-4 Cigar Factory 21, **102**
Suncook, New Hampshire 127
Sweeney Park 109

Taber, Willard G. 54, 80, 81, 96
Taunton, Massachusetts 48, 50, 71, 73, 74, 75, 183
Textile Field 1–9, 17, **60**, 72–74, 76, 87, 88–98, 99, 109, 112, 113–17, 119–20, 121–22, **123**, 124–25, **126**, 127–31, 133, 134, 141–44, 147–52, 154, **155**, 157, 158, 160, 163 164, 167, 169–77, 178, 183, 187, 188, 189, 192, 193, 198, 199, 201, 202, **203**, 207, 208, 209, 210, 212, **213**, 214; scoreboard 142, 143, 157, 162, 188, 207; *see also* Varick Park
Third Ward 64, 77, 78, 85, 87
Thomas, Ira **155**
Tragresser, Walt 114, 118–19
Trautmann, William **28**, 45, 65, 180
Triangle Shirtwaist Factory 63
Triangular League 52
Trull, Herbert A. 93
Turner Club 103
Turner Hall 159
Tyler, George "Lefty" 161, 162
Typographical Union of North America Local 152 27, 41, 42, 71, 96

Union-Leader Corporation 205
The United States of American v. William D. Haywood, et al 205
United Textile Workers 200, 204

Valley Grounds *see* Whittemore Flatts
Vance, Edward 201
Varick, Thomas R. 22, 45, 49, 67
Varick Park 22, 49, 50, 51, 52, 53, 55, 57, 66, 67, 68, 70, 71, **72**, 88, 91, 96, 111, 112, 114, 129, 142
Varney School 104

Wagner, Adolph 6, 105, 106, 107, 108
Walker Park *see* Sweeney Park
"The War of the Classes" 21
Ward Eight *see* Eighth Ward
Ward Five *see* Fifth Ward
Ward Three *see* Third Ward
Warren, George 82
Webster, Harold 79, 85

Wenzel, Gustav 100, 104, 107, 139, 206
Werner, Tom 176
West End Grounds *see* 'Squog Grounds
West Manchester 6, 20, 21, 44, 45, 55, 66, 68, 99, 100, 104–11, 122, 133, 139, 149, 176, 183, 206; *see also* Eighth Ward
West Manchester Improvement Association 107
West Side *see* West Manchester
W.H. McElwain Shoe Company 21, 34, 44, 54, 55, 69, 75, 93, 94, 99–100, 105, 109, 117, 127, 130, 132, 133, **134**, 135, 136, 139, 140, 141, 142, 145, 152, 160, 175, 176, 180, 201, 206, 211
Wheat, Zack 207
Wheeler, John S. 85
Whittemore Flatts 107, 108, 144
Wilson, Ben 21
Wilson, Woodrow 64, 105
Wobblies *see* Industrial Workers of the World
Wolf, Fred 30, 32, 33, 62

Wolfe Park 100, 103
Wolfeboro, New Hampshire 77
Women's Trade Union League 27, 28
Wood, Pete 113
Wood, "Smoky" Joe **112**, 113, 118, 154
Woodbury, Edward B. 22
Woodbury, Gordon 79, 85, 86, 87
Worcester, Massachusetts 5, 22, 52, 66, 85, 130, 162, 168, 170, 171, 175, 195, 196
World Series 3, 58, 59–62, 89, 94, 111, 114, 118, 121, 122, 150, 154, 157, 161–62, 194, 195, 196, 201
World War I 6, 10, 109, 153, 159–60, 161, 162, 166, 167, 177, 181, 183, 186, 189, 190, 200, 201, 202, 214

Yankee Stadium 5
Yerkes, Steve 59, 118
York Beach, Maine 193
Young, Cy 111
Young Men's Christian Association 117, 119, 151

www.ingramcontent.com/pod-product-compliance
Ingram Content Group UK Ltd.
Pitfield, Milton Keynes, MK11 3LW, UK
UKHW041939140426
5217IPUK00014B/568